Bridges of Friendship

Bridges of Friendship

Reflections on
Indonesia's Early Independence and
Australia's Volunteer Graduate Scheme

Edited by Ann McCarthy and
Ailsa Thomson Zainuddin

This publication has been supported by Australian Volunteers International.

inviting change

https://www.avi.org.au/

© Copyright 2017
Copyright of this publication in its entirety is held by the editors.
Copyright of the individual writings produced/reproduced in this book is held by the respective author/s.
All rights reserved. Apart from any uses permitted by Australia's Copyright Act 1968, no part of this book may be reproduced by any process without prior written permission from the copyright owners. Inquiries should be directed to the publisher, Monash University Publishing.

Monash University Publishing
Matheson Library and Information Services Building
40 Exhibition Walk
Monash University
Clayton, Victoria 3800, Australia
www.publishing.monash.edu

Monash University Publishing brings to the world publications which advance the best traditions of humane and enlightened thought. Monash University Publishing titles pass through a rigorous process of independent peer review.

www.publishing.monash.edu/books/bf-9781925495225.html

Series: Herb Feith Translation Series
Series Editor: Jemma Purdey

Text design: Les Thomas

Cover and imageblock design: Suyin Lim

Cover image: Staff at the English Language Inspectorate (IPBI), Jakarta c.1955 (left to right): Thelma Ashton, Harumani Rudolph-Sudirdjo, Frits Wachendorff, Betty Feith, Kurnianingrat Ali Sastroamijoyo and Ailsa Zainuddin. Photo courtesy of Ailsa Thomson Zainuddin.

All images courtesy of Ailsa Thomson Zainuddin unless otherwise stated.

National Library of Australia Cataloguing-in-Publication entry:

Title:	Bridges of Friendship: Reflections on Indonesia's Early Independence and Australia's Volunteer Graduate Scheme
ISBN:	9781925495225 (paperback)
Series:	Herb Feith translation series.
Subjects:	Volunteer Graduate Scheme (Indonesia)
	Volunteer workers in community development--Indonesia.
	Women--Indonesia--History.
	Indonesia--History--20th century.
Other Creators/Contributors:	
	McCarthy, Ann, editor.
	Zainu'ddin, Ailsa, editor.
Dewey Number:	307.1409598

Printed in Australia by Griffin Press, an Accredited ISO AS/NZS 14001:2004 Environmental Management System printer.

The paper this book is printed on is certified against the Forest Stewardship Council ® Standards. Griffin Press holds FSC chain of custody certification SGS-COC-005088. FSC promotes environmentally responsible, socially beneficial and economically viable management of the world's forests.

CONTENTS

Foreword vii
Preface xi
Acknowledgments xiii
Introduction xv

    The Authors xix
    About the Volume xxi
    Archival Sources xxii
    Note on Spelling xxiii
    Variations of Personal Names of Authors xxiv

PART ONE 1

Introduction 2
    Editorial Changes 8

Thesis: An Episode in Education for International Understanding:
The Volunteer Graduate Scheme in Indonesia 1950–63
"Putting in a Stitch or Two" 11
    Betty Feith

    Contents 11
    Introduction 12
    Part I: Origins and Ethos of the Volunteer Graduate Scheme . . . 16
    Part II: The Volunteer Experience – Problems and Perspectives . . . 48
    Conclusion 61
    Appendices 68

Opinion Piece: An Indonesian Opinion on the VGS 91
    Jo Kurnianingrat

Part Two 95

Introduction 96

Reminiscences: Other Worlds in the Past 105
Kurnianingrat Ali Sastroamijoyo

    Contents 105
    1. Early Childhood 106
    2. Life in the *Kabupaten* 108
    3. Primary School Days 114
    4. High School and Teacher Training 122
    5. Schoolmarm 127
    6. The Japanese Occupation 131
    7. The Early Years of the Republic 138
    8. Australian Experience 152
    9. Building the Future 164

Part Three 171

Introduction: A Friendship in Writing 172

Correspondence: "A Conversation Without Words":
Extracts of Correspondence between Kurnianingrat Ali Sastroamijoyo,
Ailsa Thomson Zainuddin and Harumani Rudolph-Sudirdjo,
1990–1993 177

Epilogue 203

In Memoriam: Jo Kurnianingrat Sastroamijoyo
September 14, 1919 – October 18, 1993 205
    Ailsa Thomson Zainuddin

Glossary 211
About the Authors and Editors 213
Bibliography 217
Index 223

FOREWORD

International volunteering has for decades been a valued component in international development thinking and practice. It emerged in the post-Second World War era as a response to skill shortages in developing countries and as a vehicle to express a new internationalism. Naturally enough, each country's international volunteer organisation reflected the unique characteristics of that country. The British Voluntary Service Overseas, now known simply as VSO, began life in 1958 as a program for school leavers and was at least partially informed by a sense of obligation and opportunity as former British colonies claimed their independence. The United States Peace Corps, from its inception in 1961, was a program of the State Department and has always been an expression of American foreign policy and its interests. But, in different ways and to varying degrees, international volunteer programs all share in the multiple aims of providing cost effective know-how in places and communities where it is needed and engendering mutual understanding across cultures through respectful personal relationships.

Without suggesting that the global enterprise of volunteering owes its existence to Australia's Volunteer Graduate Scheme (VGS), it was clearly the progenitor. The VGS was not just the first scheme of its kind, but was also the standard bearer for a particular philosophy and ethos vividly displayed in this volume. It combines Betty Feith's story of the thinking behind the establishment and the practicalities of running the Scheme with Kurnianingrat's reflections on it and her recollections and correspondence. In this way the book, which features Betty Feith's history of the VGS and Kurnianingrat's personal reminiscences, showcases both the intentions and the outcomes of the Scheme in bringing about deep interpersonal understanding, respect and friendship.

The VGS had many unique characteristics. In the first place, it was initiated by students at Melbourne University in the immediate post-war environment. There is probably nothing like war to stimulate students' international awareness. Furthermore, personal experiences of the world at war were injected into campus life by personnel who had recently returned and whose presence narrowed the social distance between lecturers and students. It was also a campus where spirited debating of issues of substance was pursued in both the Labor Club and the Student Christian Movement.

But perhaps the most defining characteristic of the VGS is that it was co-created by Indonesians and Australians. The idea surfaced at an international student conference in Bombay where the invitation for Australians to work alongside Indonesians and under their direction was first issued by an Indonesian student leader, Abu Bakar Lubis, who later went on to be a career diplomat in the Indonesian Department of Foreign Affairs. As Betty relates, a small but determined group, mainly in Melbourne, rallied support for the concept amongst students, national organisations, civil servants and politicians in both Australia and Indonesia, eventually securing an inter-governmental agreement. This too was unique in that it provided for operational costs to be shared between the Australian and Indonesian Governments, while leaving the liaison, publicity, coordination and administration to the honorary organisers in the Scheme's committees in Melbourne and Jakarta, acting under the auspices of the National Union of Australian University Students.

The ethos of the Scheme was also co-created, with the volunteer graduates being very much influenced by the thinking and behaviour of the Indonesians they worked with. This is one of the reasons why Kurnianingrat's memoirs are so priceless. She reveals her lived experience as an aristocratic girl in late colonial times, a young professional woman in the Japanese Occupation and a participant in the Revolution and its aftermath. Her stories, even the humorous anecdotes, serve to bring the dramas of colonialism and liberation into clear light, particularly her experience of social division and the impact of her awareness of not belonging to "the ruling race". As the experience of a professional and a nationalist, it translated into an understandable sensitivity to and a determination to avoid paternalism of all kinds. After reading her story it is easy to see why she would have been initially cautious, if not reluctant, to take on the services of volunteer graduates who were offered to her workplace.

There is an echo here of Herb Feith's observation that Molly Bondan, his initial sponsor and mentor, had needed to accustom herself to the idea of having him work with her. "Molly, I realised, had hesitated before offering to help me to work in Jakarta. She had tested me in a long correspondence before taking that decision."[1]

In the straitened circumstances of Indonesia in the 1950s, the Indonesian civil servants who were the colleagues, mentors and supervisors of the

---

1   Herb Feith. "Molly Bondan: Pioneer, Mentor and Role Model", in *Half a Century of Indonesian-Australian Interaction*, edited by Anton Lucas (Adelaide: Flinders University, Dept. of Asian Studies and Languages, 1996), p. 12.

volunteers necessarily had modest lifestyles. The volunteers insisted on a moral decision to identify as far as possible with their Indonesian friends, to live in a style as close to them as possible, even to earn the same money as similarly qualified Indonesian civil servants. They were determined to demonstrate that they were not colonial in their attitudes or demeanour in the workplace, in homes or in public. This conscious rejection of what others took as the entitlements of race meant eschewing expatriate lifestyles and, with notable exceptions, expatriate company.

Molly was also a powerful demonstration of how to live modestly and avoid giving offence and she had a powerful influence on the volunteers, much to the dismay of Australian Embassy officials who described her attitudes as "anti-Australian and anti-white".[2]

The volunteers' identification with Indonesia went further than issues of lifestyle and took on a distinctly political edge. It is clear that Indonesian supervisors and colleagues of the early volunteers not only talked the nationalist talk; through demonstration and collegiality they showed that nationalist pride was something one lived, and the volunteers embraced this challenge. Their wholehearted embrace of Indonesian nationalism was very much of the era. There was a romance in identifying with the Indonesian Revolution and relishing the opportunity to be part of nation-building.

Indonesia did not have a good press in Australia, which became increasingly the case as Indonesia moved towards Guided Democracy. The volunteer graduates found strength in each other and increasingly closed ranks against critics of Indonesia, striving to at least make Indonesia more understandable to Australians. But there is no doubt the wholehearted identification with the direction of Indonesia's politics became more difficult, as did the administration of the Scheme.

As Betty points out, one enduring legacy of the VGS has been the influence of people who drew on their first-hand experience of living and working in the country to help inform Australians better about Indonesia and the circumstances of its people. The VGS had another impact, which is at least as far-reaching. Betty's story of the VGS ends in 1963 when its administration was taken over by the Overseas Service Bureau (OSB), but it continued to exist as a scheme separately funded by the Australian Government to the end of 1969 (at a scaled back level) until it was absorbed into the OSB's global Australian Volunteers Abroad program.

---

2   Molly Bondan. *In Love With a Nation: Molly Bondan and Indonesia – Her Own Story in Her Own Words*, edited by Joan Hardjono and Charles Warner (Picton, NSW: C. Warner, 1995), p. 220.

The continuities were crucially important. The people involved in establishing the OSB and designing its programs had been intimately involved in the running of the VGS, most notably Jim Webb, Frank Engel, Herb Feith and Hugh O'Neill. This ensured that much of the ethos and principles of the VGS were preserved in the OSB's DNA. Over recent decades there have, of course, been changes. The Overseas Service Bureau changed its name to Australian Volunteers International and there have been shifts in the details of its relationship to government, but throughout these changes there has been constancy in upholding the values first enunciated and put into practice by the VGS.

Around the globe, and in Australia, diverse approaches to managing international volunteer programs have emerged. Within Australian Volunteers International, principles originating in the VGS continue to be maintained. Volunteers are professionals selected for both their skills and their personal competencies; they are assigned to positions only at the request and on the approval of the agency they are to work with; their remuneration is more in line with local than expatriate conditions. There is a clear understanding that the benefits are mutual, and the entire operation is founded on establishing respectful relationships across cultures and across social and economic divides. The impact of the VGS continues to inspire people who are active in the area of international volunteering. It deserves to be more widely known, and *Bridges of Friendship* is an invaluable contribution to that end.

Peter Britton

Former Executive Manager,
Programs and Deputy CEO,
Australian Volunteers International

Founding Member,
Herb Feith Foundation

Melbourne, 3 May 2016

PREFACE

Some years ago, when I was at Monash researching my biography of Herb Feith, Ailsa Zainuddin asked for my help to make good on a promise she had made to her former colleague and friend, Jo Kurnianingrat. Jo was a senior member of staff in the Ministry of Education in the English Language Inspectorate, where in 1954, Ailsa and Betty Feith worked as volunteer graduates. Herb, Betty and Ailsa went up to Indonesia as a trio, Herb returning to his former position in the Ministry of Information where he had worked from 1951 to 1953. Jo quickly established a rapport with the Australian women, as she had spent a year studying and touring in Australia in 1950 as one of the first Indonesians to receive a scholarship from the Australian Government.

As this book reveals, the Australians formed lifelong friendships not only with each other, but also with their Indonesian colleagues. This was helped by the fact that many of the VGS crew, including (especially) Ailsa, were fabulous letter writers. Over years of corresponding, during which they shared views on family life, gender equality, politics and all manner of things, Ailsa had encouraged Jo to write her memoir and was closely involved in its drafting. Jo died quite suddenly in 1993 and, although her memoir was incomplete, Ailsa was very aware that what Jo had recorded of her early childhood, family life and education, life under the Japanese Occupation and her work for the Revolution and in the newly independent Indonesian Government was important testimony and accounting of this period in Indonesia's history, imagining and formation as a nation.

In 2008 Ailsa and I began to cast around for ideas about how to best present and publish Jo's work, which was short of being a complete book manuscript yet much longer than a journal article. We spoke with the journal *Indonesia* who had earlier published Ailsa's obituary of Jo (reproduced with permission in this volume) about publishing it in two parts. At that time, however, Ailsa decided she needed to consult with Jo's family again to ensure that they were indeed supportive of her moves towards publication. This began a process of close consultation with members of Jo's family, which, importantly, coincided with Ailsa's working together with Ann McCarthy to organise her personal archive, which included significant correspondence with Jo over many years, including during the period she was writing the memoir. As is apparent in the letters reproduced in this volume, there was an expectation that Ailsa would eventually be involved in publishing the memoir.

So, when Ailsa and Ann invited me to meet them some years after we'd made our initial inquiries with *Indonesia*, we quickly agreed that Ailsa's correspondence with Jo was also valuable and somewhat precious documentation both for contextualising Jo's memoir and for depicting a friendship based on mutual respect and values.

Once the decision was made to frame Jo's memoir within the context of how it came into existence, by recording the part played by Ailsa and their friendship which began with the VGS, a further decision was made to include Betty Feith's seminal early history of the Scheme, hitherto unpublished. As Herb's biographer, I was extremely lucky to have access to Betty and her fabulous memory first-hand, but her thesis has also been, without question, a vital resource for my own research. Very early on I was given a precious rare copy of it and got my first glimpse of some of the wonderful historical documents contained in its Appendix – the first letters written by the Student Christian Movement group at Melbourne University (not yet VGS) and so on. The thesis, "Putting in a Stitch or Two", and its full Appendices are reproduced in this volume for the benefit of many more readers and researchers than the few of us who have had access it to date. Publication of Betty's thesis is, therefore, a significant complement to the archive of VGS documents held at the National Library of Australia in Canberra.

A highly valuable accompaniment to this collection of historical documents is Ann McCarthy's insightful introduction to each of the works. As Ailsa's archivist and researcher, Ann has worked side-by-side with Ailsa and Betty. In doing so she has developed a deep knowledge of the writings and their authors. When reading these introductory sections, it is clear that Ann, Betty and Ailsa have discussed the works at great length, considered deeply the time and context in which they were written, and cast a critical eye over how each might be read many decades later. She has provided a significant additional resource and useful guide for readers of this collection.

Assembling this collection, including the digitisation and reproduction of "Putting in a Stitch or Two" and its Appendices and the transcription of the letters, has been a mammoth task undertaken with much love by Ann, Ailsa and Betty together. I commend and congratulate them on their efforts.

Jemma Purdey

Herb Feith Publications Committee

Melbourne, 29 April 2016

ACKNOWLEDGMENTS

Compiling this book has been a collaborative effort involving a wide range of people in Melbourne, Jakarta and elsewhere. Former volunteer graduates Thelma Rungkat, John Gare, Ann Pryosusilo and John Foster shared their memories and knowledge of living and working in Indonesia under the Volunteer Graduate Scheme, or, in John Foster's case, under the equivalent New Zealand scheme. Ann Pryosusilo also forwarded to us invaluable biographical information about Harumani Rudolph-Sudirdjo, which she received from Marya Kristi Rudolph, Harumani's daughter. Thelma's daughter, Sari Baird, drew our attention to Thelma's photographs and letters from VGS days, which would make rich source material for future projects. Sari also helped organise a convivial lunch in June 2015. Sadly, Thelma passed away on 25 May 2016, before the completion of this book.

In Jakarta, Goenawan Mohamad and Widarti Gunawan put us in contact with Kurnianingrat Ali Sastroamijoyo's niece, Hadayanti Jayusman. Hadayanti Jayusman gathered together family photographs of Kurnianingrat, Harumani, and other friends and family members, and went out of her way to get copies of them to Melbourne, with help from Ailsa Zainuddin's daughter, Nila.

Two graphic designers lent their technical expertise and creative talents to the photographs which feature in the book. Suzanne Pascoe carried out most of the improvements to the image quality of the photos, using Photoshop and other software, and Suyin Lim provided the original design of the book's front cover and photograph pages.

Sjahisti Abdurrachman and Anton Alimin provided translations of a number of Indonesian and Dutch words and phrases used in "Other Worlds in the Past".

Peter Britton, former Deputy Chief Executive Officer of Australian Volunteers International, shared his historical knowledge about the VGS, and both he and Ruth Oliphant, Executive Coordinator, provided useful information about the historical records held by AVI. Suggestions and comments received from Peter, John Gare, Jemma Purdey, Ailsa Zainuddin, Betty and Annie Feith and Suyin Lim also helped improve the introduction and other front matter to this book.

Grateful thanks to Joe Arthur and the team at the University Digitisation Centre at the University of Melbourne, who very kindly agreed to scan and convert the hard-copy archival material that features in this book, through their Re-Born Digital service. In particular, thanks to Stacey Zarifopoulis, Imaging Officer, who carried out the work.

This book was made possible by Monash University Publishing and the Herb Feith Foundation. For their prompt, informative communication during the editing process, thank you to Kate Hatch, to Joanne Mullins, Coordinator, and to Nathan Hollier, Director at Monash University Publishing. Many thanks to Rachel Salmond, copy editor and indexer, for her work on the manuscript.

A special acknowledgment to Paul Bird, Chief Executive Officer of Australian Volunteers International, for providing a substantial financial contribution towards the publication cost of this book.

Sarah E. M. Grossman, Managing Editor of Southeast Asia Program Publications, Cornell University granted us permission to republish "In Memoriam: Jo Kurnianingrat Sastroamijoyo, September 14, 1919 – October 18, 1993".

Throughout the project, my conversations with many of the people identified above have been a very enjoyable part of my task – special mention to Sue Pascoe and Suyin Lim, who did such a fabulous job on the photographs. To Ailsa, Jemma, Betty and Annie, who have been involved from go to woe, thank you for putting your trust in my editing and compiling skills, it has been a pleasure working with each of you.

Ann McCarthy

18 November 2016

INTRODUCTION

In September 1959, *Djembatan*, the quarterly newsletter of the Volunteer Graduate Scheme for Indonesia, published an opinion piece by Kurnianingrat Ali Sastroamijoyo, writing as Jo Kurnianingrat, about the approach adopted by the Scheme. Then in its fifth year of official operation, the Volunteer Graduate Scheme (VGS) provided opportunities for Australian graduates to work on assignments for the Indonesian Government, earning the same rates of pay as similarly educated Indonesians. Kurnianingrat Ali Sastroamijoyo was formerly deputy head of the English Language Inspectorate (IPBI (Inspeksi Pengajaran Bahasa Inggeris)) in Jakarta where a number of Australian volunteers had worked. Familiar with the difficulties inherent in the giving of aid, in her article Kurnianingrat observes the potential for paternalism and misunderstanding of the needs and conditions of the recipient culture. The VGS, she concluded, had successfully steered a path around such obstacles:

> Summing up, I can only say that I have a deep appreciation for the Volunteer Graduate Scheme and the way it tries to establish friendly relations with Indonesia. No matter how important knowledge, experience, and money are, in establishing good relationships it is the attitude of the people which counts most, and the Volunteer Graduate Scheme has been very wise in making this a point of consideration in their selection of people.[1]

Helping to establish friendly relations with Indonesia was a defining objective of the VGS, which pioneered a model of volunteering based on salary equality and other expressions of identification by volunteer graduates with Indonesia and Indonesians. Between 1950 and 1963, forty-two Australians worked in Indonesia under the Scheme, carrying out a variety of roles and in some cases completing multiple assignments. These modest beginnings laid the foundations of a volunteer programme which continues today; since 1951, when the first volunteer, Herb Feith, arrived in Jakarta to work for the Department of Information, over 10,000 total volunteer placements have been completed by Australians in numerous

---

1   "An Indonesian Opinion on the VGS" by Jo Kurnianingrat, published in Part One of this volume.

countries round the world.² The VGS has been recognised as an influence on the establishment of both the American Peace Corps and the United Kingdom's Voluntary Service Overseas organisation.³

As well as giving Kurnianingrat's professional opinion on the Scheme and issues surrounding foreign aid, her article also bears out the lasting friendships established among the author and her colleagues at IPBI during the mid-1950s. Australians Betty Feith (née Evans) and Ailsa Zainuddin (aka Tommy) worked at IPBI as volunteer graduates for eighteen months from July 1954. In the course of advancing the Inspectorate's role, namely to establish English as Indonesia's first foreign language, friendships formed among Betty, Ailsa, Kurnianingrat and another colleague, Harumani Rudolph-Sudirdjo (who also went by the name Nini). Later in the 1950s, Kurnianingrat studied at Cornell University at the same time that Herb and Betty Feith were living there; of the Feiths' arrival in Ithaca in upstate New York Kurnianingrat wrote to Ailsa, "it's nice to have people from 'home' here".⁴ In subsequent years in Jakarta, Harumani and Kurnianingrat were part of each other's immediate circle of friends, as was the case for Melbourne-based Betty and Ailsa, who had known each other prior to their stay in Indonesia. Ailsa and Kurnianingrat exchanged regular letters from the 1970s, and Ailsa also corresponded with Harumani, and with Kurnianingrat's sister, Yetty. Additionally, the Australians and Indonesians saw each other during visits Betty and Ailsa made to Indonesia, and during a number of trips Harumani and her children made to Melbourne, when they would sometimes stay with the Zainuddins. The diverse writings brought together in this book offer a window into the friendships among the four women, their respect, affection and mutual interests and outlooks.

---

2   The figure of 10,041 assignments was provided by Australian Volunteers International and pertains to placements arranged between 1951 and 2015. The number would be much higher were other partners in the Australian Government's *Australian Volunteers for International Development* program (Scope Global, and, until recently, the Red Cross) taken into account. Additionally, New Zealand's Volunteer Graduate Scheme, which was established in 1959 and modeled on the Australian Scheme, has seen over 3,000 New Zealanders work in volunteer roles in the Asia-Pacific region, the majority of them through Volunteer Service Abroad. (See the website of Volunteer Service Abroad (http://www.vsa.org.nz/about-vsa/, accessed 9 September 2016).)

3   See, for example, Peter Britton's Foreword to this volume. See also "An Australian Peace Corps?", a memorandum issued by the Overseas Service Bureau in March 1964, which is reproduced in Part One ("Putting in a Stitch or Two", Appendix D).

4   Letter from Jo to Tommy, 21 October 1957. From a transcribed extract, in a file of biographical notes and extracts entitled "Kurnianingrat Ali Sastroamijoyo" (1919–1993), Papers of Ailsa Thomson Zainuddin, privately held.

Introduction

The first of these writings in the present volume is Betty Feith's study of the VGS, entitled "An Episode in Education for International Understanding: The Volunteer Graduate Scheme in Indonesia 1950–63 – 'Putting in a Stitch or Two'" (referred to in the text of this volume as "Putting in a Stitch or Two", as Betty also referred to it). Betty's history shows the aims of the Scheme to have encompassed both supporting the goals of the newly formed Indonesian Republic and helping to inform and engage Australians about their nearest northern neighbour. The conception of aid-giving advanced by the Scheme, Betty writes, was one that many volunteers perceived "quite deliberately and self-consciously as a 'New Direction' for a relationship between Australians and people of non-Western societies who had recently won political independence". "Putting in a Stitch or Two" includes discussion of some of the problems encountered by the early volunteer graduates as they set about their tasks. A lack of suitable work was one difficulty faced by some volunteers, while other issues were broadly associated with culture shock. Betty relates such difficulties to the ethos of the Scheme as a whole, and, specifically, to certain complexities and tensions inherent in the aims of the VGS. Additionally, she considers the lasting effects of volunteering, both upon volunteers themselves and upon Australian society as a whole, in areas such as the teaching of Indonesian Studies and Asian Studies in high schools and universities and the actions of pressure groups seeking reform of immigration policies, in particular the White Australia policy. The establishment of the VGS, historian John Legge has written, can be understood in relation to Australia's "developing ties" with Indonesia in the 1940s–1950s, together with other contemporary developments such as the extension of aid to Indonesia (among other countries) under the Colombo Plan and the strike by Australian waterside workers in support of their Indonesian counterparts.[5] "Putting in a Stitch or Two" is followed by the full text of Kurnianingrat's opinion piece, "An Indonesian Opinion on the VGS", introduced above.

Also published in this book is Kurnianingrat's previously unpublished memoir, entitled "Other Worlds in the Past". Kurnianingrat was teaching psychology and English in government schools in Yogyakarta for most of the period of the Japanese Occupation and war for independence against Dutch rule. A supporter of the nationalist cause, the courage and initiative she demonstrated during this time would later be commended by historian

---

5   Foreword by John Legge, in Molly Bondan, *Spanning a Revolution: The Story of Mohamad Bondan and the Indonesian Nationalist Movement* (Jakarta: Pustaka Sinar Harapan, 1992), p. 11.

and political scientist George Kahin, to whom she passed banned speeches by nationalist leaders amidst Red Cross casualty lists, while in the presence of Dutch soldiers. Additionally, Kahin identifies her as one of the Indonesian women who established "rice kitchens" in occupied Yogyakarta. Following independence, and after a year living in Sydney observing the school system, Kurnianingrat worked extensively in the field of English language education, and in 1961 she became head of the English Language Department at the University of Indonesia. "Other Worlds in the Past" spans her early years, growing up in a Sundanese *bupati* (Regent) family, and her schooling and training as a teacher, through to her experiences of the foreign occupations and revolutionary struggle of the 1940s, as well as the establishment of the Indonesian Republic. The memoir includes an account of Kurnianingrat's time at the English Language Inspectorate, where she worked with Harumani, Betty and Ailsa. Aware that past events, and in particular the Revolution, could seem remote to a younger generation, Kurnianingrat dedicated "Other Worlds in the Past" to her grandchildren.

Additionally, this volume includes transcripts of personal correspondence salient to Kurnianingrat's memoir writing, which took place during her retirement. Kurnianingrat, then in her 70s, had virtually lost her eyesight and was facing growing limitations in her daily life associated with her advancing age and physical frailty. Kurnianingrat could no longer write without assistance from others, let alone continue teaching, and her reading was done with audio books. In a letter from 1990, Harumani Rudolph had put to Ailsa her idea that Kurnianingrat write about her life, a suggestion largely motivated by a desire to help her friend address the frustrations inherent in her circumstances at the time. Ailsa responded enthusiastically to Harumani's idea, having also previously encouraged Kurnianingrat to document her past. Over the two and half year period between January 1991 and June 1993, a steady flow of letters, some including draft chapters of the memoir, were exchanged between Kurnianingrat's home in Cipinang Muara, Jakarta, and Ailsa's home and workplace in the southeastern suburbs of Melbourne. The task proved to be a rewarding one for Kurnianingrat. Kurnianingrat's correspondence with Ailsa, together with the letters exchanged between Ailsa and Harumani at the beginning of the project and at the time of Kurnianingrat's final illness, provide a record of the writing process in relation to Kurnianingrat's memoir, in the context of the lasting ties and shared loyalties among the three friends.

Together, the writings published here demonstrate a number of different dimensions to friendship: between individuals, and also between cultures, as a decisive aspect of people's everyday lives – in particular accenting the interwoven threads of our lives – and as an ideal symbolising human mutuality and equality, as embodied in the Volunteer Graduate Scheme. Of the social and political impact of the VGS in the context of political events in Indonesia at the time, Molly Bondan, an Australian whose abiding political and personal commitments to the Indonesian Republic are documented in a biography, *In Love With a Nation*, among many other writings, concluded:

> The Volunteers did a lot in the way they used their knowledge to help others, but what they did in promoting friendship between Indonesia and Australia in those difficult early days cannot be measured.[6]

This passage suggests the lasting, positive contribution made by the VGS in "those difficult early days" of independence in Indonesia. Additionally, a passage in a letter from Kurnianingrat to Ailsa poignantly expresses the shared understanding, respect and affection intrinsic to friendship. In this letter, Kurnianingrat describes a dream she had had of the two of them sitting together, silently enjoying each other's company – as Kurnianingrat puts it, "I fully understood you and felt very close to you".[7] She refers to their "conversation without words", a phrase that eloquently conveys their close friendship, notwithstanding the wealth of expression that actually passed between them over the years.

The Authors

Common life experiences undoubtedly contributed to the development of lasting ties among Kurnianingrat, Harumani, Betty and Ailsa, beginning with their shared commitments as teachers and educators working at IPBI during the mid-1950s. English teaching and training were the focus of Harumani's working life, as they were of much of Kurnianingrat's. Both women were educated at Dutch schools during the 1920s-30s, becoming proficient in several languages, including Dutch, Indonesian, Javanese, English and, in Kurnianingrat's case, Sundanese. Both would take up scholarships to study at American universities (Harumani at Barnard College, Columbia University, and Kurnianingrat at Cornell University),

---

6   Molly Bondan. *In Love With a Nation*, p. 109.
7   Letter from Jo to Tommy, 16 October 1988, in "Jo – Correspondence and Autobiography/Biography" (1955–1993), Papers of Ailsa Thomson Zainuddin, privately held.

and would go on to gain further qualifications at, and also teach in, tertiary education institutions in Indonesia, including the University of Indonesia.[8] Harumani and Kurnianingrat were among a generation of educators whose work in the area of foreign language training contributed to a vital area of national development; the two women were part of what has been described as "a small, educationally privileged generation of teachers who played a key role in the great democratising wave of increasing education for all".[9] Like Kurnianingrat, Harumani supported the Republic at the time of the civil war with the Dutch. In Dutch-occupied Jakarta, Harumani taught in SMP I, a Republican school that held classes in private dwellings in order to avoid detection by the Dutch authorities and, at the time of the Japanese Occupation, she combined teaching with working for the Red Cross in Bandung. Kurnianingrat was a close personal friend not only of Harumani, but also of her husband, Chris Rudolph, whom she had first met in 1950 when they were both working as school heads in Jakarta.[10]

As with Kurnianingrat and Harumani, there were many similarities between the educational and social backgrounds of Ailsa and Betty. Both Ailsa and Betty attended Methodist Ladies' College in Kew, Melbourne, and would later go on to be actively involved in Australian Student Christian Movement (ASCM) circles. Upon arriving in Jakarta, the two women, together with Betty's husband Herb, shared a house. (A photograph of the new arrivals taken outside their new home at Jalan Halimun appears in this volume.) Their lives have been intertwined in one way or another ever since, with their experiences in and ties to Indonesia an integral part of their friendship.

Betty and Ailsa both have unique matrimonial ties to Indonesia. Betty and her husband Herb Feith, who became an internationally acclaimed scholar of Indonesian politics, were two of the Melbourne University students who initially pioneered the VGS. Ailsa met her Minangkabau husband,

---

8   Harumani Rudolph-Sudirdjo graduated as a Bachelor of Education (Sarjana Pendidikan) at the University of Indonesia in 1967. She taught full-time at the Faculty of Social Sciences at the University of Indonesia between 1970 and 1978, and in later years, during which she was, officially at least, retired, taught English language courses at the university on a part-time basis (among other roles).
9   Gillian Belben, "Harumani Rudolph-Sudirdjo: 'Learning and Teaching through Changing Times'," *Network*, Vol 2, Issue 1, July 1995.
10 The main sources of biographical information about Harumani Rudolph-Sudirdjo used for this book are Belben, "Harumani Rudolph-Sudirdjo" and Harumani Rudolph's curriculum vitae, dated 1992. Copies of these documents are in a file entitled "Harumani Rudolph-Sudirdjo – Biographical Documents (CV; Belben Article)", Papers of Ailsa Thomson Zainuddin, privately held.

Zainu'ddin, in Canberra during the early 1950s when he was working in the diplomatic service of the new Republic and she was working as a research assistant for Manning Clark while writing her MA thesis on the *Bulletin* and Australian nationalism. After Betty and Ailsa returned from Indonesia in 1956, they went on to teach Indonesian studies and Southeast Asian history at universities in Melbourne; Betty at Burwood and Toorak Teachers' Colleges (later part of Deakin University), and Ailsa at Monash University. Among other subjects, both Betty and Ailsa taught their students about Indonesian national heroine R. A. Kartini, and her pioneering work in the area of education for girls. Betty was a member of the History of Education for Girls discussion group (HEGG) at Monash University, a group which Ailsa co-founded and co-convened. In her capacity as Senior Lecturer in Education at Monash University, Ailsa supervised Betty's dissertation on the history of the Volunteer Graduate Scheme, as published in this book. Ailsa and Betty remain members of a reading group that meets once a month for discussion on topics broadly focused around the history of education. In a letter from Ailsa to Harumani dated 5 January 1990 (reproduced in Part Three), Ailsa wrote that she thought of Betty as a sister, "just as I think of you and Jo as very like sisters (to each other and to us)."

About the Volume

Bridges of Friendship brings together a diverse set of writings whose common thread is the lasting friendships formed among these four women in Jakarta in the 1950s. Part One of the book features Betty Feith's thesis on the VGS, "An Episode in Education for International Understanding: The Volunteer Graduate Scheme in Indonesia 1950–63 – 'Putting in a Stitch or Two'". It narrates the historical development of the Scheme over its first thirteen years, recording the web of people, events and ideas integral to that development, as well as the daily experiences of the first generation of volunteers. In writing her thesis, Betty was informed by her extensive first-hand knowledge and understanding of her subject, as a co-founder of the VGS and a volunteer. Also in Part One is an opinion piece by Kurnianingrat about the approach adopted by the Volunteer Graduate Scheme.

Kurnianingrat's personal reminiscences and part-memoir make up Part Two of this book. Kurnianingrat's memoir includes a detailed and moving account of life in occupied Yogyakarta during the Revolution, as well as recollections of the author's childhood and an account of her experiences living in Sydney in 1950. Part Three of this book documents the background to

Kurnianingrat's writing of her reminiscences in 1991–1993, through extracts of her personal correspondence from that time. As the letters show, Ailsa and Harumani played a part in encouraging Kurnianingrat's memoir project, and they also assisted with the writing process. This transcribed correspondence forms part of the rich historical and archival content of *Bridges of Friendship*, which will be of interest to researchers in fields such as the social history of Indonesia during the turbulent middle decades of the twentieth century, international volunteering, and Australia's engagement with Asia, particularly its ties with Indonesia. The book closes with Ailsa's obituary for Kurnianingrat after her death in 1993.

This book is the result of a meeting between Ailsa Zainuddin and Jemma Purdey in July 2014, at which Ann McCarthy was also present. Ailsa had among her personal records the memoir by Kurnianingrat and a copy of Betty Feith's thesis. The letters are also among Ailsa's personal records, which, at the time, Ann was engaged in arranging and describing. The compilation and editing of these texts was carried out between July 2014 and July 2016. The first step in bringing these texts into print was digitising the four main documents ("Putting in a Stitch or Two", "An Indonesian Opinion on the VGS", "Other Worlds in the Past" and "In Memoriam: Jo Kurnianingrat Sastroamijoyo"), which was followed by checking, editing, standardising and formatting the digitised texts. The bibliography and the glossary of this volume have as their basis the bibliography and glossary of "Putting in a Stitch or Two", but both have been extensively enhanced by additional terms and citations relevant to the other components of the volume.

Archival Sources

Many diverse archival records are referred to, cited or reproduced in this book, especially in "Putting in a Stitch or Two". Many of them are held in several different Australian archival collections and repositories, but the location of some records remains unknown. In general, for archival material pertaining to the VGS, there are two key collections, both of which are held in the National Library of Australia in Canberra: Records of Australian Scheme for Graduate Employment in Indonesia, 1950–1968 (MS 2601); and Papers of Herbert Feith, 1946–2001 (MS 9926).

Readers interested in the archival material in this book are advised of two particular personal collections of importance. The first of these is an assorted set of records of the VGS which were gathered, used and, in some cases, also created by Betty Feith. These records came to light during the compilation of this book and include letters pertaining to volunteer applications to work in Indonesia, NUAUS reports and publicity material about the Scheme, publications and talks. They also include the copy of Betty's thesis that was converted into digital form for this volume. (These VGS-related records gathered by Betty Feith include some but not all of the archival material that she identifies in her introduction to her history of the Scheme.) These records, which are currently being boxed and listed, are to be housed together with the Papers of Herbert Feith (MS 9926) at the National Library of Australia, Canberra.

The second of these two particularly important collections is Ailsa Zainuddin's personal archives among which are many original records salient to this book, including the original of "Other Worlds in the Past", and the original correspondence reproduced in Part Three. Ailsa Zainuddin's personal archives, which at the time of writing remain in private hands, are to be deposited at the National Library in Canberra.

In the footnotes and bibliography of this book readers will find references to a number of original, unpublished documents held in the two archival collections identified above. The list of citations does not constitute an exhaustive lising of all the relevant material in these two collections. Priority has been given to referencing the main documents published in this book, as well as archival material cited in the book's introduction.

Some of the archival material relevant to Betty's Feith's study of the VGS is among archival records held at the Melbourne offices of Australian Volunteers International (AVI). They include volunteer correspondence and minutes of meetings of the Melbourne Committee dating from the 1950s and 1960s. For more information or to enquire about viewing these records, contact AVI in Melbourne.

Note on Spelling

In general, current Indonesian spelling and naming conventions have been adopted throughout this book, for instance "Jakarta" is used rather than "Djakarta", "Sanusi" instead of "Saneosi", and "Sastroamijoyo" replaces "Sastroamidjojo". Old spelling and naming conventions have been retained in the correspondence and other primary material cited or reproduced in "Putting in a Stitch or Two", and in the letters reproduced in Part Three. Additionally, they have been retained in "Other Worlds in the Past" in cases where this was called for by historical context or other factors.

While variations in spellings were mostly standardised in favour of the new spelling, there were exceptions to this. For instance, Kurnianingrat's friend, Soemarsono, is also referred to as "Soen" in the text. In the interests of clarity this name is spelt the old way, rather than as Sumarsono. Additionally, the spelling of "Soedjatmoko" has been retained unchanged, in accordance with accepted usage in relation to this historical figure.

Variations of Personal Names of Authors

Multiple spellings or versions of personal names exist for some of the authors whose writings are published here. Kurnianingrat Ali Sastroamijoyo was known to her friends and family as "Jo". From 1970, she took on the name of her husband, Ali Sastroamijoyo, whom she married that year. In a letter to Ailsa from 1980, Kurnianingrat specified that she be referred to as "Kurnianingrat Ali Sastroamijoyo" for publication purposes, with "Kurnianingrat" to be used in shorter pieces therein, such as the introduction.[11]

Some published references to Harumani Rudolph also include her maiden name, Sudirdjo. In her immediate circle, Harumani was known as Nini. Additionally, for some years Ailsa has used her maiden name, Thomson, as well as her married name. In 2015, Ailsa changed the spelling of her surname from Zainu'ddin to Zainuddin.

Ailsa and Betty chose to be referred to by their given first names in the front matter of this book. In the correspondence published in Part Three, Ailsa is referred to as "Tommy" (her more usual moniker among her Indonesian circles), while Betty Feith is usually referred to as "Bett".

---

11   Letter from Jo to Tommy, 31 July 1980, in "Jo – Correspondence and Autobiography/Biography" (1955–1993), Papers of Ailsa Thomson Zainuddin, privately held.

PART ONE

INTRODUCTION

"An Episode in Education for International Understanding: The Volunteer Graduate Scheme in Indonesia 1950–63 – 'Putting in a Stitch or Two'" is the thesis Betty Feith submitted for the degree of Master of Educational Studies at Monash University in 1984. It consists of two parts: an in-depth discussion of the development of the ethos and philosophy that became characteristic of the Scheme, followed by analysis of a number of difficulties experienced by some volunteer graduates as they set about realising their aims. While Betty situates her historical analysis in the context of the VGS's relationships with Australian educational and religious organisations such as the ASCM, NUAUS and the OSB, she focuses primarily on the experiences and points of view of volunteers, especially those in Jakarta and Melbourne.

The part of the title of the thesis that Betty chooses to refer to her thesis by, "Putting in a Stitch of Two", picks up a phrase from a statement made by Herb Feith stemming from his stay in Indonesia in 1951: "It's just [fine] being here and watching the various strands coming through in the fabric, and putting in a stitch or two oneself where one can." The thesis makes apparent a set of interlinked objectives central to the VGS as a model of aid-giving. These aims centred on, in Betty's words, "racial and financial equality as expression of identification", that is, identification by volunteers with Indonesia and its people, particularly in relation to national independence and the objectives of the Indonesian Republic. The contemporary political circumstances in Indonesia, which had won independence from Dutch rule in 1949, served as important context to this aim, as it did to the VGS as a whole. Betty shows the strong support of the Indonesian Government characteristic of the first generation of volunteers. Many of the volunteers felt, as she puts it, "a sense of shared pride in the progress of the newly independent country, and further, a desire to be part of and to share in that nation-building, albeit as short-term guests." Betty cites letters and reports home to Australia which reveal this stance, including the detailed accounts by Ollie McMichael, one of the first three volunteers to work in Indonesia. McMichael wrote, for instance: "Every Indonesian I've met has a pride and enthusiasm in the revolution and in the new society. ... It's a desire for revolution in standards of living, health, education and they are determined to be democratic." The assistance which volunteers could provide was vitally necessary, McMichael continued, in order to address "the economic position and the education problem" as well as problems of poverty and illiteracy.

The Scheme focused not only on the technical skills volunteers brought to their work, which could be essential in light of the critical shortages of trained people in many fields at that time in Indonesia, but also on rethinking the philosophical grounds on which such help was provided. In particular, the existing conventions then dominant among Westerners living and working in Indonesia were rejected as vestiges of colonial hierarchies. It was common for Westerners to keep within expat circles, and to receive high salaries and other benefits not enjoyed by the majority of Indonesians. As Betty's study demonstrates, the category of the "foreign expert" influenced in negative terms how volunteers tended to define their own roles. In the salaries they earned, and in areas such as housing, diet, social interaction and language, volunteers set out to participate in Indonesian society on equal terms with their Indonesian counterparts.

The energy and idealism integral to the VGS – including a steadfast conviction about putting into practice a model of aid and development based on principles of international unity and cooperation – comes across strongly in "Putting in a Stitch or Two". Betty describes a sense of excitement bound up with being "part of the making of history", both in the possibility that individuals could help to lay "the first foundations in your field for this huge new country" (as it was put to would-be volunteers) and also in the goal of advancing "a radically new method of aid-giving, a new way of relating to the needs of Third World people and nations." Betty also discusses the influence upon volunteers of the "sincerity and zeal" which was not uncommon among the senior civil servants they worked for, many of whom were "genuinely dedicated idealists". The element of equality the VGS embodied was widely perceived as its most consequential aspect, among participants of the Scheme and commentators. Betty quotes Dr R. H. Tirtawinata, Indonesia's Ambassador to Australia at the time. Observing volunteers' willingness "to live among us on our own standards of salary and living, to share family life with us, to become in truth real members of our community", Tirtawinata commented that "[s]uch a contribution is worth immeasurably more to us than the rupiahs it saves our treasury".

Many of the early volunteers were conscious "of having been part of a radical new direction in aid, of having done something revolutionary", and this consciousness contributed to a proliferation of writing about the Scheme and about conditions on the ground in Indonesia. Betty refers to "a constant urge to write and then extend, with new chapters, the history of the Scheme as the participants saw it". Volunteers' letters to friends and family in Australia were relevant in this respect. Key early publicity reports on the VGS, which were distributed on university campuses and elsewhere, were substantially made up of reworked versions of volunteers' letters home, as Betty discusses, citing extensively from the reports in question. Among volunteers, weekly correspondence home served functions over and above the usual ones of keeping the travellers in touch with their friends and family and sharing their experiences – the latter of particular significance in light of the unique and unprecedented nature of the Scheme and what the volunteers were doing. Most Australians at the time knew little about Indonesia, Betty writes. The information communicated both privately and publicly about the VGS and about volunteers' experiences in Indonesia also served as a crucial means of publicising the Scheme. It offered a way of demonstrating the strengths and merits of the Scheme as a "unique approach to working in Asia", based on "racial and financial equality".

The stories, descriptions and reports from volunteers about their activities and about Indonesian culture and politics more broadly also highlight the way the VGS engaged with issues and problems in Australian society, in particular Australia's isolationism in relation to Asia. The main aims of the Scheme included presenting a view counter to "the stereotype [of Indonesia] popularly accepted in Australia at the time". For instance, in an article in *Djembatan* entitled "It's dangerous to go to Indonesia", Ailsa Zainu'ddin wrote that visiting did indeed pose a threat – not that one would "be stabbed, stoned or toppled over in a car", but rather would be changed by the experience, specifically by the lasting effects of contact with Indonesians, "their hopes and aspirations, their hospitality, their culture, the warmth of their friendship and the beauty of their countryside". The need felt by many volunteers "to explain, expound and defend Indonesian Government policy", Betty writes, gained further importance from the late 1950s on account of political events occurring at that time, such as the campaign in West Irian (West Papua).

Looking back, Betty Feith is circumspect and somewhat critical of the strong moral tone apparent in some of the literature of the VGS regarding the Scheme's objectives and methods. She identifies a "note of confident, even arrogant Australian nationalism" among the writings in question in regard to the urgency of supporting Indonesia's development as a nation, and their own part therein. She is similarly cautious about the firm beliefs evinced by some volunteers as to what constituted the "wrong attitude" as opposed to the "right" one among those who wished to join the VGS. In general, her analysis explains the extent of volunteers' enthusiastic endorsement of the Indonesian Government by contextualising it within the history of the Scheme as whole. A range of objectives, personalities and conditions evidently converged in that history, perhaps most importantly a group of young people with the courage and resolve to put into action their vision of a more just and equal relationship between those providing aid and assistance and those receiving it.

The VGS's links to ecumenical traditions is one salient factor in this respect. Writing about the beginnings of the secular volunteering movement in Australia, Justice Michael Kirby has referred to the importance of spiritual feelings expressive of an ethos of human unity, harmony and compassion.[1] "Putting in a Stitch or Two" speaks to this issue in many ways. Betty records the importance of the ASCM post-war conferences as forums where the aims and direction of the fledgling VGS were discussed and advanced. Many volunteers, she writes, were members of, or otherwise associated with, the Protestant or Catholic church. A strong Puritan work ethic is shown to have decisively shaped many volunteers' attitudes towards their work tasks. Related themes are apparent in Betty's concluding remarks about the long-term effects of volunteering upon the values and outlooks of those involved, and the consequences of these changes for them and for their community following their return to Australia.

Additionally, "Putting in a Stitch or Two" also casts light on how the day-to-day activities involved in running the VGS were instrumental in consolidating its ethos and philosophy as a whole, and how those shared activities helped foster a sense of common purpose and community among its members. The chief activities undertaken by volunteers in this respect were making the initial enquiries with officials and contacts in Indonesia on behalf of applicants and interested correspondents in Australia and processing those applications that had already progressed along the pipeline. This work was done by the Scheme's committees in Melbourne and Jakarta (the latter being composed of volunteers living in Jakarta at any given time). For each new applicant, committee members conducted "a long period of 'informal inquiry'" which began long before the application reached the stage of an "official 'request' from the Indonesian Ministry [in question] and 'acceptance' by both governments for the applicant to work as a volunteer under the Scheme".

---

1   Introduction by Michael Kirby, in *A Place in the World: Stories from Australian Volunteers International*. Melbourne: Melbourne Books, 2007.

From as early as 1952, before the VGS even came into existence officially, "there was always an agenda of current business, including letters to be answered, ministries to be visited, informal contacts already established to be followed up, and a great deal of routine 'chasing about' which usually had to be accomplished before any enquiry could be answered". These tasks brought volunteers into contact with each other, working closely together during weekends and holidays; over time, such shared activities helped to cultivate a sense of "solidarity, of community, and as time went on, of mutual support and personal friendships". As Betty writes, a growing consensus – though "never a party line" – emerged among the volunteers, many of whom were of a similar age and shared backgrounds as members of the ASCM or Labor Club at university. The coherence of the group, Betty comments, "depended more on mutual acceptance of their interdependence in this strange environment than on any religious or political agreement".

Such observations make apparent the grass-roots nature of the VGS and its organic development as an initiative based on the efforts of individuals of good will who saw Australia's nearest northern neighbour not as a foreign and hostile culture to be feared or mistrusted, but rather in terms of realising the potential for an abiding friendship between two peoples. As well as being conveyed throughout the narrative of "Putting in a Stitch or Two", this also comes across in the eleven documents that feature as appendices to the study, along with an annotated list of volunteers who served under the Scheme between 1951 and 1963. Among the appendices is an early letter from the Melbourne Committee (which included Betty) to Ollie McMichael advising of the progress made in getting the Scheme off the ground, both in Australia and in Indonesia. The writers outline those student groups, politicians and public officials so far contacted about the Scheme; the response received thus far, they report, is positive but as yet without any firm commitment to the ideas proposed. A concluding comment speaks to the early volunteers' confidence and faith in their project: "In the meantime: we will try and move the Powers as fast as possible". The appendices also include six further letters to individual volunteers drawn from the VGS committee files, as well as literature about the Scheme distributed in Australia by NUAUS and the OSB.

Betty's study ends at 1963, when additional government funding saw OSB director Jim Webb's role expanded to full-time, which placed the Scheme on "a sound organisational and financial basis under the Overseas Service Bureau umbrella". The new arrangement helped facilitate recruitment of new graduates in the numbers required on the ground in Indonesia, which had often proved difficult in the past.[2]

Betty Feith is uniquely placed to document the beginnings of the Scheme and the evolution of its ethos and philosophy, having been closely involved in its establishment and operation. She was the secretary of the initial committee set up in 1950 to investigate the feasibility of the Scheme, and, following official recognition of the Scheme by both governments in 1954, was closely involved in its development and operation.[3] She volunteered in Indonesia in 1954–56, when she worked at IPBI and at a teacher training college. (In the 1990s she returned for a further four years, teaching English at the University of Atma Jaya in Yogyakarta and at Andalas University in Padang, West Sumatra.) "Putting in a Stitch or Two" attests to her familiarity with the archival records documenting the Scheme and its activities. In the introduction to "Putting in a Stitch or Two", Betty discusses issues arising from her role as a participant observer in the events and developments she narrates. The care with which she distances her own viewpoint is in keeping with the tone of the study as a whole, and its representation of different points of view on the VGS and its methods and objectives.

"Putting in a Stitch or Two" can be seen to establish a narrative about the task of bridge-building and about some of the ways that endeavour was perceived and articulated by volunteer graduates. For Betty, as for many others who participated in the Scheme, volunteering in Indonesia was the

---

[2] Frank Engel made this point in his talk on the establishment of the OSB and the role played therein by the ASCM; see "The Origins of the Overseas Service Bureau – An Address by Frank Engel – Australian Volunteers Abroad Briefing, Jan. 1983", Papers of Herbert Feith, National Library of Australia, MS 9926 (transfer pending). Hugh Collins has made a similar comment in relation to the transition from the OSB to AVI in 1999, referring to OSB's "mature manifestation" as AVI as evidence of the organisation's "institutional trajectory"; see his Foreword, in Renate Howe, *A Century of Influence: The Australian Student Christian Movement 1896-1996* (Sydney: University of New South Wales Press, 2009), p. 13.

[3] Betty's role in the initial Melbourne Committee is discussed in Betty Feith, "History of the Volunteer Graduate Scheme – Talk for AVA briefing – January 1983", Papers of Herbert Feith, National Library of Australia, MS 9926, (transfer pending); see also Jemma Purdey, *From Vienna to Yogyakarta: The Life of Herb Feith* (Sydney: University of New South Wales Press, 2011), pp. 75–76. For more on the beginnings of the Scheme, and on Herb Feith's role in particular, including his trip to Indonesia in 1951–53, and the involvement of Professor W. McMahon Ball and Molly Bondan in that visit, see Purdey, *From Vienna To Yogyakarta*, pp. 55–56, 70–79, *passim*.

beginning of a relationship with that country – its culture, history and people – that would continue long after she first worked there as a volunteer graduate.

In Betty's case this has been an involvement shared with Herb and their family. Jemma Purdey has described the "common values and sense of moral obligations" essential to Betty and Herb's marriage – a merging of Betty's ecumenical Methodism and Herb's syncretistic Jewish faith.[4] Values important to both of them and which they have actively worked towards include respect for the dignity of the individual and commitment to pacifism and international unity.[5] A desire to help break down barriers between people and between cultures has informed Betty's work in teaching and lecturing (about which more information is included in the conclusion to "Putting in a Stitch or Two") and her lifetime involvement in church and other service. Another publication by Betty Feith, entitled *Women In Ministry: The Order of Deaconesses and the Campaign for the Ordination of Women within the Methodist Church 1942–77*, echoes "Putting in a Stitch or Two" in its spirit of inclusiveness, critical enquiry and dedication to the cultivation of social, educational and religious institutions that foster human flourishing, regardless of gender, nationality, ethnic group or other such factors.

Editorial Changes

The bibliography of Betty's thesis is not included in Part One, but forms the basis of the bibliography for the volume as a whole, as does its glossary. Bracketed references giving the year in which Betty completed her study have been added to sections of the text written in the present tense. Additionally, a number of minor adjustments and corrections have been made to quotations cited in the text, bringing them into line with the original documents (especially in a section of Part I of the thesis featuring extensive quotations from NUAUS publicity reports on the VGS). In the process of editing the appendices to Betty's thesis, fonts and formatting were standardised; data contained in text boxes (signatures, official insignia, etc) was not reproduced.

---

4   Purdey, *From Vienna to Yogyakarta*, p. 53.
5   Discussions on this topic can be found in Purdey, *From Vienna to Yogyakarta*; see also Margaret Coffey's interview with Betty Feith, Ailsa Zainuddin, Don Anderson, Frank Engel, Alan Hunt and others, "In Memory of Herb Feith", *Encounter*, Radio National, 9 March 2003.

A number of relatively minor changes were made to the narrative in the interests of clarity of argument and narrative flow. These changes were in the nature of revising a word, phrase or sentence here and there, relocating a sentence or sentences from the main text into a footnote and *vice versa*, adding or removing paragraph breaks, and revising some of the work's titles. Text about the church backgrounds and humanitarian motivations that were not uncommon among the early volunteers was one area subject to such revision. A number of sentences contained in Betty's thesis abstract were included in the introduction in "Putting in a Stitch or Two". Finally, some editing was done to ensure consistency of spelling and grammar throughout the narrative, all the while respecting Betty's distinctive form of grammatical argumentation, involving her use of inverted commas, capitalisation and underlining/italics to highlight particular words and phrases. Throughout the editorial process, changes to the manuscript, especially regarding revisions of any substance, were first discussed with and approval sought from Betty.

"Putting in a Stitch or Two" is followed by the full text of Jo Kurnianingrat's opinion piece, "An Indonesian Opinion on the VGS", originally published in *Djembatan*, Vol 2, No 4, Special Issue, September 1959. Editorial additions to the text are enclosed in square brackets.

THESIS

AN EPISODE IN EDUCATION FOR INTERNATIONAL UNDERSTANDING

The Volunteer Graduate Scheme in Indonesia
1950–63
"Putting in a Stitch or Two"

by Betty Feith

Contents

Contents 11
Introduction 12
Part I: Origins and Ethos of the Volunteer Graduate Scheme 16
Part II: The Volunteer Experience – Problems and Perspectives 48
Conclusion 61
Appendices 68

Introduction

This study narrates a history of the Volunteer Graduate Scheme from its initial planning in 1950 until its administration by the Overseas Service Bureau in 1963. Under this Scheme, which was run under the auspices of the National Union of Australian University Students (NUAUS), graduates from Australian tertiary institutions worked in Indonesia on local salary schedules. The majority were teachers in tertiary institutions. The philosophy of the Volunteer Graduate Scheme was one of sympathetic identification with Indonesian nationalism. Its sponsors pursued goals of racial equality and justice towards Asian nationals, and the teaching of these ideals to fellow Australians.

The aim of this study is *not* to examine the influence and effect of the Volunteer Graduate Scheme (VGS) upon any educational or social institution in Indonesia, or upon Indonesian people, least of all the colleagues and friends of those involved. Such an aim is beyond the scope of this exercise. In any case, that aim would more appropriately be the task of an Indonesian. An Indonesian researcher would be better able to assess the Scheme, as one small entity among the many and varied educational and social projects implemented in Indonesia from the early fifties, involving the presence and contribution of many foreigners from a range of aid institutions, educational foundations, and government bodies.

The purpose of this study is much smaller: it is to narrate a history of the Volunteer Graduate Scheme in Indonesia from its beginnings in 1950 until 1963 when its funding, administration and the organisational arrangements for the selection of future volunteers were merged into the overall responsibility of the newly established Overseas Service Bureau (OSB). The Scheme then formally ceased to exist. Its successor, which became known as Australian Volunteers Abroad (AVA), still sends volunteers to Indonesia via the Overseas Service Bureau, but they are a small proportion of the annual total number of volunteers leaving Australia. [1984]

This study outlines the chronology of the events, developments, and plans which brought the Scheme into being. Its history is seen as falling into four distinct periods. The first was that of the initial planning (1950–1953). The second (1954–1957) was a period of rapid expansion after the Scheme's official acceptance by both governments. The third period (1957–1960) was that of an active publicity campaign to promote the Scheme and increase the numbers of potential volunteers. This period saw the publication of *Djembatan*, the quarterly journal published from Melbourne by the Volunteer Graduate

Association for Indonesia (VGA), the formal body established in 1957 for the purpose of administering the VGS. *Djembatan* sought not only to maintain the morale of volunteers and increase the interest and sense of involvement of their circle of friends and acquaintances, but also to explain and analyse the aims and basis of the Scheme, and to justify its stance. The fourth period (1960–1963), that of assessment and reconstitution, is dealt with only very briefly, as the events of the early sixties led to a new chapter in the history of aid projects – that of the establishment of the Overseas Service Bureau and Australian Volunteers Abroad, which sees the whole of the "Third World" as its concern. The contributions and points of view of volunteers serving under AVA after 1963 have not been included in this study.

In the first part of this study, the philosophy and ethos of the Scheme as developed by the first volunteers is discussed, and the process described by which the ideas and attitudes of the "founders" were transmitted to later arrivals and to a network of friends and relatives in Australia. The basic stances of the early volunteer graduates involved sympathetic identification with the goals and aspirations of Indonesian nationalism. One key element of this was the need to establish racial and financial equality not only as a valid mode for Westerners working in Asia, but as a more valid code than others. Another was the importance of demonstrating, by their own practical alternatives, the limits of the European-centric view held by many fellow-Australians. Particular reference is made in this study to official statements expressing this radically different and innovative philosophy of aid-giving, which its authors believed to be characteristic of the Scheme and which was seen to be as important as any practical aid which might be given.

The development of a "consensus", or "common front", in the thinking and attitudes about the Scheme, and about the philosophy of aid in general, among the Scheme's Jakarta and Melbourne Committees from 1951 to 1963, is discussed in some detail. This was possible because I was personally involved at the policy-making and administrative level first in Melbourne from 1950 to 1953 and as a volunteer from 1954 to 1956, then as a member of the Melbourne Committee from 1962 until 1964.

The second part of the study attempts to discuss major problems faced by the volunteers – particularly the problem of finding suitable work in sufficient quantities to satisfy people imbued with the Puritan work ethic not only from their secondary and tertiary education, but in some cases, also imbibed from family backgrounds of service to church, state, or community. The problem of culture shock is also discussed. This problem is seen in part as the discovery that the Puritan work ethic was not necessarily shared by all Indonesian colleagues! The problem of coping with feelings of guilt and a sense of failure, inevitable for all volunteers at certain times as they perceived the gap between the ideals of the Scheme and the reality of their own personal lives, tastes and preferences is also discussed in some detail.

Ivan Southall's contribution is then briefly discussed. My conclusion attempts to identify the main influence of the Scheme: not in Indonesia, but in Australia, in the actions taken by returned volunteers, both personally and in groups and organisations, the aims of which were to change attitudes within Australia.

The primary source material for this study consists partly of personal letters, collections of newsletters, and reports written by the first participants of the Scheme from 1950 until the early sixties. It also includes personal letters, official "business" letters and reports from Jim Webb, for some years the honorary secretary of the Volunteer Graduate Association, and then full-time director of the Overseas Service Bureau. I wish to acknowledge also the generosity of Mrs McMichael in making available the entire collection of her son Oliver's personal letters and his "Indonesia file" after his death in 1978. Oliver McMichael, known as Ollie, was one of the first three volunteers in Indonesia. On hearing of this collection, Gwenda Rodda, another of the initial volunteers, also kindly collected her remaining letters and papers and forwarded them to me. Additionally, Ailsa Zainu'ddin also made available on loan her complete set of Bulletins – letters intended for a wide circle of family and friends, written from the start of Ailsa's first journey to Jakarta as a volunteer in 1954 through her period of working in Jakarta, and some subsequent visits. Most of the issues of *Djembatan* from 1957 to 1963 are still in my possession. [1984]

When searching through old files I found to my surprise that some of the original letters written by me in the early fifties in my capacity as the first secretary of the Melbourne Committee from 1950 are still extant. Many of my husband's letters, written first from Indonesia, then while in the United States from 1957 to 1960, and later in Canberra, Jakarta, and Melbourne, until 1965, have been kept and were available for checking and re-checking. Also copies of correspondence between Jim Webb and members of the Scheme in Indonesia which were sent to the Melbourne Committee for members' information and reference have been kept and are still in my possession.

It was only after having got this study well under way that I became aware of the difficulties imposed by the nature of my role in the enterprise which is the subject of this study, and by my relationship to the other key figures, including my husband, Herb Feith. The role of "participant observer" is a new one to me. Thus I was not initially aware of the inhibiting effect that the re-perusal and study of this material would have upon me even thirty years later. For fear of undue bias and clouded judgment, I find myself in danger of continually retreating into the ironic "after all we were all very young" stance which is neither fair to the concept of the Scheme, nor to the Indonesian administrators who trusted its advocates and members and became its staunch supporters. Some of these supporters are now dead, and some are very elderly and in poor health. It is unfortunate that this account does not do justice to *their* part in the story.

Another limitation of this study is, of course, that it represents the partial view of *one* participant observer. Inevitably this view is Melbourne–Jakarta-centric. Appendix A, a list of all volunteers who served under the Scheme from 1951 until 1965, shows that some volunteers, particularly those originally from states other than Victoria, corresponded regularly with the Melbourne Committee during their terms in Indonesia, contributed to *Djembatan*, and after their return to take up new jobs and in some cases to start new families remained in contact with the Melbourne Committee for a short time only. A future researcher would need to renew those contacts where possible. Perhaps upon investigation it will be found that ex-volunteers in other centres in and outside Australia, along with families and friends and perhaps colleagues, students, and fellow class-mates, have, as in Melbourne, joined with academics and other professionals in attempting to strengthen those webs and bridges of relationships and understandings of perceptions and empathies, with communities "there" and "here".

Any future study would also need to include the involvements of volunteer graduates serving in various parts of Indonesia since 1963. It would need to include also the participation of those who began their stay in Indonesia as volunteers, and through matrimony, long-term professional duties, or both, have become long-term residents of Indonesia, though maintaining close ties with Australia. Their insights and their willingness through the years to share their homes, their time and their concerns with succeeding volunteers, students, teachers, researchers, aid personnel and also "ordinary tourists", have enriched the "Indonesian experience" for many.

The correspondence, both private and official, and the various reports which I have used in this project are a rich and varied primary source for any future student. I hope that my introductory study will form a useful starting point.

Part I

Origins and Ethos of the Volunteer Graduate Scheme

In August 1950 the World University Service (WUS) Assembly met in Bombay, and John Bayly, then still an architecture student, and the Chairman of WUS in Australia, was one of the two Australian delegates.[1] This meeting and his involvement in it turned out to be pivotal in the events leading up to the formation of the Scheme, and indeed a milestone in the history of aid programmes in education between Australia and Third World countries. Bayly explained the significance of the Assembly some years later as follows:

> The most important item on the agenda was the re-orientation of international student relief work, and the result of the deliberation was, from the Australian point of view, a shift of interest from the programmes of the World Student Relief Organization to the broader field of World University Service.[2]

He commented on the controversy over where priorities should lie in future: "material relief, in goods and money, was then as now a basic necessity", but members of the Assembly became convinced that something more was needed, with "education for international understanding" being seen as part of that "something more". Some receiving groups among student delegates were wary of programmes that could be interpreted as charity. One delegate went on record as saying "We don't want boxes of boots. Teach us how to make them for ourselves".

Bayly identified what to him years later was the most important contribution of the conference:

> *"Education for international understanding"* is a somewhat nebulous idea, but its expression in the organisation of meeting between people from different parts of the world can generate a sense of identification with a real international community.

---

1 The second delegate was Alan Hunt, who later became a Victorian Liberal Party politician. John Bayly later became a lecturer in Town Planning, Architecture School, University of Melbourne.

2 John Bayly, "Foreword – Full Circle", *Djembatan*, Vol 2, No 4, Special Issue, September 1959, p. 2. *Djembatan* was the name of the more-or-less quarterly newsletter of the Volunteer Graduate Association which began publication in 1957, edited by A.G. Zainu'ddin. This Special Issue was funded by UNESCO and W.U.S.

> For me, as for anyone privileged to take part in such a gathering, *this sense of identification* was the most challenging outcome of the Bombay Assembly ... Once, over a cup of tea or at a street corner (I forget just where), an Indonesian delegate, spoke to us of the value that could accrue if technical experts in underdeveloped lands were able to enter into the whole life of the society in which they worked, not merely contributing their knowledge but committing themselves to the solution of problems with which they had become identified. This could be help to self-help at its best. (emphasis mine)[3]

The concept of a Volunteer Graduate Scheme developed from a small group of students at Melbourne University who heard John Bayly's report immediately after his return. This concept of equality and sharing; that of sharing work skills and work experience on the same rates of pay as local Indonesian Government public servants, became the basis of the Scheme. Right from this first beginning, this concept was seen quite deliberately and self-consciously as a "New Direction" for a relationship between Australians and people of non-Western societies who had recently won political independence, and who were at this time beginning to express, though polite and muted the tone, a feeling of rejection of any concept involving their area becoming the objects of paternalistic planning, no matter how well-intentioned the planners. Ibu Jo Kurnianingrat, one of the senior educational administrators in the Ministry of Education of Indonesia in the early fifties, when directly asked to give her opinion, expressed this rejection perhaps more firmly than most would have been prepared to do publicly:

> To be frank, we were very hesitant about taking in two foreigners without knowing much about them ... there is often so much misunderstanding between Indonesians and foreign "experts" that foreign aid, which I'm convinced is offered with the best of intentions, can become quite a burden, especially when people have the bad taste of trying to impress upon us how valuable this aid is, whether in manpower or in money. It is often forgotten that we certainly cannot have fought for our independence to be dictated to again in building up the

---

[3] Bayly, "Full Circle", p. 2. Bayly's final comment is of particular significance: "The seed for this enterprise (i.e. the Volunteer Graduate Scheme) was sown within W.U.S. Many people, most of whom may never have heard of W.U.S., have brought it to fruition. Now, in this record of what has been achieved so far, W.U.S. has been able to play a part in telling the story. The original idea has made a full circle. If this publication sows one or two more seeds, who can say what may grow out of them?"

country, no matter how well meant this dictatorship may be. It would also be nice if clever people tried to remember that we are not entirely bereft of common sense and experience, and that we at least know the conditions and the needs of our own country, though the majority of us have not got the proper training for our jobs.[4]

There was a sense of excitement among the first members of the Melbourne Committee emerging from the discussion and planning resulting from John Bayly's report.[5] The committee saw as one of its first tasks, that of publicising the idea as a possibility, at the forthcoming conferences of the National Union of Australian University Students (NUAUS) and the Australian Student Christian Movement (ASCM) in December and January. As war-time travel restrictions had forced cessation of inter-state gatherings, these immediately post-war federal student conferences were big annual events in the life of student organisations, attracting large numbers of students from universities and teachers' training colleges in every state. The idea of the Scheme, its possible development, and strategies for future implementation were fully discussed at both these gatherings during conference time by the small group so far involved, and there was an enthusiastic response particularly from students attending the ASCM conference.[6]

Through initially chance personal contacts which later developed into regular correspondence and personal friendship, three individuals managed to get promises of work within three Indonesian Government ministries

---

4   Jo Kurnianingrat, "An Indonesian Opinion on the V.G.S.", *Djembatan*, Vol 2, No 4, Special Issue, September 1959, p. 15. Ibu Jo Kurnianingrat first heard about the Scheme from Gwenda Rodda whom she met by chance, since Gwenda lived for a time in a room at the back of the pharmacy where Miss Kurnianingrat was a regular customer! She was the deputy head of the English Language Teaching Inspectorate of the Indonesian Ministry of Education in the early fifties, and became a close friend of several of the Australians employed by her Ministry. She then completed postgraduate studies in English literature and language at Cornell University. She has maintained contact through the years and now lives in retirement not far from the University of Indonesia campus, where she taught till the end of her professional career. Jo Kurnianingrat, along with other young women named by George Kahin, had played a critical role in the national struggle against the Dutch police action in December 1948. See George McTurnan Kahin, *Nationalism and Revolution in Indonesia* (Ithaca, New York: Cornell University Press, 1952), pp. 337–39, 397. Professor Kahin is one of the few *Western* historians to have acknowledged the existence of women in the nationalist independence movement 1945–1950. It was freely acknowledged by Indonesian chroniclers. [1984]

5   [For more on the formation, membership and activities of this committee, see Jemma Purdey, *From Vienna to Yogyakarta: The Life of Herb Feith*, pp. 75–79.]

6   "The Origins of the Overseas Service Bureau – An Address by Frank Engel – Australian Volunteers Abroad Briefing, Jan. 1983", p. 2.

on the understanding that their positions as employees of the Indonesian Government would be regularised later. Their status was seen by themselves and their respective employers as an *ad hoc* individual arrangement pending the establishment of agreements between the two governments. The details were to be worked out in the future. Herb Feith left Melbourne in July 1951 with a scholarship from the Political Science Department, University of Melbourne, and with permission from Professor McMahon Ball to work as an Indonesian Government public servant in the Ministry of Information, while enrolled as an MA student. He had been able to secure the promise of employment as the result of a lengthy correspondence with Molly Bondan, a Sydney woman married to a senior administrator in the Labor Ministry in Jakarta, who herself worked in the Ministry of Information.[7] As the Jakarta bureaucracy at senior level was not so rigid then as it later became, and the senior people were more accessible, Herb's informal contact and discussion with Dr Leimena, Minister for Health, and other senior administrators enabled Gwenda Rodda and Oliver McMichael to follow within twelve months. Both paid their own fares with the understanding that the agreement currently under negotiation between the two governments would be ratified and would result in the refund of their fares and eventually the payment of their fares home![8]

By 1954 the Scheme was officially recognised by both governments, and its conditions were clearly set down: graduates were to work for Indonesian employers in places nominated by Indonesian requests, on local public servant rates of pay. The Indonesian Government, through the employing ministries, was to be responsible for accommodation, as well as pay – the usual responsibility at that time.[9] The Australian Government was to pay

---

7   John Coast's *Recruit to Revolution* (London: Christophers, 1952) gives an early account of Molly Bondan. The early correspondence between the volunteer graduates is full of references to visits to her house, and appreciative acceptance of her advice. She was a woman of very sharply expressed views and with a very strong personality, and some of the younger girls amongst the volunteers were rather in awe of her. A much later account can be found in Ivan Southall's *Indonesia Face to Face* (Melbourne: Lansdowne Press, 1965), with a photograph.

8   The funds in fact were forthcoming just in time for Ollie McMichael to clear his debts before flying home to spend Christmas with his recently widowed mother after his time of 18 months. His last few letters home are full of his anxiety as to whether the money would come through in time. A copy of an early letter to O. McMichael from the NUAUS office, 19 September 1951, is included in Appendix B.

9   At that time, the finding of accommodation was probably a bigger challenge to employing ministries than finding the modest cash monthly salaries. Accommodation of *any* kind was extremely short, and both the Feiths and Professor Kahin had to make their own arrangements, briefly, in October 1954, when the

the fares and an initial clothing allowance and bicycle allowance, and committed funds for any emergency such as illness requiring hospitalisation. It was expected that volunteers would work in Indonesia for about two years.[10]

Philosophy and Ethos of the Scheme

Although the basic philosophy of the Scheme was discussed, aired, formulated and reformulated over a number of years, it did not change substantially from its initial formulation. An important strand was a sense of shared pride in the progress of the newly independent country, and further, a desire to be part of, and to share in, that nation-building albeit as short-term guests. The early letters home show not only acceptance of the patriotic feeling and indeed nationalist emphasis of their colleagues and acquaintances, but enthusiastic endorsement:

> ... when they see you are not another "colonial" they become terrifically friendly and will laugh at you in sheer delight ... there's not much anti-Dutch feeling, and thousands of Dutch still work here undisturbed.
>
> But they have bitter memories of the colonial time and they are always delighted to hear you are an Australian, and not Dutch or American ...
>
> ... The revolutionary spirit is another thing. Every Indonesian I've met has a pride and enthusiasm and faith in the revolution and the new society. If only they could be shown how to put it into practice. They are desperately keen to build a free, prosperous and independent country. Politics are taken very seriously indeed ... freedom here is very real ... this revolutionary spirit was only started by the bloodshed, and is now a most wonderful thing. It's a desire for revolution in standards of living, health, education, and they are determined to be democratic ... Still the people greet each other *"Merdeka"* meaning "Freedom"! The national anthem is most inspiring and has a thrilling tone.[11]

    Ministry of Information was unable to organise anything at the end of a three-month period of temporary accommodation in a Ministry house. It was a time when Indonesian families of public servants, with numerous small children, were squeezed into very inadequate rooming houses, old hotels, and ex-colonial army barracks, so the volunteers were hardly in a position to complain!

10 A complete list of volunteers from 1951–1963 has been compiled – see Appendix A. Sometimes personal circumstances necessitated earlier returns, sometimes illness. Ollie McMichael returned earlier partly because of his mother's recent loss. Ian Doig developed an incapacitating illness which left him with a permanent limp.

11 Letter from Ollie McMichael to his parents, 9 July 1952. This unguarded expression of enthusiasm was part of a private letter and was never included in any of the printed in-

Along with the sense of enthusiastic nationalism conveyed in this letter home by volunteer Ollie McMichael is a belief that time is short, and that everything must be done quickly. There is a sense of fervent conviction about this expression of fear that time is running out. A note of confident, even arrogant Australian nationalism is also detectable.

> But this revolutionary spirit might die unless the government can do something about the economic position and the education problem. There is still terrible poverty ... there is still disease and terrible illiteracy. And if the people lost hope they'll turn to the Communists – like China. The need is for 1/ Economic aid without strings – they *won't* tolerate military [indecipherable] strings. 2/ Technical help – free or cheap like us. 3/ Understanding and friendship from *Australia*. No country matters more to Indonesia than we do. Britain and Holland – No – colonial countries. America – No – imperialist. Russia – No – imperialist. If Australia fails – they'll turn to CHINA. ... The time limit is generally agreed to be three to five years – if no war or world economic collapse comes before then! Gosh it's important.[12]

The above comments were never intended for public consumption. However, the message of these private letters home was transmitted to formal and "semi-official" publicity about the Scheme which was mailed out to

---

formation about the Scheme later distributed by NUAUS. Ibu Jo Kurnianingrat would probably have accused its writer of paternalism just as arrogant as that of the Dutch administrators of an earlier era! The letter is quoted without reference to its accuracy or lack thereof, but as a typical example of the state of mind of the writer! It should also be noted that Ollie had been in the country less than two weeks at the time of writing this third letter, and that his command of the Indonesian language would have still been very basic. However, he can be seen as reflecting the views of Mollie [Molly] Bondan and Herb Feith, as well as that of his own section head, who had studied in Sydney, and of other English-speaking public servants, to whom he had been introduced. Dr Johannes Leimena was probably the most influential and most keenly interested of those senior Cabinet Ministers with whom Herb Feith had been in contact since his arrival in 1951, although Dr Roem of Foreign Affairs had shown a friendly interest in the initial stages. Dr Leimena gave Ollie and Gwenda Rodda an interview on their second day, and talked to them about the potential importance of the Scheme and of young Australians as "ambassadors of goodwill". [For Ollie McMichael's letters home from Indonesia, as cited in this volume, see "Ollie McMichael Correspondence", 1952–1982 [2002], Papers of Ailsa Thomson Zainuddin, privately held.]

12   Letter from Ollie McMichael to his parents, 9 July 1952. Ollie quoted in the same letter, a comment from the Australian *Chargé d'Affaires*: "If only the people at home realized this they would empty their pockets to help! Because if Indonesia fails, Australia is sunk!" The timing of this letter, during the Cold War, should be noted.

interested enquirers and available freely on university campuses, from 1952 onwards. One such report reads:

> This country *has gone through* and is going through *revolution* – democratic national revolution. The revolution didn't finish when the fighting stopped – it moved into a higher realm, and you find it here now as social revolution. You find creative thinking surging up in newly-won freedom – bringing political idealism, cultural renaissance, and a thirst for education. You find a determination to progress independently towards peace, security, prosperity. But you still find the remnants of the colonial consciousness. And you find irresponsibility. These two different pictures are real, and you find the two thought patterns often alongside one another – or even in the one person.[13]

The significance of the Independence Day celebrations was not lost on the new arrivals:

> I've never seen so many flags in my life. Every tiny *kampong* produced dozens of flags ... red and white flags – the city was just festooned in two colours. Bikes, *betjaks*, cars, buses even *trains* were flying flags. Ceremonial gates were erected everywhere ... we had a ceremony of hoisting the flag on a new flag pole [at the Airport Technical School] (erected the day before!) It was entirely organised by the boys. First a speech by the president of the as-yet embryonic Student Union ... then the solemn reading of the Proclamation – the hoisting of the flag, the National Anthem, silence for the heroes of the revolution. Then I was asked to speak in English which I did for a few minutes, and speeches followed by various class leaders ... each speech was started with the revolutionary greeting *"Merdeka!"* (Freedom) It was very impressive and had a sense of reality that I've only noticed occasionally in Australian national ceremonies (probably the things which Anzacs feel on Anzac Day). It's unique to be here during these first years following a country's liberation. It is still very real – the sense of achievement and freedom. (Ten more years and it will be conventional I guess).[14]

Another important aspect of the enthusiasm of the first volunteers, and in the building of the "ethos" of the Scheme, was a sense of being part of the

---

13 "P.E.G.A.W.A.I. (Plan for the Employment of Graduates from Australia to Work as Indonesians) i.e. Graduate Employment Scheme for Indonesia – Report to Intending Pegawais under P.E.G.A.W.A.I. (pegawai – employee)", August 1952.

14 Letter from Ollie McMichael to his parents and Don, 18 August 1952.

making of the history of a new nation, of being part of the "first act" – of laying the foundations of something very important. Many events and situations contributed to the absorption, and, later, the reinforcement of this heady idea: for instance the fact that busy Cabinet Ministers such as Dr Leimena found time to talk to them at length in their first few days in the country – about the possibilities of the Scheme, what the Indonesian administrators hoped to gain from it, and what the volunteers could do in "nation-building". Even President Sukarno himself once took time off to talk to newly arrived volunteers at almost a moment's notice![15]

Many of the administrative heads of the newly formed Indonesian ministries in Jakarta were genuinely dedicated idealists, and were not at all embarrassed to break into patriotic and nationalistic "national upbuilding" discourse, quite unselfconsciously, as part of their everyday conversation. Their sincerity and zeal about seeking the resources needed to implement their goals, and their apparent willingness to fit these young Australians into their plans for "building the world anew" – all this inevitably made an impact on people still very recently embarked on their professional careers, and used mainly to hearing the typical monosyllabic and business-like approach of even the most conscientious Australian administrators.[16]

The transmission of this sense of making history, of being on the stage for the Opening Scene, began with the very first letters home. These letters were later edited and put into the form of reports and newsletters by the first three volunteers, working together in committee, mainly on Sunday afternoons in Jakarta. They were then typed up at the NUAUS office to be given to "interested persons and enquirers" with the imprint of NUAUS, so attaining a "semi-official" status.

The first report gave a brief account of the settling in of Ollie McMichael and Gwenda Rodda, each from a different capital city although they had travelled together on the same ship, the *Roma*, paying their own way.[17] The detail given about "how we managed to actually arrive" strikes a quaint

---

15 "Lemonade with the President", Noela Motum, *Djembatan*, Vol 1, No 1, July 1957, p. 2.

16 The writer still remembers her disappointment when the first piece of information offered her by the Education Department Careers Officer in Melbourne in 1949 was about the extent of the future salary and the rapidity of rise in pay and promotion!

17 See "P.E.G.A.W.A.I. (Plan for the Employment of Graduates from Australia to Work as Indonesians) i.e. Graduate Employment Scheme for Indonesia – Report to Intending Pegawais under P.E.G.A.W.A.I. (pegawai – employee)", August 1952, p. 1. This clumsy heading was dropped when the original newsletter, slightly altered, was published as part of the larger 21-page "Account of the Scheme and a Letter from Indonesia to Interested Volunteers" (first edition 1953; second 1954; third 1956).

note to readers of later decades used only to ever more rapid air transport, and to tourists freed from the former necessity of obtaining visas for short-term visits to Indonesia. It is understandable now only in view of the horror stories circulating at the time in the Australian press, on the difficulties of even getting to Jakarta, and coping with its celebrated problems once there.[18]

Then followed a brief survey of the people, language, politics, religion, racial problems, education, music, health, Jakarta, housing, food, laundry, servants, accommodation, transport and traffic, climate, cost of living, working conditions, personal problems, and categories of people thought by their informants to be needed at once – and all this in nine closely-typed single-spaced duplicated pages. The final paragraph reads as follows:

> The rewards of work here are many – in the warmth of friendship – in the interests you find in this different society, in the music, the colour. But above all you find a sense of fulfilment. The feeling of being needed, of being useful, can be most satisfying. You will meet Cabinet Ministers (sic) and discuss all sorts of problems with them, and you may be laying the first foundations in your field for this huge new country. This sense of service and creation can be exhilaratingly tangible and absolutely real. You may be faced with great temptations due to great power, but if you can retain your identity with the people around you, your life will be one of the most satisfying and integrated you could choose. History is being made here, and you can help make it.[19]

---

18 See the first chapter of Southall, *Indonesia Face to Face* for an entertaining account of this problem. See also *Indonesia Face to Face*, pp. 15–17 and 112–13.

19 The first draft included the exuberant words "and even change it". These were omitted (perhaps with the modesty of second thoughts) in the version first sent out to interested volunteers. See "P.E.G.A.W.A.I. (Plan for the Employment of Graduates from Australia to Work as Indonesians) i.e. Graduate Employment Scheme for Indonesia – Report to Intending Pegawais [etc]", August 1952, p. 9. Later volunteers stressed this sense of privilege at "being in on the ground floor" of the building of a New Society. See for instance the following statement by Hugh Reeves: "At times one felt depressed by the overcrowding, poor equipment, and administrative inefficiency, but always there was the feeling that this was only the beginning, as well as the satisfaction of helping even in a very small way to make a better future for Indonesia". *Djembatan*, Vol 2, No 4, Special Issue, September 1959, p. 8. See also a statement by Harry Whitfield: "At times I was disheartened by the slow progress made in obtaining equipment and building up laboratories; then I would think of the words of an Indonesian friend: 'Harry, it's precisely because there are so many frustrations, lack of administrative experience and financial difficulties that people like you are needed in Indonesia'. Indeed, in

For Herb Feith the question of the survival of political democratic institutions in the Western sense was particularly important; he was fascinated to be in the wings of the political stage, watching the drama of the creation of a new society with the possibility of having an occasional small part on stage or, to use his own metaphor, to watch the fabric of a new society being woven, and having a part in the making of the garment:

> Will democracy prove transplantable? Will the social servility bred of feudalism and colonialism be broken? What are the chances of the third force policy as a means of keeping the peace? Will a new culture emerge from the combination of the traditional religious culture of the villages, and the Western culture of the Dutch-educated revolutionary intellectuals? Or how will the more or less static village culture respond to the impact of the dynamic new industrialism? Will the emancipatory nationalism become aggressive and chauvinistic or will its internationally conscious elements gain the ascendancy? What will be the result of the meeting of Christianity and Islam? Will the gigantic tasks in health and social affairs be able to be carried through and universal compulsory education be enacted? I could go on listing many more such fascinating problems. It's just [fine] being here and watching the various strands coming through in the fabric, *and putting in a stitch or two oneself where one can.*[20] (emphasis mine)

Linked with all this interest in observing, watching, and participating is a strong moral note. The early volunteers were optimistic believers in the new Scheme rather than detached scholarly observers, and they firmly believed that people who came with the "wrong attitude" would be better not to have come at all. They were also quite confident that they knew what the "right attitudes" were. Only certain qualities were suitable for volunteers who wanted to "put a stitch or two in" to the fabric of the new society. Herb Feith, for instance, wrote:

> The crucial question would be – would you come here with a desire to help, with idealism, with an attitude which enables you to overcome

---

retrospect, it was a privilege to have worked with such an idealistic, enthusiastic group of students and professors and to have had some part in helping to build a university which surely will be a leading university of Southeast Asia". *Djembatan* Vol 2, No 1, September 1958, p. 11.

20 "Report by H. Feith to Students and Graduates Interested in the NUAUS Scheme for Graduate Employment in Indonesia", September 1951, p. 7. This report was distributed by NUAUS.

personal difficulties and inconveniences? Everybody to whom I have talked about our scheme has stressed just this question. Naturally you wouldn't come here for idealistic reasons alone, but you'd have to have an idealistic streak in you somewhere I think, some "hope for the future" as one of the men in the Ministry of Health put it. You'd have to be free from any colour superiority notions, obviously. And you'd have to have a desire to give help (and instruction too perhaps) on a basis of equality without taints of paternalism. I think too you ought to have *political* idealism and interest in politics. Without that I doubt whether you'd be able to identify yourselves at all with the young intellectual nationalists you'd be working with. The people I've talked to are very anxious about this side of it because they say that if just a few of our group were unhappy here and unable to adapt themselves and to overcome the practical difficulties by their own attitude towards them, the whole scheme would be a failure. There have been cases, or at least one case, where a foreigner has been unhappy working for the Indonesian government and left it before his time was up. This obviously shouldn't happen again.[21]

---

21 "Report by H. Feith to Students and Graduates Interested in the NUAUS Scheme for Graduate Employment in Indonesia", September 1951, p. 7. The volunteer graduate who is referred to in this quote was a certain Stan Cory, who had appeared without warning, in Jakarta, having read something in an NUAUS newsletter, and had asked Herb to find him a job. Herb and various senior ministry staff, including Sugarda of the Ministry of Education, went to some trouble for him. Then Stan Cory left after a very short time, causing annoyance and embarrassment and resulting in Sugarda later being initially unwilling to consider any more Australians. This was in 1951, before the arrival of anyone from Australia who could be regarded as having been sponsored by NUAUS or the Australian Government, so perhaps no great harm to the Scheme had been done. But this early "failure" cast a long shadow, and there is no doubt that later arrivals under the Scheme felt under strong pressure to "give it a go", even when ill and when no real work seemed available. Ian Doig's case comes to mind. His illness, combined with the lack of suitable work, would have made it easy for him to have obtained an "honourable" early retirement, but with stoic grim determination and wry humour he "stuck it out". All the early volunteers must have felt that the future success of the Scheme depended very much on them, and at times it must have seemed a heavy burden. Ian Doig commented wryly: "One of the basic aims of the Scheme is to give technical assistance … but frankly I found this aspect of my stay the least satisfactory … in my case, as an industrial chemist, I hastened to Indonesia in the hope that I would be in time to help in the construction of a proposed pharmaceutical factory, and that was the last I heard of the project – another Indonesian plan that failed to materialize. So when I arrived I was merely an embarrassment to the man I was seconded to, and he passed me on to a medical research institute where my training was of little use. Eventually, however, I extricated myself from there and found satisfying work designing pilot

The evangelical moral tone fitted the themes: the need for Australians to adapt to non-Western society and culture, the importance of genuine racial equality. The significance of the Scheme in its rejection of "Experts' Salaries" with their drain on scarce foreign exchange, of its rejection of the usual paraphernalia of Experts' conditions, particularly special housing – these themes are recounted again and again.

Indonesian society is seen as more tolerant than Australian society:

> Then there is next to no racial feeling here. The explanation given [to me] is that this is due to the long co-existence of different racial groups but it doesn't altogether satisfy me. Still whatever the explanation the fact is real and significant. In your work you see Dutchmen, Indo-Europeans, Chinese and Indonesians mixing completely freely and naturally. Where there is antagonism it is only on political grounds inasmuch as one racial group identifies itself with a particular political tendency. But this antagonism is definitely not felt on the level of personal relations.
>
> ... And again there is here a wonderful degree of religious tolerance. ... it is an undoubted fact and quite striking to one coming from a place as full of petty sectarian suspicions as Australia.
>
> ... be very chary of the sources of information about Indonesia available in Australia – some of it is so misleading as to look more like wickedness than stupidity. Beware particularly of people who've spent one horrid week in a Djakarta hotel, five days of it mucking about with the inefficient harbor or airport or immigration authorities![22]

The early volunteers believed it particularly important that they present a counter-view, an alternative, to the stereotype popularly accepted in Australia at the time. They themselves had been warned about the possibility of being stabbed in the back by *betjak* boys in a dark street, or being robbed of all their worldly goods at the port, or of even worse fates likely to befall travellers.[23]

---

    plant equipment for the manufacture of dextrin and rayon. ... a visiting American journalist, when asked what Indonesia needed most, replied 'Ulcers!' It may take hours to contact a person by telephone, weeks to receive a letter from within Indonesia, and years to obtain some vital piece of equipment". *Djembatan*, Vol 2, No 2, December 1958, p. 7.

22   "Report by H. Feith to Students and Graduates Interested in the NUAUS Scheme for Graduate Employment in Indonesia", September 1951, pp. 8, 9.

23   See Southall, *Indonesia Face to Face*, pp. 145–147 and 17.

... I'm convinced that Indonesia's good name abroad is being made by people who come and live here for anything more than three months, and being lost or destroyed by those who pop in for three days. So it is essential that they meet somebody who can explain certain peculiarities (such as the atrocious customs procedures which some folk encounter...[24]

As part of "doing their bit" to provide an alternative view to the more aware and intelligent tourist who might be calling in for only a couple of days *en route* to Europe, volunteers living in Jakarta in the early and mid-fifties would go to enormous lengths to meet ships and take their friends and acquaintances (including "friends of friends", who had perhaps written anxious letters asking could they please be met at Tanjung Priok, the major port some weary miles out of the city). Sometimes volunteers would even obtain leave with the blessing of section heads and come to Jakarta especially to meet a ship and take a tourist around Jakarta on a quick guided tour! Alas, such plans sometimes came to nought, because some shipping lines (the Italian line was one) were so fearful of these travellers' tales and the anxieties aroused thereby among some intending tourists, that they were found more than once to change their advertised route at the last minute, not calling at Jakarta at all, or if stopping, staying only for a few hours, instead of the advertised two days. If they had travellers disembarking, then of course they had to stop, but sometimes very briefly and sometimes, as it were, they surreptitiously crept in to Tanjung Priok a couple of days before (or after!) the advertised date of arrival, foiling would-be tourists and intending welcome committees of new volunteers alike![25]

It must also be remembered that the moral tones and moral themes of financial and racial equality, and the need to provide guidelines for an alternative method for Westerners to work in Indonesia from that followed by "Experts" were partly at least learned by the first few volunteers from their Indonesian Department heads, some of whom had suffered at the hands of paternalistic administrators and Western bureaucrats in charge of aid arrangements between Indonesia and Western countries in the early fifties. One such said:

---

24 Letter from Ollie McMichael to his mother, 3 August 1953.
25 A. G. Zainu'ddin, *Bulletin* No. 9, 5 February 1955, entitled "Travellers' Tales" and written especially to reassure intending travellers.

> Do I sound very bitter and aggressive? It is not meant that way at all. I do welcome all people who want to help us build up the country; there is still so much to be done, and there is a job for everybody – however, the cooperation should be based on mutual appreciation. Of course I do realise that the agencies who give us support want to see their money and staff used as efficiently as possible, which may account for their tendency to "guide" us. I am sure that everything could be settled in a much more satisfactory way if both parties could arrive at a better understanding. We certainly need to learn quite a lot yet, but learning from other people is quite a different thing from being told to do things.[26]

Along with the belief that volunteers were to be given the opportunity of "making history", as part of nation-building, went a growing conviction that the Scheme itself was part of this making of history, in its role in establishing an alternative path in the tortuous journey of aid to the Third World.

This sense of being part of a radically new method of aid-giving, a new way of relating to the needs of Third World peoples and nations, was basic to the Scheme from the very beginning. The first reports proclaimed it with confidence. In December 1954 NUAUS issued a report entitled "The Scheme for Graduate Employment in Indonesia: An Account of the Scheme, and a Letter from Indonesia to Interested Volunteers". The letter from Indonesia referred to in the title was signed on behalf of the eight volunteers then working in Indonesia, by Herb Feith. The first section of the report is entitled "What is the Scheme?", and the very first sentence lays claim to a revolutionary approach to the giving of aid, and in international relationships:

> The Scheme for Graduate Employment in Indonesia is an attempt to work out a new approach to the post-war situation in Asia – as it exists in the Asian country nearest to us – Indonesia.[27]

The first paragraph goes on to explain that the need for experts continues to exist, but that positions are also open for volunteers. The reason given is

---

26 Jo Kurnianingrat, "An Indonesian Opinion", p. 15.
27 "The Scheme for Graduate Employment in Indonesia: An Account of the Scheme, and a Letter from Indonesia to Interested Volunteers", Second Edition, December 1954, p. 1. The first edition of this report (not for publication) roneoed by NUAUS and issued in November 1953 had begun with the same statement. The 1954 edition of the report follows the 1953 version exactly, word for word, for most of pages one and two, explaining what is new in this approach to aid.

that the Indonesian Government cannot afford the foreign currency needed to pay a large number of experts, the implication being that volunteers can be used as a money-saver. "With the government-to-government machinery now established, the way is open for an annual ten or so trained people from Australia to go to work in Indonesia."

The argument then goes on to claim that, in any case, finance aside, "the need is not primarily for foreign experts. More particularly it is for people on the middle level of skill". The question is then put: "What can these people hope to achieve?" (i.e. volunteers working as teachers, engineers, doctors, etc as "middle level" people). Thus the volunteers are by implication included in this "middle level" category, though the former implication remains that some at least of these could be claimed to be "experts" if funds, and particularly foreign currency, could be found to pay for them, or if they *wished to go* to Indonesia under the "Expert" category.[28]

> What they do in their actual work is important. Inevitably they will be entrusted with more responsible work than they would do in Australia. They can help in overcoming a critical shortage at a time when new foundations are being laid in a very great number of fields.

Then comes the nub of the argument, the factor on which the whole rationale of the Scheme's claim to be doing something new and different in international relationships depends:

> But more important perhaps is the fact that these young people assert by the way they live, that racial equality is real. By having natural and friendly relations with Indonesians on a basis of mutual respect, they help to do away with the colonial legacy of mistrust and misunderstanding, which to so large an extent continues to affect relations between coloured people and white.[29]

---

28 "The Scheme for Graduate Employment in Indonesia: An Account of the Scheme, and a Letter from Indonesia to Interested Volunteers", Second Edition, December 1954, pp. 1–2.

29 "The Scheme for Graduate Employment in Indonesia: An Account of the Scheme, and a Letter from Indonesia to Interested Volunteers", Second Edition, December 1954, p. 2. Gwenda Rodda explained this point as follows: "To me, the most important thing in living in Indonesia was that I could speak to people on a basis of equality. If a friend reported that the price of a certain kind of material had gone up 4 *rupiahs*, I knew what the implications were. Friends could chat, knowing that I lived the same sort of life as they did. That sort of conversation is impossible where the participants come from different economic backgrounds although they may live in the same town." Gwenda Rodda, "Hidup Sederhana", *Djembatan*, Vol 2, No 4,

By December 1956 the NUAUS office had assembled a third edition of the report, slightly expanded and changed, and the alteration in the opening paragraphs is significant:

> A limited number of opportunities still exists for foreign personnel to work in Indonesia at an expert or semi-expert level on wage-scales higher, sometimes substantially higher, than those of Indonesians. The Volunteer Graduate Scheme (VGS) represents an *alternative opportunity. This Scheme enables young Australians to work on a basis of salary equality with Indonesians, thereby symbolising a new relationship of equality between Australians and Asians.*[30] (emphasis mine)

Later in the report this claim is spelled out as follows:

> And now for some problems peculiar to us as *"pegawais"*. We are "Europeans" but we live in an Indonesian milieu. Both Indonesians and Europeans think us a little queer and hard to account for. But Indonesians are happy that we are glad to live with them and like them, and Europeans often a bit envious of the extent to which we can be at home in the Indonesian situation – or alternatively, scornful of our attitude.
>
> In one sense our most important job in Indonesia, more important even than what we do at work, is just to live normally and naturally in the Indonesian world, and to make friends among Indonesians, without standing on any superiority ideas. We aim to be orientated and integrated as members of an Indonesian society, and not to live as members of a foreign clique seeking its own business and pleasure irrespective of the environment, which happens to be Indonesia. In small ways, such as by friendly conversation with the *betjak* driver

---

Special Issue, September 1959, p. 10. My own view on this subject of the Scheme as an attack on neo-colonial racist attitudes was published in an article entitled "Colonialism Dies Hard" written for *Djembatan* Special Issue, and later reprinted in *Indonesia Face to Face* in Chapter 15 "'No Natives or Dogs'", pp. 156–161. Though my views on other subjects have changed or at least modified over the years, I see no reason to alter any of what was written there, though I am aware that it smacks somewhat of the "Holier than Thou" attitude validly complained of by Elaine Wills (see below, footnote 36). In the light of what has surfaced within Australian society recently, and previously within American society during the Vietnam War, I see this aspect of any volunteer scheme as more important than ever. See below (Conclusion), pp. 61–67.

30 "The Volunteer Graduate Scheme for Indonesia – An Account of the Scheme and a Letter from Indonesia to Interested Volunteers", Third Edition, December 1956, p. 1.

or by giving up a seat in the bus, one shows that whites are very ordinary people. By sharing in manual work, washing dishes, splashing down muddy *kampong* tracks and so on, one silently protests against the perpetuation of hierarchies fostered by both feudalism and colonialism.[31]

One result of this consciousness among the early volunteers, or *pegawais* (the Indonesian term for public servant came to be used interchangeably with "volunteer graduate" by those involved in the Scheme), of having been part of a radical new direction in aid, of having done something revolutionary, was a constant urge to write and then extend, with new chapters, the history of the Scheme as the participants saw it. From the first open letter of Herb Feith, August 1951, written only just after his arrival in Indonesia, and the report of Ollie McMichael written a very short time after arriving, to the more formal reports, then to the beginning of the Volunteer Graduate Association in Australia in 1957, with a newsletter, *Djembatan* – which periodically published a brief history of the Scheme – from then on readers were provided with continually updated versions. This was done informally by *Djembatan*'s editor, Ailsa Zainu'ddin, who "looked back" from time to time, and also more formally and precisely by office bearers of the Association. Jim Webb, the long-time and for some years almost full-time secretary, and Don Anderson, the chairman of the VGA's Melbourne-based committee, both contributed survey-type "Let's Look Back" articles in early issues of *Djembatan*.[32] All these attempts to explain the chronology, to summarise events from 1950 up till the time of writing, and to pin-point the difference about this Scheme stressed racial and financial equality as key-notes. Ollie had claimed right from the start that anti-racist attitudes were one of the key differences between volunteers and experts, as well as their different earning capacities:

---

31   "The Volunteer Graduate Scheme for Indonesia – An Account of the Scheme and a Letter from Indonesia to Interested Volunteers", Third Edition, December 1956, p. 16. The third edition shows careful editing throughout and is more formal and less chatty in tone. A general "Toning down" is evident. For instance a lengthy section on "laziness" under "Problems at work" is omitted altogether, and the problem of comparative lack of work ethic of local staff is referred to more indirectly.

32   Jim Webb's tightly written crisp piece, "A new approach to Asia", was in *Djembatan*, Vol 1, No 4, June 1958. Don Anderson's piece, entitled "Backstage", was in *Djembatan*, Vol 2, No 1, September 1958. He noted that by September 1958 the number of volunteers reaching Indonesia was twenty-six and fifteen of these had come from Melbourne, that a large proportion had come through ASCM channels and that he expected the proportion to decrease as the Scheme expanded.

It is senseless coming up here unless you are free from colour barriers or race prejudices. ... I have found little necessity for entertainment of the film, dance, sport, party type. All this assumes you live on Indonesian food in your mess and have many Indonesian friends, not mixing with whites here most of whom spend quickly the hundreds they earn per week.[33]

In 1959 NUAUS printed a hand-out entitled "A Pilot Project in Southeast Asia" and the claim is made succinctly therein:

The Volunteer Graduate Scheme is primarily a venture in international friendship and understanding, an attempt at a practical demonstration of racial equality. In addition the aim is to provide technical assistance in a small way.[34]

The Ambassador had made the same point in 1956: "Such a contribution is worth immeasurably more to us than the *rupiahs* it saves our treasury".[35]

By late 1957 and into 1958 a new note can be detected in the material. Added to the early exuberance and confidence, to the sense of being part of history, of boundless optimism and earnest moral tone, the conviction of having done something radically different and really important for international relations in general and for the development of closer ties between the two countries in particular – added to all of that and mixed in with it can be found various expressions of having to explain, expound and defend Indonesian Government policy. The public campaign within Indonesia to wrest West Irian (West New Guinea) from the Dutch Government began, and rapidly got into full swing. There had been nasty public incidents, including attempts upon the life of President Sukarno. The Indonesian press reported anti-Dutch slogans and the enforced migration of people legally Dutch but born in the Indies. Both the volunteers in Indonesia from 1957 on and those already returned and contributing to *Djembatan* from outside

---

33 "P.E.G.A.W.A.I. (Plan for the Employment of Graduates from Australia to Work as Indonesians) i.e. Graduate Employment Scheme for Indonesia – Report to Intending Pegawais [etc]", August 1952, pp. 7, 8.

34 "A Pilot Project in Southeast Asia – The Australian Volunteer Graduate Scheme for Indonesia", NUAUS, 1959. This document is reproduced in Appendix C (i).

35 Speech delivered by His Excellency, Dr R. H. Tirtawinata, Ambassador for Indonesia, to the Volunteer Graduate Scheme Conference at the University of Melbourne on Thursday, 23rd August 1956. The full text of the speech was roneoed by NUAUS.

Indonesia felt it necessary to explain the situation as they saw it and to comment on the official government policies and attitudes.³⁶

For example, Ailsa Zainu'ddin contributed an article to the first issue of *Djembatan* entitled "It's dangerous to go to Indonesia", the main point of which was to correct the stereotypes of horror stories of *betjak* boys knifing tourists in the back or mobs overturning the cars of foreigners, and then concluded:

> But in fact, these people (i.e. the circulators of such traveller's tales) have said the right thing for the wrong reason. It *is* dangerous to go to Indonesia. You won't be stabbed, stoned or toppled over in a car. The danger is not a physical one, but a matter of the mind and the spirit. They saw that three weeks is too long and a lifetime too short. Once you have lived in Indonesia with Indonesians and have come to know something of their hopes and aspirations, their hospitality, their culture, the warmth of their friendship and the beauty of their

---

36   It is interesting that Arthur Feith, Herb's father, wrote a letter published in *Djembatan*, criticising some of what he regarded as needlessly crude anti-Dutch sentiment expressed in its pages, while commending other contributions expressing some concern for Dutch civilians. (As a former Jewish refugee he had ever been suspicious of official government "propaganda" and also of course unofficial, from whatever nation!) See *Djembatan*, Vol 1, No 4, June 1958, p. 14. The selection of "more or less" suitable articles for *Djembatan* was among the topics discussed at a meeting of the Melbourne Committee in February 1960. The minutes of the meeting in question record the viewpoints expressed: "Editorial Policy for *Djembatan*: The editor asked for guidance as to what sort of articles she should print in *Djembatan*. As a starting point for discussion she circulated the following comments she had received on previous issues: 1. Ken Thomas ... Volunteer Graduates are employees of the Central Government ... we should certainly not endanger the Scheme by writing 'difficult' subjects in our official newsletter [e.g. central government/rebellion]. He does not say we should never criticise the Indonesian government but rather that certain subjects should be tabu (Chinese traders being another such subject). 2. John Gare and Hugh O'Neill felt that articles were written too much with 'tongue in cheek' and presented too rosy a picture. 3. Elaine Wills complained of a 'holier than thou' note in the Special [issue of] *Djembatan*. 4. Eric Campbell objected to Molly's article in the Special *Djembatan*. The editor asked for guidance on the question of editorial censorship, on what subjects are tabu, to what extent should we try to educate our Australian public and to what extent can we criticise the Indonesian Government. It was decided that in general articles may be somewhat critical as long as they are basically sympathetic, but that individual articles must be considered on their merits and Ken and Thelma were appointed advisers in this matter." The minutes also record the names of those present at the meeting: "Mesdames Zainu'ddin, Cleland and Rungkat, Messrs. Anderson, Webb, Whitfield, Cleland and Doig. Apologies: Dr and Mrs Mylius." See Minutes of Volunteer Graduate Association for Indonesia National Committee – Special Meeting, held 20 February 1960, Kew, Melbourne.

countryside, you will find yourself a changed person in many ways, and you may find, as I have, that you are as homesick for Indonesia when you return as you were for Australia when you were there.[37]

In the same issue of *Djembatan*, Herb Feith contributed a piece on the political scene. Writing in June 1957, he noted that events which had occurred since the previous December

> ... and in particular the so-called revolts in the islands outside Java, represent a major crisis in the workings of the new Indonesian democracy. ... the fact is, that in all of the developments of this six-month-old crisis, there has not been a single shot fired. ... From a personal point of view, the point of view of the person living here, the most important thing to be said about Indonesian politics is that despite these crises, everything goes on normally. ... There is never anything like an atmosphere of political fanaticism, never the slightest reason for an Australian to be thinking about his personal safety. Perhaps there is a point for *pegawai* parents here. If your letters from Indonesia are delayed, don't worry. It won't be because anyone is afraid to write or because communications have been cut or anything like that. Almost certainly it will be just another case of administrative muck-ups.[38]

To readers of the eighties, the strength of support by these writers for the official Indonesian Government policy may seem excessive. (Our newspaper-reading public has after all developed a scepticism of *all* government policies, including perhaps our own.) [1984] But it must be remembered that all those involved in this campaign (and perhaps that is not too strong a word) to defend, interpret and explain were writing from the viewpoint of those who had been subjected to very strong anti-Indonesian writing in the Australian press from 1946 on.[39] Also it was felt necessary to reassure parents and friends that none of the volunteers then in Indonesia were under attack, or in danger of being mistaken for Dutch colonials. Several letters from various places outside Jakarta were published in *Djembatan* during

---

37 Ailsa Zainu'ddin, "It's Dangerous to go to Indonesia", *Djembatan*, Vol 1, No 1, July 1957.
38 Herb Feith, "The Indonesian Political Scene", *Djembatan*, Vol 1, No 1, July 1957, p. 8.
39 See Rodney Tiffin, *The News from Southeast Asia: The Sociology of Newsmaking* (Singapore: Institute of Southeast Asian Studies, 1978) for a detailed study of the slanted reporting of Southeast Asian news in the Australian media.

this period, saying specifically that there was no need for anyone to worry, and that everything in day-to-day life was normal.[40]

The sheer number and weight of letters written by early volunteers, and the importance attached to them by their authors and recipients, might seem surprising to readers of the current age of the STD phone call and the picture postcard. The continual flow of long detailed letters, sagas almost, of daily events, scenes, food, trips, friends met and adventures experienced were sent to family and friends, sometimes even to younger brothers and sisters and children of friends. A break in the weekly flow was a cause for concern among the family circle at home. This persistence in a semi-public form of correspondence can be explained partly in terms of novelty. After all, this was the period when very few Australians visited Indonesia for more than a few days *en route* to Europe. More importantly the writers and readers saw the letters as an important part of the sharing of the volunteer experience, of conveying its message – that of a unique approach to working in Asia.

How Had the Rationale for the Scheme Emerged?

It is important to stress that newsletters for publication or even just private circulation did not just "happen". The volunteers got into the habit of meeting regularly to discuss the best ways of carrying out immediate chores and "nuts and bolts" items of business – basically "How to get the Application Papers through" for intending volunteers, as well as trying to find niches for a growing list of interested people who had not yet formally applied, but who wanted to know if there could be a chance for them to work somewhere in the country. Officially, volunteers could only be accepted if they were requested by a specific ministry of the government. But what

---

40 *Djembatan*, Vol 1, No 3, February 1958 is a typical example: "Some concern has been expressed in Australia about the position of Australian graduates in the present Indonesian situation. So far the 'emergency' has made no difference to the life and work of volunteers personally, who unanimously advise intending Volunteers to continue with their plans ... Those who are anxious on behalf of the Volunteers may also note the comments of Sir Richard Boyer – that he saw no sign of violence in Indonesia during his visit, which included four ports and found Indonesians very friendly towards Australia". (p. 14) The Number 2 issue of Volume 5 of *Djembatan*, dated October 1963, contained a further explicit reassurance to allay possible concern at this later period in the Scheme's history: "Last month's developments in Indonesia have produced a number of enquiries about possible effects for the Volunteer Graduate Scheme. As we see it, the situation is very much 'business as usual'. It is clear from a number of letters from Volunteer Graduates in Indonesia that they have not been personally affected by the recent events, and one letter emphasises that the need is as great as ever for the sort of work that Volunteer Graduates can do. [signed] D. S. Anderson, Betty M. Feith, 15th October, 1963" (see "Editors' Postscript").

happened in practice, long before the application was anywhere near the official "request" from the Indonesian Ministry and "acceptance" by both governments for the applicant to work as a volunteer under the Scheme, was a long period of "informal inquiry" on behalf of a particular interested correspondent by one of the volunteers in Jakarta. Whether the enquirer was a teacher, an engineer or a doctor he or she had usually heard about the possibility of working in Indonesia not through any professional journal, but through NUAUS, the SCM, Newman Society channels, perhaps through a chance article in a daily paper featuring the Scheme, through chance personal contact with a returned volunteer, through friendship with the small but growing number of Indonesian students living in the capital cities and attending a variety of tertiary institutions under the Colombo Plan.[41]

Accordingly letters came from them, as suggested by the NUAUS handouts, to the Melbourne Committee which passed them on to Jakarta, or to the Jakarta Committee direct. Thus, from the time that the first three volunteers were working in Jakarta in 1952, and so even before the Scheme was officially established, there was always an agenda of current business, including letters to be answered, ministries to be visited, informal contacts already established to be followed up, and a great deal of routine "chasing about" which usually had to be accomplished before any enquiry could be answered. So from the very beginning, the first three volunteers, despite other interests and preoccupations, and not necessarily through personal friendship, were very much thrown together through the sheer necessity of carrying out these chores. Time and time again Ollie's letters mention the frequent holidays (due to religious festivals for either the Islamic or Christian calendar) being substantially taken up with committee meetings to get through the ever-increasing pile of urgent business. Once further volunteers arrived to swell the numbers, the habit of meeting over holiday time grew – partly for business, but also increasingly for social get-togethers as more brought Indonesian friends along, and later, fiancés and inevitably, Indonesian relatives. Also the regular Sunday afternoon get-togethers of the few who happened to be in Jakarta at the same time reinforced the sense of solidarity, of community, and as time went on, of mutual support and personal friendships. The Jakarta dwellers were joined very frequently by

---

41   The obituary for Noela Powell (née Motum) (1984) mentions that she first heard about the Scheme and became interested in the possibility of working in Indonesia as a teacher, as a result of hearing Herb Feith's report at a Newman Society conference. Ann McDonald and Thelma Rungkat heard an earlier report from Herb at an ASCM conference in Armidale, New England, 1954.

those living within travelling distance; those further afield, e.g. in Menado joined the nucleus in Jakarta at holiday time or during the occasional Minute Conference.

Out of these regular and at first *ad hoc* business meetings called to discuss new applications and unfinished business developed the longer weekend get-togethers out of town, when rationale, policy, "aims and basis" were thrashed out, argued over, and formulated and reformulated. There was never a "party line" and there was never absolute unanimity. A consensus did eventually emerge on some important matters however, and certainly a sense of community developed. Perhaps this was because during the mid-fifties there was a sizeable group of volunteers who were more or less the same age, some of whom had come from similar backgrounds in SCM or Labor Club or both, at university. They were all going through the inevitable culture shock of young people from a relatively sheltered prior existence, as most of them had never, or only briefly, travelled outside Australia before coming to work in Indonesia. (This was, of course, because they were the immediate post-war generation). It was inevitable, that for at least some, there were problems coping with a certain amount of disillusionment about work placements, even if no other problems developed.

One of the most critical of these difficulties, which are discussed at length in the next chapter, was when the promised job for which a certain volunteer had been invited never did eventuate, and more than once people in their twenties, absolutely inexperienced in coping with any sort of ambiguity in the job situation, had to live through weeks and months of "grey area" in the office where they were expected to appear daily, before it became clear to everyone that the volunteer concerned was in fact literally free to create his or her own job. In some cases this clarity was never to emerge, due to an apparent lack of planning in some government departments where people had been placed, but were given no work at all. The apparent lack of dismay and absence of concern on the part of some (but by no means all) Department heads, that this planning had not been done, and would possibly never be done, and the seeming lack of interest in the future alternative tasks and prospects for the unfortunate volunteer was perhaps one of the severest aspects of culture shock that the work-oriented and relatively well-disciplined, or in other words, conventionally work-habituated, young Australians had to face. Very few of them, moreover, in their career training, had been taught, trained, or encouraged, to create their own jobs!

One particularly memorable example was of concern to the Jakarta Committee in 1955. It gradually became clear that the volunteer had been placed in an office where there really was nothing that she could usefully do. As she had been assured that her presence was necessary and that a job would be found for her the effect on her morale was devastating. A conscientious Indonesian Ministry senior level administrator went to considerable trouble to obtain a transfer for her to a different section, in a different part of the city, where the situation was such that she *could* do "something useful". This transfer took some time, however, and meanwhile she had to carry the load of frustration and sense of failure. The committee – which had accepted part of the responsibility for finding her work in the first place, and all of the responsibility for her arrangements in arriving in Jakarta in the second place – had to carry it also. The writer believes that it was through these "defeats" as well as the more happily remembered "successes" featured in *Djembatan*, through the difficulties as well as the excitements and delights of all the new experiences to be shared with this "community", and through the process of working through the problems and anxieties, including the illnesses of Indonesian friends and colleagues as well as their own, that the members of the group that was meeting together in Jakarta were welded into a team.

The editor of *Djembatan* commented in the first issue that the members of the Scheme had developed this sense of "belonging together" so that in some ways the Scheme could be compared to a family. Volunteers certainly argued amongst themselves about the "aims and basis" of the Scheme, about its implications, and at times the extent of its legitimate demands on their free time, just as people did and still do about their own family. For that reason this writer agrees that the analogy of the family is a helpful one. The coherence of the group did not depend on personal friendship or choice of companions – just as brothers and sisters cannot choose their own siblings, so volunteers could not choose to be associated with fellow Scheme members as persons. Its coherence depended more on mutual acceptance of their interdependence in this strange environment, than on any religious or political agreement. Ken Thomas perhaps expresses this sense of group loyalty most fully in his article in *Djembatan*:

Reflections on Going Home

… What is it, I wonder, that attracts us? … it is as well to emphasize that the Scheme means something different to us all … not only were we unable to agree on what the Scheme really is (at a previous lengthy meeting) but we can't sit down together for five minutes before we fall out over an interpretation of the Australian scene! It's really bewildering for an Indonesian family to have us to tea and get us talking on Australia. But I think this merely shows that we are first and foremost individuals who have, beneath that surface, *some fundamental areas of agreement.*

There is plenty of surface agreement too. From the moment a graduate lands in Djakarta he becomes a full member of the group. This is something I can never really understand. We come from different backgrounds and states, but when we sit down for our first meal together at *"Anedja"* well, the fun starts and the stranger is no longer a stranger. I must tell you that *"Anedja"* is the restaurant we have adopted for introducing the new *pegawai* to Indonesian food as cooked on home ground ... (the real Djakarta flavour – dust, sultry weather and the unfortunate beggars) ... if you come, you must be prepared to leave part of yourself behind when – or if – you go "home".[42] (emphasis mine)

What Were the Fundamental Areas of Agreement?

It is clear that a common front or consensus emerged through the fifties and into the sixties among the "new generation" of volunteers, on various matters. Firstly, whatever was said within the group there was a "closed front" presented to the outside world which to the writer's knowledge was never breached. There was an unwritten agreement that no one member should ever criticise views expressed by another either at a public meeting (obligatory once back home) when called upon to speak about "Life in Indonesia as a Volunteer" or in print. Secondly, no-one should publicly criticise the Indonesian Government, upon returning. The common task was seen as that of interpreting, explaining, making comprehensible; there was no shortage of negative criticism and comment from others!

And even at the personal level, despite the inevitable disagreements in private and the personal tensions which arose from time to time, volunteers refrained from criticising each other, or their own or each other's Indonesian colleagues, or their immediate superiors. Admittedly, they were working in professions where this sort of loyalty was expected. But it went beyond the usual professional etiquette. Thus in that sense they remained a "family" – through several years they maintained this solidarity with each other and with their Indonesian colleagues; they closed ranks. For instance, again and again in letters the statement recurs: "Don't tell my parents", "Don't tell my family" about a serious illness, some accident, some bad

---

42 Ken Thomas, "Reflections on Going Home", *Djembatan*, Vol 1, No. 3, February 1958.

problem in the office, some personal temporary disaster until it could be "shrugged off" or seen in context.

Such warnings were necessary because a support group had developed in Sydney and Melbourne of friends and especially parents; "friends of the Scheme" met frequently in each other's homes, exchanged letters and photographs and welcomed travellers going through either way. The family-and-friends network became an important aspect of this sense of solidarity – rightly or wrongly, older family members were known to rush into print to criticise some anti-Indonesian statement in the press, and some would dare to contradict professional journalists or debate with public speakers at public meetings of the Australian Institute of International Affairs or perhaps the Australian Indonesian Association, on the basis of "My son (or daughter) is a volunteer in Jakarta (or Yogya or Bandung) and they tell it differently …". One mother even volunteered to address the Country Women's Association! And volunteers sometimes wrote to aunts or parents of *other* volunteers to reassure them that it was not such a hare-brained scheme after all … So if information were not to be passed on to this growing social and educational network, warnings had to be specially given.

Also there was in some way a closed front on policy matters once they had been thrashed out over many weekends, Sunday after Sunday and on holidays, through the fifties and into the early sixties, both in Jakarta and back in Melbourne. This early sense of solidarity was reinforced by the production and distribution of *Djembatan*, very much a cooperative enterprise, and the active participation even to the extent of "busy bodying" of the Melbourne Committee of the Volunteer Graduate Association through the early sixties.

The history of the Scheme can be seen to fall into four stages. The first stage, 1950–1953, was that of the initial careful planning and inevitable delays and disappointments and difficulties inherent in the delicate negotiations. The second stage, 1954–1957, can be seen as that of rapid expansion. Then came the period of sustained publicity of the Scheme, with many contributors to *Djembatan* assuming the role of expounder and re-assurer during its first two years, in 1957–1958. For if not actively defending the Indonesian Government, the aim of both the editor and many of her contributors was to make the government's actions at least *comprehensible* to Australian readers who were mainly friends of the volunteers and ex-volunteers, and also to relatives, who were always inclined to be over-anxious, and who in most cases would not have been trained political observers! Next came the fourth stage – that of stock taking.

By June 1960 the Melbourne-based Committee noted that ten years had elapsed since the Scheme was first envisaged. In the fourth issue of *Djembatan*'s third volume, the editor mentions that a *pegawai* (Lance Castles) had recently departed for Indonesia, and that he was the first volunteer to leave Australia for over a year.[43] There had after all been armed rebellion in Sumatra and East Indonesia, and though the casualties had not on the whole been heavy by modern civil war standards, it was still armed rebellion. In some quarters this political situation had put a strain on the Indonesian Government's legitimacy and credibility, and many potential enquirers had ceased to enquire.[44]

In 1959–1960 the editor of *Djembatan* was referring to 1955–1956 as "the golden years". It was actually the numerical peak, with nine people leaving Australia for Indonesia in one year. Also by 1960, a new group of Indonesian students had graduated from courses in Australia and were beginning to return to Indonesia. Some volunteers, particularly those working in technical areas such as health and medicine, argued that the Scheme should be redefined and radically altered; given that the early acute shortage of trained personnel in Indonesia was no longer apparent, they argued, Australian volunteers might even be in danger of putting Indonesian colleagues out of work.

It was therefore decided by the Melbourne Committee to send out a questionnaire to all volunteer graduates, and *Djembatan* featured a review in a couple of issues, resulting from the replies received. The editor noted in the June 1960 issue that all current volunteers had returned answers to the questionnaire and commented, "The encouraging thing is that every *pegawai* at present in Indonesia is firmly convinced that there is still a place for the Volunteer Graduate Scheme". Indeed their main concern was rather to ask, where are the volunteers for the jobs? They believed that it was still possible, despite inflation, to satisfy physical and psychological needs on an Indonesian civil servant's salary, certainly for anyone without dependents. The subsequent issue of *Djembatan* summarised the points made by respondents, noting twenty-three volunteers in all had expressed comments. Some volunteers had felt that the concept of equal pay was less important either than the actual work done or the ability to "mix and make friends and take an interest in their security and culture". One

---

43 *Djembatan*, Vol 3, No 4, June 1960, p. 1.
44 Cindy Adams' hilarious book *My Friend the Dictator* (Indianapolis: Bobbs-Merrill, 1967) accurately conveys the attitude of the West and its press to an unreliable regime and an unreliable President!

had stated quite bluntly that "the receipt of an Australian income (over and above the local salary – the usual arrangement for foreign contract staff) would not have made any difference to his relationships with his Indonesian acquaintances".

Others saw the equal pay aspect as central, "... for me the whole Scheme would lose its point and uniqueness if this expression of our aim had to be dropped. Then we might as well direct enquirers to the foreign aid schemes and be done with it". It was noted that "the majority of replies were in the affirmative – there was only one clear negative".

The decision emerging was that in view of the continuing and in some ways increasingly urgent need to maintain an open door between the two countries, in the face of an increasingly difficult political situation and the resulting hostile press in Australia, the Scheme was as important as, and in fact more important than before. Lance Castles and John Forster wrote from Jakarta:

> It's not yet time for us to think of withdrawing. There is no need to pull out now. If the V.G.S. could ever have achieved anything, it still can, and its need to do so is probably greater than ever.[45]

During the same period, 1957–1960, Herb Feith had been publicising the Scheme during his three years of post-graduate study at Cornell University. He had been urging its adoption or at least adaptation, to enable young Americans to work in Indonesia, or, if that proved impracticable due to the current political international situation, in Burma or in the "new emerging nations" in Africa. In a letter to the American Committee on Africa he wrote:

> My concern with the possibility of American-African parallels to the Australian-Indonesian Volunteer Graduate Scheme has arisen from a number of considerations. It seems to me that the African countries which have recently achieved independence, or are about to in the near future, are in a similar situation to the one Indonesia was in, when the Australian Scheme began in 1951–1952. There is

---

45 For material relating to these re-appraisals, see Foreword, *Djembatan*, Vol 3, No 4, June 1960; *Djembatan*, Vol 4, No 1, September 1960, pp. 1–3. Harry Whitfield, writing from Yogyakarta where he was teaching at Gadjah Mada University, shared this view very emphatically and made very derogatory comments about European "experts" in Yogyakarta whose personal qualities were such as to lose the respect of Indonesian colleagues. See Harry Whitfield, "The Old Ways and the New", *Djembatan*, Vol 3, Nos 1/2, December 1959, pp. 17–19.

a similar lack of trained persons, a similar scope for persons of a wide range of occupations to work in government services, a similar tendency for government services to be seen as the spearhead of national aspirations, and a *similar idealism with which it is possible for the idealistic young American to identify himself.* Finally it seems to me that an American-African scheme of the type I am envisaging would draw its strength in part from *a sense of guilt about the national past* which is similar to that felt by young Australians who have gone to Indonesia under the Volunteer Graduate Scheme.[46] (emphasis mine)

… Our Australian-Indonesian scheme works through the Indonesian civil service, the advantage here lying partly in the symbolism of salary equality and partly in the fact that, once the trust relationship is established, it is possible for suitable work to be found for persons of almost any occupational category.[47]

Perhaps the early sixties could be seen as a further phase – that of gradual re-expansion. The numbers began to increase again, and the editorial of the December 1961 issue of *Djembatan* was optimistic about a further increase in numbers of volunteers:

We expect a number of new volunteers next year. By December 1962 the number of Australians who have participated in the V.G.S. may well have reached a grand total of 40, including at least six who have served there for two terms.[48]

The acceptance by the Melbourne Committee of Michael Rubbo's offer to spend the next summer taking photographs and gathering material for the purpose of subsequent visits to university campuses as field officers,

---

46 Letter from Herb Feith to American Committee on Africa, April 23, 1959.
47 This writer believes that Herb Feith had a continual tendency to be over-optimistic about the availability of "suitable work". Others were also over-optimistic – e.g. Sylvia Graham wrote concerning the Tondano PTPG (College of Education): "… two-thirds of the English staff was provided by the Volunteer Graduate Scheme, but, of course, in the total educational picture our role is infinitesimal. For the English Language teaching programme of the Ministry of Education sixty or more teachers under the Scheme could be absorbed without difficulty. Each Australian Education Department complains of shortage of staff and lack of buildings. In relation to their aims this is true, but the gap between the two seems almost non-existent when compared with that in Indonesia". Sylvia Graham, "Teaching in Tondano (Sulawesi)", *Djembatan*, Vol 1, No 2, November 1957, p. 12.
48 *Djembatan*, Vol 4, No 4, December 1961.

to publicise the Scheme further, seemed to anticipate a further large expansion.[49] By December 1961 it was possible to organise a conference of then current volunteers, in Jakarta. The Australian Government provided the fares for volunteers working outside Jakarta to travel to the capital, and also for Michael Rubbo and Jim Webb to attend.[50] Herb Feith was a research fellow at the ANU and happened to be in Jakarta, so he was able to continue "putting in a stitch or two" to the fabric of planning, and to report on his American contacts and negotiations. From these small beginnings the plans for the Overseas Service Bureau developed. Further Australian Government funding enabled Jim Webb to work full-time for the OSB in 1963, bringing the Volunteer Graduate Scheme to a sound organisational and financial basis under the OSB umbrella.

With the new bureaucratic structure of the Overseas Service Bureau and the streamlining of administrative channels for enquiries and potential volunteers and actual applications, the need for an active committee in Melbourne was less acute. Until the beginning of 1962 *Djembatan* had been appearing four times each year. There were no issues through 1962 until December, when a small two-page issue appeared to explain:

> ... now it is proposed to circulate a less ambitious news-sheet ... usually a few pages of news ... rather than articles as provided formerly ....
>
> At the end of last year the Association announced plans for an expansion of publicity about the Scheme and asked for assistance to make this possible. The generous response to this appeal enabled the Association to carry out its plan to send Michael Rubbo to Southeast Asia during the long vacation and to appoint him as a Field Secretary for the first two terms this year. In this capacity Michael visited all

---

49 The idea of sending speakers around the campuses was of course not new. Don Anderson had been the first, supported for a month, by NUAUS and ASCM jointly after his visit to an SCM conference at World Student Christian Federation (WSCF) level in Yogya, December 1952. Several volunteers subsequently called in at different university and other tertiary campuses either on their way home or soon after arrival back home, on visits arranged by NUAUS, and sometimes, ASCM. Some had their fares paid, some paid their own. To the writer's knowledge this was the first paid appointment. Michael Rubbo represented a new generation of students, and not having previously heard of the Scheme, he found it necessary to re-invent it.

50 Jim Webb was at this time Warden of the Union of the University of Melbourne, a job which enabled him to use his organisational administrative skills to further the secretarial tasks of the Volunteer Graduate committee. His abilities were recognised by the Department of External Affairs, and in fact he seemed at times to be their unpaid administrative officer!

the mainland universities between March and August and displayed in each place his very effective paintings and photographs.

This new venture in publicity by the Association brought the volunteer graduate idea actively before a large cross-section of a new generation of students and has resulted in new interest in and enquiries about the Scheme. We are indebted to Michael for his enthusiastic and imaginative work.[51]

With the ceasing of *Djembatan* as an official publication, the task of "networking" and passing on specific necessary information was taken up by the smaller and more informal newsletter mentioned above.[52] From the time of the return of the Feiths to Melbourne in 1962 this newsletter was edited firstly by myself, and later by Janice Forster, ceasing only in 1965 when a regular newsletter intended to include news of Indonesian volunteers was compiled regularly by the office of the Overseas Service Bureau. Information about the OSB, from 1962 on, and of current, former and intending volunteers was regularly given in this newsletter. Minutes of the early OSB meetings also contained detailed reports.

The burden of following up enquiries in Jakarta became even greater during the early sixties, for there were times when there was only one

---

51 *Djembatan*, Vol 5, No 1, December 1962, p. 1.
52 The final *Djembatan* in its normal 16-page cyclostyled format was probably Vol 5, No 2, October 1963. The cover of this issue of *Djembatan* bears the usual identification – "*Djembatan*, Newsletter of the Volunteer Graduate Association for Indonesia". The inside cover bears the usual explanation about the identity of the VGA, including the role it was soon to lose: "The V.G.A. maintains a liaison with the Australian and Indonesian governments, keeps abreast of developments in Indonesia, publicises Indonesia's needs and the opportunities which exist through the Volunteer Graduate Scheme". The Editor's column outlines the position of the Scheme as of October 1963, as follows: "'The First Ten Years' – The first official Volunteer Graduates arrived in Jakarta in June 1953. In the following decade more than 40 Australians have worked in Indonesia under the scheme. Despite an earlier optimism, there has been no recent increase in the average of four or five applicants a year. The potential for the scheme throughout Australia must, however, be much greater than this. The principal limiting factor has been the amount of promotional work which the Committee has been able to undertake. The prospects for the next decade are much brighter. The Secretary, Jim Webb, has resigned from his job as Warden of the Union House, University of Melbourne, and is now full-time Director of the Overseas Service Bureau. In this role he will be able to give much more time to administering and developing the Volunteer Graduate Scheme. Already we have received considerable publicity in the Bulletins of the Bureau. ... The Volunteer Graduates Committee has agreed to accept the Bureau's offer to conduct day-to-day administration of the Scheme. The Bureau will also carry the normal administrative costs and will provide an annual V.G.A. budget to cover any special projects devised by our Committee." See "The First Ten Years", *Djembatan* Vol 5, No 2, October 1963, p.1.

volunteer working there and thus only one person able to do the chores involved before each application could be finalised. This involved getting time off from one's own work to chase about the various buildings of Officialdom in Jakarta to visit office after office to make polite informal enquiries, to follow up application papers (which occasionally could be mislaid, as can even happen in government offices in Melbourne and Sydney!), to make appointments – and in the event of last minute cancellations due to the unavoidable absence of a senior administrator unexpectedly called "upstairs", or literally overseas, remaking them – and above all to keep in touch with the sometimes despairing would-be-volunteer waiting in Australia. Lance Castles was at one stage this sole representative, and he agreed upon reflection many years later that at this time there seemed to be increasing difficulty in finalising enquiries, let alone applications. When asked to reflect upon the possible reasons for this he replied:

> Well, don't forget that many government public servants were in an increasingly difficult economic situation, and were out of the office trying to find means just to subsist from day to day – "*tjari uang*" (literally searching for cash!). When you were lucky enough to find someone in his office, he was finding it increasingly difficult to make any decision at all, in case it should turn out to be "incorrect" in an increasingly unstable political situation, and thus get him into trouble later.

He saw the problems within the administration as inseparable from the overall economic and political situation throughout Indonesia in the early sixties, which with constant rumours of President Sukarno's declining health and erratic performances as Principal Actor in the State Theatre, and with galloping inflation, was confirming the old stereotype in the Western press of Indonesia as unstable and a potential "trouble-maker" among the New Emerging Forces.[53]

---

53   Conversation between Lance Castles and the writer, January 1983. Lance also made the point that life was not as "grim" for volunteers as Western observers such as Cindy Adams would see it; they had the support of their Indonesian friends and hosts. Lance lived with an Indonesian family, the Ramelans, "and they became very adept in coping with all these emergencies". Ivan Southall accurately recreates the style and mood of the meetings called both in Jakarta and Melbourne to consider the progress or non-progress of the chores involved in volunteer applications. He also gives a realistic portrayal of the "filtering" or "self-selection" process which continued as enquirers and would-be volunteers either stayed with the Scheme still waiting – or became weary of the delays and wrote to say they had taken other jobs, or decided to go to another Third World country. See Southall, *Indonesia Face to Face*, especially Chapter 7 "He who chooses himself".

Part II

The Volunteer Experience – Problems and Perspectives

Reflecting with the advantage of hindsight on the past thirty years and more, it now seems to me that at least *some* of the problems encountered by the volunteers were inherent in the ambiguities of the early statements and enunciations of the Scheme itself.

This is true in particular of the problem of "finding something useful to do". Certainly volunteers were recruited right from the beginnings in 1951, and before the "official statements" had begun to emerge, *partly* simply to have a share in *being there* – to have a place in this "New Approach to Asia", in building up a radically different way for Australians to inter-relate with Asians. There was a dilemma within the concept of the Scheme itself. In one sense, to fulfil the aims of the Scheme, all the volunteers needed to do was just to arrive and become part of the local landscape and become integrated into the local society. Yet that was initially only one "main plank" of the aims and basis of the Scheme. At least in its formative first stage, the second fundamental plank was the opportunity to *do something useful*. Volunteers from the very beginning were promised this.[54] They were told "your contribution is *needed*" *urgently*.

In August 1951 Herb Feith wrote, as a new arrival in Jakarta:

> I was very very happy to hear that there are now more than thirty – I think nearer forty – of you interested in working for some time in Indonesia. It's indeed very difficult to explain to anybody who hasn't seen at first hand the terrible social misery which results directly from a lack of administrative and technical skills, just how valuable trained people can be in this country. ...by far the most important of the "pros" [of being a volunteer graduate are] the wonderful opportunities here to do a useful job. With the tremendous shortage of trained people [in Indonesia] ... there are lots of ways cropping up every day in which one can be useful.[55]

---

54 See subsection of Part I entitled "Philosophy and Ethos of the Scheme".

55 "Report by H. Feith to Students and Graduates Interested in the NUAUS Scheme for Graduate Employment in Indonesia", September 1951, pp. 1, 7. And note the stating of the promise succinctly in *Djembatan*: "*The aim of the Scheme is threefold – to provide technical aid; to be a symbolic gesture of identification; and to 'build bridges of friendship' between the two countries.* ... On an average, four persons per year have gone to Indonesia as *pegawais* since the Scheme's inception, although it would be possible to send 15 a year if they were to be found. *In a Scheme numerically so small,*

However, by 1959–1960 it is possible to detect a less optimistic note in the hand-outs distributed by NUAUS on the usefulness plank – for instance, a hand-out of this period entitled "A Pilot Project in Southeast Asia" summed up the rationale of the Scheme thus:

> The Volunteer Graduate Scheme is primarily a venture in international friendship and understanding, an attempt at a practical demonstration of racial equality. In addition the aim is to provide technical assistance in a small way.[56]

Such a modification came too late to help heal the bruised self-esteem of some volunteers of the fifties, and to reassure the anxious committee members continually gathered in Jakarta to help boost the morale of particular individuals. Lest it may seem that this writer is overstating the case of this theme, she points out that many of the volunteers had come from Protestant or Catholic church backgrounds where, at church and in school, children were exhorted to "work, for the night is coming when no man (sic) can work", and where hymns such as "Awake, awake to Love and Work the Lark is in the Sky" constituted almost weekly musical fare. The galaxy of role models available to these young Australians were of older men and women within church life, or school teachers or older members of their own families, whose whole life was a living example that to Live is to Work, and those without work are to be pitied. It should also be remembered that some at least of the volunteers had clerics, either Catholic or Protestant, and including missionaries in Foreign Lands, as part of their own family myths and legends; in their case, the perhaps unconscious aim of the volunteer was to see oneself as a "new-style missionary" – with a different message, a new Gospel (i.e. that of racial and financial equality as expression of identification), but the same dedication and commitment to just as honourable a cause. But how to be true to such an ideal without work each day as the expression of such a goal?

The problem of a lack of work became especially acute for one volunteer, herself the unlucky one with "nothing at all to do in the office", who saw luckier ones in Jakarta and out of it, "busy, busy night and day", to

---

then, the actual technical aid given is not of primary importance, although, for the gesture to have any value, the aid given must be worth giving." (emphasis mine) *Djembatan*, Special Issue, pp. 5, 6. In the writer's opinion, the latter two aims outlined are part of the one objective – that of identification, without which no real friendship is possible. In this very formulation of the promise of useful work, a problem is implied.

56   "A Pilot Project in Southeast Asia", NUAUS, 1959.

misquote the Jakarta pop-song of the day. They were *obviously* purposefully engaged in something *they* saw (whether validly, in the long term, or not, would be impossible to determine, but the lucky busy ones were usually *too* busy to worry much about long term results!) as *"useful"* and *enjoying it*, and *sometimes doing "really important things"*. Thus the sadly idle observer could see all around her (or him) their peers and fellow *pegawais* enjoying all the satisfactions of *"putting in a stitch here and there"* to the many-coloured and many-stranded fabric and social history of the nation; or if less ambitious, at least into the new fabric of an office section or a recently created technical department.

It became apparent that the inevitable problem of the gap between expectations and reality, when confronted with difficulty in finding "real work", was one of the most serious that many of the volunteers had to face. Time and time again letters are preoccupied with it, and in the newsletters of the early sixties it is a constantly recurring theme – "so-and-so hasn't found enough to keep him (or her) busy but the Jakarta Committee is hoping that things will improve soon".[57] The personal sense of frustration was perhaps greatest when the volunteers had been trained in a highly specific technical capacity, and believed that they had been hired for the same capacity, only to find that the equipment for which they thought they had been employed to use not only had not arrived, but was never in fact likely to do so. Ian Doig's case was perhaps one of the most depressing for all concerned. It must also be remembered that the technically trained Australians were graduates of institutions where, even where the training given had been routine, it provided career opportunities with rapid advancement and promotion at least at the technical and professional level (at least for the males of the early fifties). (Skilled labour was also at that time highly in demand in Australia and relatively highly paid!) Also these graduates had come out of the "straight" secondary schools of the forties, not the "alternative" schools of the seventies, which have to a later generation provided excellent training for a depressed economic climate – i.e. in the social and human skills involved in learning "how to do nothing at all, all day".[58]

---

57 The writer remembers several agonising sessions in Jakarta about whether a committee member should intervene, or do nothing for fear of being thought interfering!

58 Some volunteer graduates were in fact given research jobs by their ministries which left them to construct their own agendas. They were left very much to their own devices on a day-to-day basis. The University of Melbourne Honours History School perhaps provided some basic training for future volunteers in grappling with the tasks of constructing one's own professional agenda as a graduate research student.

This problem was compounded by one which is in some sense the reverse side of the coin. Some volunteers were *extremely* busy – either through good fortune (for the busier you were, the more likely you were to feel you were fulfilling the requirements of the scheme)[59] or because of the circumstances of the job in hand (the doctors, for instance, were usually "run off their feet"!) And to such really busy people, and both Gwenda Rodda and Herb Feith were amongst that number, it came as a shock and a real source of difficulty to find local staff, certainly more of them in the "lower echelons" of the hierarchy of the administration, literally sitting about all day in the office with nothing to do, or, whatever there *was* to do, just not doing it. In all the early reports, what seems remarkably like "laziness" is mentioned repeatedly.[60]

The medicos – Vern Bailey, Keith Lethlean and Ray Mylius – were also subject to the frustrations discussed above. Similar problems faced Indonesian graduates from technical institutions and universities' engineering faculties, who returned after a lengthy stay in Australia as Colombo Plan students, only to find that in many cases they were not able to use the skills they had acquired. (Personal conversations with former volunteer Lou Eakins through the seventies. Lou, an engineer, continued to work in Indonesia on engineering contracts and became acquainted with several frustrated Indonesian engineers!)

59   Perhaps it was partly a matter of temperament. Ollie McMichael *enjoyed* being constantly required to go hither and yon, and his very busy schedule was undoubtedly a cause of his sense of fulfilment. His file of letters sent to the writer by his mother after his death reflects this sense of fulfilment throughout, and the following quotation from his last letter written just before his departure is perhaps an indication: "...the Group Scheme has required my solid work and worry and the whole process of identification has not been a light task. There have been weeks of frustration and worry and agonising misunderstandings and mistakes ... to penetrate and get stuck into life here requires lots of mental effort. But it's more worthwhile than words can ever express. I feel myself part of Indonesia, and Indonesia is part of me. Spiritually I've got some of Asia in my very soul now...". Letter from Ollie McMichael to his mother, 4 November 1953.

60   See for example the following passage: "...what may well be worse [for the new arrival to cope with!] is laziness and lateness and a lack of working habits. When one is aware of the critical situation that Indonesia is in, one can almost go mad when one sees some of one's workmates so casual. Sometimes it can be very difficult to be friendly and not bossy, and yet not become lazy and shoddy oneself. The fact is that the revolutionary tension which kept people working hard and selflessly five years ago is all but gone now, and the organisation is not good enough yet for the normal incentive of government departments to function monthly." See "The Scheme for Graduate Employment in Indonesia: An Account of the Scheme, and a Letter from Indonesia to Interested Volunteers", Second Edition, December 1954, p. 18. All the references to "laziness" and "lateness" were edited out of the 1956 edition of the newsletter. The first informal newsletter about the Scheme, issued in August 1952, also contained specific references to laziness, though attempts were made to explain the phenomenon! See "P.E.G.A.W.A.I. (Plan for the Employment of Graduates from Australia to Work as Indonesians) i.e. Graduate Employment Scheme for

In retrospect their sense of shock is hard to understand. After all, in Australian society, one does not expect to find the ordinary rank and file possessed by the Puritan work ethic to the extent that the senior executive level of at least an earlier and perhaps tougher generation seemed to be – or nowhere near the same extent! There is after all an Australian tradition teaching suspicion of working too hard lest you seem to be "toadying to the boss". And why should the humble Jakarta typist, or the Department's gardener, assigned the task of cutting grass laboriously by hand outside an office door (saving the cut grass carefully for the goats grazing outside the office toilet!), work harder? Why should the local equivalent of the "tea-lady" – usually in fact an elderly retainer of the male sex and pre-Independence memory and training, whose only daily task seemed to be to provide the luke-warm morning coffee or tea, carried by hand, to the more senior staff – come earlier and leave later? Why should the harassed young clerk, with middle-school secondary background, and already several young children to support on a miniscule government salary work that little bit harder, while actually in the office, to show zeal for the "upbuilding of the country"? Why indeed! (It could be said in their defense that to lower level *pegawais*, the concept of work, like that of sustenance, was that of a fixed amount – if you take too much away, like removing water from a bucket by a tin scoop by scoop, there will not be enough left for next day – so there should always be some left over!)[61]

It could be claimed that the young Australians were the victims of their own "propaganda". They saw patriotism, true nationalist feeling expressed everywhere, and undoubtedly sincerely so, everywhere about them – and never more so than at official national celebrations organised at the office level.[62] They themselves ardently believed in the social goals of the new nation and in the implications for each *pegawai* of the "nation-building" messages. They saw their own tasks, even if routine and insignificant if considered on an individual basis, as part of that Great National Effort – and they were delighted to have an opportunity of *"putting a stitch in here*

       Indonesia – Report to Intending Pegawais [etc]." I see this attitude on the part of early volunteers as a real problem for the unfortunate Indonesian colleagues, many of whom must have inwardly groaned whenever they saw one of the energetic newcomers approaching, obviously intending to ask, even if politely, "Have you done what you promised, yet?" and knowing that the inevitable answer would have to be "Not yet, I'm sorry!"

61   Now that employment is hard to keep in Australia, it is not uncommon to hear colleagues advising "save something for tomorrow" [1984].

62   See subsection of Part I entitled "Philosophy and Ethos of the Scheme".

and there" on the national or at least the office section level. It was difficult for them to adjust to the reality that though their Indonesian colleagues undoubtedly believed and accepted the rhetoric, they did not *all*, always, see a close connection between the former and their own personal routine as employees of an enormous bureaucracy. Thus punctuality at the office, keeping appointments, willingness to take work home, in fact going out of their way, either literally or figuratively, through the customary track ensuring security to all of them through the bureaucratic jungle, *was not* their way of seeing their devotion to the ideas of the nation no matter what their new foreign guests might expect.

In fact, the willingness of Indonesian *pegawais* to take the risks of the unusual, to undertake an extra or unexpected task should have been interpreted as part of their innate courtesy and unwillingness to offend the incomprehensible busy-bodies who *seemed* to mean well. It was part of an agreeable willingness to accommodate visitors and so avoid giving offence, rather than as part of a determination to achieve rational goals and reform a colonial society. After all Rome had not been built in a day, and *they* were not here for just a couple of years to "*make their mark*" as guests, pioneers of a new ideology for Aiding the Third World, in unknown territory. They had been born in Indonesia. Local staff accepted the realities of daily existence – to live and work there, if work came to hand; if pressing work were not pushed into one's hand there was a paper to be read, and news to be shared with colleagues and friends in other offices. There was a very small salary at the end of the month, and much more importantly, a large bag of rice, part of their government servant allowance, and of crucial importance in feeding their families.

And, perhaps most important in the Indonesian *pegawai*'s view of their daily round, and *unlike* these busy young Australians, *they* had other work waiting for them at home – several young children perhaps, needing to be fed and their schooling paid for. Many Indonesian *pegawais* had additional jobs in the private or informal sector waiting for them in the afternoons or early evenings which paid much better than the government ones. These ranged from hammering used cans in a *kampung* co-operative, to making recycled tin,[63] to selling anything (from tiny clothes in the local market previously run up on a battered old Singer by a sister or aunt, to home-made cakes), and to acting as night watchman for some much higher ranking

---

63   I remember a gardener who cut grass for a government department, did the ironing of our household in 1954, acted as a night watchman, helped hammer tin in his *kampung* enterprise, and always had time to give me conversation lessons!

pegawai's comfortable home. These were the second and third jobs of the lowest paid. The occupations of the better-educated in their own time were teaching at private schools sometimes for two more shifts in the day, giving a couple of hours' classes in one of the many private tertiary institutions springing up everywhere around the larger cities, or translating for rich foreign companies. All this "private work", imposed by daily necessity, was in a very real sense much more important than the time they spent at the government office, despite all the official rhetoric, because this is what kept their families and households functioning. Such a state of affairs was inevitable until a much later oil boom enabled a substantial rise in the middle level government salaries.[64]

Thus sometimes when Australians wrote home in private letters or even in semi-official reports about the "laziness" of local staff, they were guilty of the paternalistic judgmentalism shown by the former Netherlands East Indies administrators (themselves outstanding examples in their own time of the Puritan work ethic). They may not have realised at the time of writing that in some cases at least what appeared to them as laziness was a combination of acceptance that *their* humble contribution was never going to solve the problems of the infant Republic or even the crumbling building where they sat from 7:00a.m. (officially) to whenever their office truck or bus collected them, together with weariness from wakeful nights with ill relatives or babies or just "*tjari uang*" (looking for cash).[65]

Another problem must have been all-pervasive among volunteer graduates. And this was the most difficult to discuss thirty years later, because perhaps it was seldom "owned" or brought out into the open, or given accepted expression within the group: that of the need to be, and to be *seen* to be "living up to the ideals of the Scheme". All the volunteers, in their less confident moments, must have felt the difficulties of their position of being "informal ambassadors of goodwill, helping to build bridges of understanding". Some of that earlier reporting and "newsletters to interested would-be-volunteers" seemed to imply that no Australian living in Indonesia under the Scheme would ever wish to buy expensive imported canned food in the local Chinese groceries (much less sponge on a chance European, British or Australian Embassy acquaintance who had access to such luxuries,

---

64 The oil boom's beneficial effect from 1973 onwards, was noticeable to the writer in 1974 when in her first visit back for some years she was able to notice items such as a washing machine and a fridge – formerly unobtainable luxuries – in the small house of a former colleague from her office.
65 The writer's own correspondence, 1954–1956.

even including Danish blue cheese, in Embassy stores!).[66] Nor would they *want* to go for a swim in the Embassy swimming pool (after all were there not public swimming pools open, from which the colonial sign "No dogs or natives allowed" had been appropriately removed with independence?), or feel the need to save out of their tiny salaries for excursions to expensive restaurants or even want to go to the pictures. Their lives outside office hours would be filled with satisfying informal social contacts with entertaining and stimulating Indonesian friends who, being all musically gifted, could provide instant musical entertainment. Volunteers were assured that Indonesians had no racial prejudices or religious intolerance, and – as they were *Indonesians* – "*real Indonesians*" – *just being with them* would be in itself fulfilling the aims of the Scheme. Volunteers received very definite messages that too much contact with other Europeans was not desirable for *pegawais* working under the Scheme. Foreigners after all lived a different life-style – a *Colonial Life-Style* – and the whole point of the Scheme was to show a real viable alternative to anything that might even remotely resemble that life-style. The task of the volunteer was to melt into the Indonesian landscape socially as well as professionally.[67] After all, volunteers were there not only to do a specific job, but to show that white people need not necessarily live like those other Westerners – the "foreign expert":

> There is nothing extraordinary about living on an Indonesian salary in Indonesia, eating Indonesian food or speaking Indonesian – except that the majority of foreign personnel in Indonesia do not do these things. As one *pegawai* commented: "The Europeans have a fairly full appreciation of what it means, much to their general embarrassment"

---

66   Jakarta was regarded by the diplomatic community as a hardship post. Hence "goodies" from home were available to staff at their store or "canteen" which of course was not open to the general public. Probably the most expensive items would have been hard liquor.

67   In fact of course many volunteers *did* make friends with other Westerners, including diplomatic staff, many of whom turned out to be not particularly colonial in their attitudes, but in some cases had joined up to "see the world". Two male volunteers eventually married girls from European Embassies – and one woman volunteer married an Indonesian diplomat. The "ideology" however was such that people often felt the need to be apologetic, even if they did not actually feel guilty, about their associations with "colonial-style" fellow Europeans. Yet some made enduring friendships with fellow-members of church congregations – Americans or Europeans, whose lifestyle was certainly within the "luxury" class – and with a completely new group of foreigners, researchers and graduate students, mainly Americans, who began to arrive on Rockefeller and Ford Foundation grants. But always the message was part of the background of the daily life for volunteer graduates – they were there mainly to meet Indonesians, not other foreigners however attractive!

> ... it is reward enough when Indonesian colleagues talk about "these foreigners" and obviously exclude you.[68]

Perhaps an unconscious warning could be read into this comment; it is true that many volunteers were included by their Indonesian colleagues in such conversations, and were genuinely excluded from the inevitable talk about "those foreigners". "Us and them" was a genuine distinction between, on the one hand, volunteers working closely in a team with Indonesian colleagues, to whom they were usually junior in both rank and age and who felt comfortable with these enthusiastic but very young "younger brothers and sisters", and, on the other hand, "experts" in the same field, e.g. English language teaching and teacher-training. The latter were ultimately responsible to *other* employers and funding agencies and their loyalties were quite properly elsewhere both professionally and personally. Inevitably, too, the whole life-style of the "foreign experts" meant distancing themselves from even the most senior and most responsible Indonesian colleague. However, *nothing* could alter the reality that after all the volunteers were also foreigners. Most of them knew that they would eventually return to Australia to make another professional and personal life there. Thus the responsibility,

---

68 "Invitation to Adventure – A History of the V.G.S.", *Djembatan*, Vol 2, No 4, Special Issue, September 1959, p. 6. On the attitude of volunteer graduates to Australian Embassy staff, see the following extract from a letter written from Herb Feith to Jim Webb, 16 November 1961 (written during Herb's temporary visit to Jakarta as a research fellow of the ANU, August to December 1961): "... it's the old situation of conflict with the embassy. P... (one of the Embassy staff) feels that V.G.S. go out of their way to have nothing to do with the embassy, they just collect their bike money and return tickets home and have no other connection. They never think it's worth their while to talk to the cultural attachés about Indonesian–Australian relations, and on the other hand, sit at Molly's feet. Why can't the relationships be as with the Peace Corps, whose members are proud to be American, and whose impact will be the impact of a group acting concertedly, not just of a few isolated individuals? Is it necessary for people to turn their backs on their own country in order to practise their belief in humanity? and so on. Nothing at all new, yet the emotional intensity of it all surprised and shocked me – particularly coming from P. who, on his own testimony and from what I can observe, is nearer us in spirit than most other members of that embassy ... As P. pointed out, most Indonesian officials one speaks to, even ones relatively near to the Volunteer Graduate Scheme, have never heard of the existence of the Scheme ... I should add that the present Volunteer Graduate Scheme, at least the ones I know, Lance, Peter and the New Zealanders, are not at all strongly anti-Embassy or anti-Australian government. Apparently some *Djembatan* articles, including Bett's one in the Special Issue if I interpreted the hint correctly, have been important in arousing this highly emotional reaction in P. ... and perhaps also in others". In the article mentioned, the Scheme had been approvingly described as "an institutionalization of protest". See Betty Feith, "Colonialism Dies Hard", *Djembatan*, Special Issue, p. 19.

ultimately, for decisions taken by any volunteers, no matter how seriously and responsibly taken, *must be* inevitably less, as it was the Indonesian colleagues of both high and lower rank who would have to live with those decisions once the volunteers had cleared their desks and made their last farewells.

In some important sense, even for those who married Indonesian nationals, and indeed just as much for them too, total identification with their friends and relatives (no matter how close) would always be impossible, for after all they were not Indonesian citizens. Thus perhaps there was a warning, at least for those able to read between the lines, against "over-identification" for those with many Indonesian friends and who seemed to be very adept at "melting into the Indonesian landscape".

For those volunteers with a natural or professional interest in either comparative religion, politics, language or ethnicity, life out of office hours eventually could become full of interest. However, even volunteers with very keen interest in all these matters were sometimes hampered, at least in the early period of their stay, by the circumstances of their hostel accommodation. One of the first three volunteers, for instance, spent some time in a hostel where she shared a room with three Javanese girls who used to speak to each other in Javanese, not Indonesian. The Australian at first could not understand why her early lessons in the Indonesian language were not helping her in her efforts to break down the language barrier! A less obvious but more absolute barrier to real friendship between herself and these girls was their socialisation as Javanese young ladies and her much freer behaviour as an independent Australian. It was not surprising that the friendships she developed were not with these girls but with young people of ethnic backgrounds whose attitudes to social behaviour was more relaxed.[69]

It is certainly true that volunteers who genuinely liked eating Indonesian food and "fitted in" to their hostels or private family accommodation did not need to spend much of their salary on imported food, and certainly there was plenty of company! But what if the volunteer happened to be not particularly interested in comparative religion or politics or "local customs", and if they liked playing or watching Aussie Rules or basketball, with their leisure time back in Australia mainly taken up in hobbies such as swimming, beaching and camping with friends and family – the activities of most young Australians! What if the volunteer found that the Indonesian language *was* very difficult – after all she had never been good at French

---

69   Ivan Southall has described this volunteer's predicament in *Indonesia Face to Face*, p. 69.

at school! – and if she was slow to make friends because of poor language ability, and week after lonely week had not one really close Indonesian friend. One early volunteer shared a hostel room with uncommunicative young ladies, public servants in another ministry who spent almost no time in their room after office hours anyway, whose only interest seemed to be clothes, who not only spoke no English but talked to each other *very* quickly, and who perhaps begrudged the newcomer's presence in an already overcrowded room with large wardrobes shutting out the light and where there was obviously no room to put the Australian's heavy ship luggage! The Australian men could at least wander off on their own but girls were expected to be with other people, especially at night!

For people in such a situation, lonelier than had ever seemed possible back home in Australia, the sense of struggling far, far behind some of the other Australians – who had turned out to be accomplished linguists or at least very adept in picking up the more informal day-to-day expressions of the language, and who seemed to be always going out with Indonesian groups or to Indonesian homes – and the sense that she must "grit her teeth and keep on keeping on" must have seemed a heavy burden. Married couples, or a pair of girls rooming together and doing similar work as in the case of the two Semarang teachers, were shielded from such experiences. Perhaps the heaviest part of the burden was the undoubted sincerity of the idealism of the others. Possibly the reasons behind the "early returns" of those few volunteers who left Indonesia earlier than they had originally intended were partly that some more isolated individuals, particularly if they lived out of Jakarta and so could not afford to go there often, felt oppressed by the group solidarity and by the optimism and what at times must have bordered on "do-goodism" of the majority, particularly those at any one time constituting the Jakarta Committee. For anyone less inclined to feel "part of the team" this may have been a more difficult problem than struggling to adapt to food or climate, though there were cases of that too – e.g. one volunteer declared "she could not bear to eat rice any longer!"[70]

Finally, for some volunteers, one more problem was to be faced, that of "reverse culture shock" on their return to Australia. The sight of the empty countryside (except for sheep), the large empty front gardens, empty noontide suburban footpaths, busy city streets full of non-smiling hurrying

---

70 Some volunteers did develop digestive problems because of the at first unfamiliar diet, though they were in the minority.

Australians – all this made many who were newly-returned long to be back in noisy bustling Java, or in whatever town had become "home".[71]

In June 1963 the Overseas Service Bureau committee was asked by Jim Webb to approve a grant to Ivan Southall to assist him in his plans to travel to Indonesia and interstate, to meet former volunteers. He wished to write "a book specifically based on the volunteers' own descriptions of their experience".[72] Jim Webb believed "the publicity value of such a volume would be a great asset at this stage of the Scheme and Bureau, with the added possibility of extensive publicity through press reviews, radio and TV".[73] The committee accepted this proposal. Ivan Southall made his plans, and armed with addresses, advice, and warnings, took himself and his typewriter to Indonesia for several weeks. The then current volunteers arranged for his accommodation and travel and helped arrange his interviews. Ivan returned with material not only for this projected book, published as *Indonesia Face to Face*, but also for a second one for younger readers, entitled *Indonesian Journey*.[74] His draft was discussed with the Melbourne Committee until 4:00a.m. one very lengthy meeting! All the volunteers at the time in Indonesia received copies and were asked for their comments. A couple expressed the concern that Indonesia is seen only as a backdrop "in which the volunteers are seen to parade larger than life".[75] There was also a query expressed by a couple of letters as to how much appeal it would have for people who did not have inside knowledge of the Scheme, and who did not know the people concerned, or who had no

---

71 See A.G. Zainu'ddin: "You may find, as I have, that you are as homesick for Indonesia when you return as you were for Australia when you were there." From "It's Dangerous to go to Indonesia", *Djembatan*, Vol 1, No 1, July 1957.

72 Memo OSB Committee, Travel Grant to Ivan Southall, June 1963. This was not an entirely new idea, as Keith Adams of the ABC had previously requested interviews with the Feiths, and Ailsa Zainu'ddin for tapes for a radio programme, on condition that they had the opportunity to listen to and make suggestions about any desired changes to the tapes. Those arrangements had proceeded satisfactorily.

73 Memo OSB Committee, Travel Grant to Ivan Southall, June 1963. The point was made that Ivan would not have been able to afford to pay for the trip without this help.

74 Ivan was not yet the famous children's author that he later became. In my opinion this second book was the better of the two – there he was able to convey vividly and empathetically his *own* impressions of his journey, without having to refer to people whom he never really got to know; though he used their material very extensively for *Indonesia Face to Face*, it was not possible for him to see *their* Indonesia through *their* eyes!

75 George Hicks to J. B. Webb, 1 November 1964. I share this concern; and of course in my case and that of the other early volunteers, there is the added personal embarrassment of having personal affairs so publicly and romantically presented!

prior knowledge of the country. On the other hand, the view was expressed that "it will do something towards filling the vacuum in the understanding of Indonesia by the general run of the people at home".[76] "The book has its uses in Australia in that it must help to increase knowledge and understanding of Indonesia".[77]

The book was for some years widely available in public and school libraries and on occasion it has led to useful class discussions. In one sense it caused a problem for those involved; Ivan Southall seemed to be speaking on their behalf, yet that was a task no-one could do but themselves. It was in no sense *their* book – it had to be Southall's, in the *Simon Black* and *Parsons on the Track* tradition.

---

76 John Janes to J. B. Webb, 12 November 1964.
77 Mary Johnston to J. B. Webb, no date but shortly after the others were received. The general response amongst the Melbourne Committee members seemed to concur with this view, and at a time when it was still very difficult to find sympathetically written material on Indonesia, it undoubtedly "helped to fill a gap"!

Conclusion

What has the foregoing discourse to do with education in Indonesia or with aid projects within its educational institutions? Perhaps Indonesian students and researchers will one day tease out what they see as "foreign influences" with either positive or negative results, in a yet-to-be written history of the Indonesian educational system.[78]

I simply want to comment on what I see as its effect on Australia and Australians.[79] What seems relevant to me, after having reflected on my own personal and professional history since the Indonesian experience, and upon that of all those volunteers with whom I am still in contact, is to attempt to assess the effect and influence of the experience of volunteering on the later lives of the people concerned and upon their immediate circle of friends and professional associates, their personal development and further education at both formal and informal levels, their professional careers and their public and community concerns.

In my own case, a brief summary may suffice. I continued with the study of Indonesian language and literature and Area Studies, for audit only, at Cornell University, while my husband was qualifying for his doctorate (1957–1960) – this was through the encouragement of Professor George Kahin. I later enrolled in the Indonesian language course when it was initially offered by the ANU with Tony and Johani Johns as teachers in 1960–1961.[80] After my return to teaching in Melbourne in 1968, I was involved not only in teaching Indonesian Studies and Southeast Asian history, but also in developing the network of people interested in continuing Indonesian studies and in maintaining a link with Indonesian friends both "here" and "there".

---

78 In 1979 the New Zealand Council for Educational Research published *Assessment of Indonesian Education – A Guide in Planning*, the result of several years' full-time work by C.E. Beeby as a consultant with the Indonesian Ministry of Education. This was a valiant attempt to describe and analyse the enormous bureaucracy which the Ministry had by this time become. Though basically sympathetic, this was inevitably written from the point of view of the outsider.

79 A quite separate study for a future scholar could be the influence of the Scheme and of Australian Volunteers Abroad (AVA) and OSB policy and that of the mushrooming non-governmental agencies of the 1970s, on the formation of Australian Government policy on aid issues.

80 I am currently attending language classes at Victoria College where I teach Indonesian history; one of the aims of the course is to encourage students to continue with their studies at post-graduate level. [1984]

My own experience is just one example of the way in which many former volunteers have developed what began as an "interest in another culture" – reinforced and strengthened by their stay as volunteers in Indonesia, and in some cases by periods of work in other Third World countries – into a major strand of their professional careers. This includes teaching and publishing and researching in the Asian Studies area or the language area, and being administrators of Asian Studies programmes.[81]

Less professional and more informal organisations were begun by ex-volunteers and their friends as part of this task of "bridge-building" and extending the knowledge of Australians and Indonesia. For instance, Don Anderson, then chairman of the VGA, and Zainu'ddin, the first lecturer in Indonesian language appointed at the University of Melbourne at the beginning of 1956, helped to form the Australian Indonesian Association (AIA) in September 1956. The committee which founded the AIA included both founding groups – the VGA and the network of Colombo Plan Students (the first batch of which had just arrived) and their friends. For many years the AIA has served an educational function in the production of journals, newsletters and occasional monographs, and the organisation of language classes and a winter series of lectures (in collaboration with the Centre of Southeast Asian Studies at Monash University). [1984] The AIA has also served an important social function, providing a network which has enabled ex-volunteers and their families to maintain contacts with Indonesian families residing in Melbourne and Indonesian students, and to meet visiting Indonesian guests. Later, Hugh O'Neill, who has continued to offer Southeast Asian Architecture among his courses taught at the University of Melbourne, formed the Indonesian Arts Society as an offshoot of the AIA. This organisation enables serious students of the fine arts and music to meet visiting practitioners and visit specialised galleries with like-minded members and friends.

Another informal organisation begun by ex-volunteers with the encouragement of sympathetic university staff members was the Contemporary Indonesia Study Group (CISG). Its aim was to provide a forum for discussion of recent events in both languages, through regular evening sessions

---

81 Three of the four doctors who gained their initial experience of tropical medicine under the Scheme continued to work as doctors in the tropical medicine areas in other countries. Beth Mylius, beginning as a social worker, assisted in the formulation of a "development agency" of such groups as Community Aid Abroad (CAA) and Action for World Development in the seventies and later returned to Indonesia with her husband as part of an ADAB Community Development Project attempting to improve the water supply in Lombok.

(initially chaired by Harry Whitfield), and for lectures from visitors and local people "just returned" from a recent study trip or from volunteering. These sessions have enabled ex-volunteers and their friends and families to "keep up" their Indonesian language skills and extend their knowledge of Indonesian conditions. The Contemporary Indonesia Study Group has served a useful function in enabling former volunteers, plus spouses, to participate in a form of continuing education in an informal and encouraging atmosphere. (This informal association has proved very valuable, just as a similar opportunity had proved for me at Cornell – domestic commitments would have made formal continued study in this area very difficult). The venue was initially the Department of Indonesian Studies, University of Melbourne, and was later switched to the Centre of Southeast Asian Studies at Monash University. Attendance has always been open, and the programme has attracted numbers of Indonesian students and longer-term residents.

Just as important in providing what became the substance of their professional lives, the volunteering experience provided the impetus for pressure group activities from time to time designed to change a situation in Australia. The "double vision" of returned visitors from another society alienated them to some degree from aspects perceived as undesirable and negative in Australian society. Hence, some volunteers joined pressure groups to change the structures of university courses to enable the development of more Asian Studies-oriented courses and more Indonesian language departments. Other volunteers joined groups designed to bury, at long last, the White Australia Policy, and to persuade enough of the "informed public opinion" among the newspaper-reading public in this country to enable a less racist immigration policy to emerge.[82] Some joined in the organisation publicising the Bali Relief Appeal at the time

---

82   The Foreword of *Djembatan*, Vol 4, No 1, September 1960, alerted its readers to the formation of the Immigration Reform Group under the chairmanship of Jamie Mackie, then head of the Department of Indonesian Studies at the University of Melbourne, and its publication of *Control or Colour Bar? – A Proposal for Change in Australia's Immigration Policy*. This document argued that the "notion of White Australia is poisoning our relations with Asia, indeed with the whole non-European world. The atmosphere of suspicion which it creates, affects even the attitudes of those Asians who came to study here." *Control or Colour Bar?*, Introduction, vi. Don Anderson, Harry Whitfield, George Hicks and Ailsa Zainu'ddin were among the group producing that pamphlet. *Djembatan* advertised it as a bargain at 3 shillings. It was enlarged and published by Melbourne University Press in 1962 as a book of 170 pages entitled *Immigration: Control or Colour Bar*, edited by Kenneth Rivett, at a cost of 12/6d.

of the disastrous volcanic eruption in 1963, and in working groups behind the "Drugs for Indonesia" appeal sponsored by the Australian Indonesian Association in Melbourne, also in the sixties. Later some joined in the formation of a group to secure funding for the Saturday community-language school in Bahasa Indonesia, for Indonesians and part-Indonesian children growing up in Melbourne. In all these pressure groups and working parties, whether long- or short-term, were to be found, along with a significant and growing number of teachers and academics whose experience of Indonesia had come through field research and study tours, a considerable proportion of ex-volunteers.

Perhaps the biggest single effect is more pervasive than these activities and less easy to define. The people who were volunteers, as with many of a later generation of students, teachers and academics, were fundamentally changed by their experience in Indonesia. They altered their "life-interest directions" even if their professional careers or their pattern of community organisation joining remained unchanged. As Jamie Mackie remarked in 1983:

> The most basic and widespread effects of our contacts with people of an utterly different culture ... is to make us aware of how culture-bound we ourselves have been in our thinking about the world ... the discovery of Indonesia is also the discovery of Australia.[83]

Ambassador Tirtawinata had predicted such a state of affairs many years ago, in his 1956 address at Melbourne University:

> I believe its [the Scheme's] effects in Australia will also be noticeable, despite the comparatively small number of persons directly affected ... its spiritual and intellectual effects [i.e. increasing mutual understanding by changing *Australian* attitudes] will outweigh the actual teaching and training which you are able to give us, and that will be reflected in many directions in the future.[84]

To identify the variety of motives underlying the initial departure of the volunteers would be a complex task – some freely admitted the mixture of motives and aspirations they saw within themselves. For some it was perhaps

---

83 Asian Studies Association of Australia Newsletter, Vol 7, No 2, November 1983, p. 30.
84 Speech by Dr R. H. Tirtawinata to the Volunteer Graduate Scheme Conference, 23 August 1956. Despite the diplomatic language, this speech contains some important points.

more simple than others – one for instance was a Quaker and saw the task of international reconciliation at a personal level, as something "laid upon him" by his religious belief. Others had ties to the internationally-minded and "Fellowship of Reconciliation"-type streams within their own church backgrounds and saw volunteering as one way of expressing that call from their churches, to "building bridges of international understanding". Some, perhaps, were looking for "a cause" into which they could throw all their energies, and could not see any gripping need within mainstream Australian society at that time.

Some were in fact migrants to Australia, and were searching for an identity which could not be contained within Australian public or professional life. As migrants they saw Australia with that terrible clarity of "double vision" which marginality and alienation bring.[85]

Some had missionary backgrounds in their own families and were searching for an alternative way to be "a missionary" – not for any religion, but for this Good News of a mode of identification.[86]

During the early 1980s it became painfully clear that the attempts of former volunteers, along with many other Australians, to change the attitudes of fellow Australians in order to bring about a non-discriminatory, truly inter-racial society had been less successful than they may previously, perhaps in moments of self-congratulation, have assumed. The extent of anti-Asian propaganda filling the capital cities in recent weeks, on street hoardings, in university toilets, and spread through the media by such organisations as the League of Rights and by the utterances of many individuals from professors to taxi drivers has been such as to provoke the following comment from a Hong Kong resident in the Letters column in *The Age*. [May–August 1984] In the letter, the author notes that the local press in Hong Kong had recently carried:

---

85 See for example the autobiography of author and political activist Amirah Inglis, entitled *Amirah: An Un-Australian Childhood*. Melbourne: William Heinemann Australia, 1983. Inglis reached Melbourne as an infant, and also a few years ahead of Herb Feith. But her family stories and attitudes about the Australians with their barbarous ways are at some points strikingly similar to his. Both those two grew up without an accent, but in fundamental ways they were and have remained undoubtedly un-Australian. Their parents saw Australian school teachers as barbarous and uncouth, Australian food as uneatable, and above all, Australian attitudes as ignorant and provincial.

86 For Beth Mylius, part of the "group feeling" of the volunteers (shared by her) was *rebellion* against that missionary background, which was sometimes of a fundamentalist evangelical nature.

... prominent news items about a survey showing that "Australians" disapprove of "Asian" immigrants, and prefer people from "Britain and Europe" ... It appears that what the survey actually shows is that white Australians prefer white immigrants and reject people of any other color ... there are many white Australians in Hong Kong and they obviously find Asians perfectly acceptable as neighbours ... and vice versa. It is not the color of the baby's skin that makes the bathwater black.[87]

Professor Wang Gungwu suggested at the 1984 Asian Studies Association of Australia (ASAA) Conference in Adelaide that "we should blame ourselves" for this spate of anti-Asian publicity.

> We have been talking to ourselves and to each other at these gatherings, and not to our fellow Australians and professional colleagues. We have assumed that they have all along accepted and understood our view ... We must now communicate our message more clearly.[88]

The task laid upon members of the ASAA by Professor Wang Gungwu – that of communicating the message of the aims of a genuinely multicultural society within Australia, and particularly the obligation to bring about "a fair go" and justice within our social structure and the opportunity of equality for Asian migrants – has now been vigorously publicised through the media. A thesis could be written solely on the implications of the racism explicit in some of the recent statements on "desirable proportions" of future Asian migrant intake and the "Australian cultural heritage".

And so the task taken up by early volunteers of creating new perceptions of Asians among Australians, of enabling new ways in which Indonesian and Australian people could relate to and view each other, has by no means become redundant. It has entered a new phase, in which academics have become prominent in their examination of the racism perhaps previously unexamined in our entire social fabric and social history. The majority of ex-volunteers, including those who went to Indonesia after 1963, and their network of family and friends are inevitably involved in this examination.

---

87 Brian van Buuren, *The Age*, 26 May 1984.
88 Private conversation with Professor Wang Gungwu, elaborated at the annual general meeting of the Asian Studies Association of Australia (1984) in a memorable speech in which he pleaded against the use of the "ugly word" "racist" by the Association as part of its condemnation of the recent "anti-Asian" debate.

For their attempts as volunteers to become part of Indonesian society made the processes of learning to live within another culture, albeit as guests, part of the search for their own personal identity. This has carried through into a continuing search for a place for themselves, once returned, as part of Australian society. This continuing attempt to interpret the thoughts and attitudes, the dreams and hopes of their friends within Indonesian society, has become part of their lives and work till the present day.[89]

---

89   This continuing task is shared by three former volunteers who continue to live in Indonesia, though visiting families and friends in Australia as often as possible. Ann McDonald married Suyono Pryosusilo, Joan Minogue married Hardjono and lived and taught in Bandung, and Mary Johnston continued to serve as a volunteer through AVA on successive terms.

Appendices

Appendix A – Alphabetical List of Volunteers Serving in Indonesia from 1951–1963

Appendix B – Early Letters from Committee Files (Transcripts):
   i. From Betty Evans *et al.* to O. McMichael, April 1951
   ii. From Valerie Wadsworth to O. McMichael, September 1951
   iii. From Embassy of Indonesia to O. McMichael, June 1952
   iv. Reference from the Director of Civil Aviation, Republic of Indonesia to O. McMichael, December 1953
   v. From *Charge d'affaires a.i.*, Embassy of Indonesia to Gwenda Rodda, November 1954
   vi. From Australian Embassy, Jakarta to Gwenda Rodda, May 1956
   vii. From Department of External Affairs, Canberra to Gwenda Rodda re Joan Minogue and Noela Motum, February 1957

Appendix C – NUAUS Material (Transcripts):
   i. "A Pilot Project in Southeast Asia – The Australian Volunteer Graduate Scheme for Indonesia", 1959 (one page hand-out)
   ii. "What is a Pegawai? Volunteer Graduate Association for Indonesia", no date (illustrated flyer)
   iii. From "Review of the Volunteer Graduate Scheme, 1960" (first page of 11-page report)

Appendix D – Overseas Service Bureau Hand-Out (Transcript):
"An Australian Peace Corps?", 4 March 1964 (one page hand-out)

Appendix A – Alphabetical List of Volunteers Serving in Indonesia from 1951–1963

(* indicates those with whom continuous contact has been maintained [1984])

*Thelma Ashton B.A., Armidale Library Assn. Cert. – Married Richard Rungkat – 1955–57 – Central Libraries Bureau, Ministry of Education, Jakarta
*Vern Bailey M.B., B.S., B.Sc., Melbourne – 1955–57 – Government doctor, General Hospital, Subang, West Java
Merle Bailey (née Day) (joint appointment) – 1957–59 – Nutrition Research Institute, Wonosari Central Java
Ian Barlow B.A., Dip.Ed., Melbourne – 1962–64 – English Lecturer, Faculty of Education, Manado, Sulawesi
Marcus Bull B.Sc., Melbourne – 1958–60 – Industrial Research Institute, Jakarta
Eric Campbell B.A., B.Sc., Melbourne – 1958–59 – Maths and Physics teaching, Faculty of Education, Bandung, West Java
*Lance Castles B.Econ., Melbourne – 1960–63 – Research Assistant in the Faculty of Economics, University of Indonesia, Jakarta
Scott Chaston B.Sc. (Sydney) Dip.Chem.Eng. – 1960–62 – Faculty of Education, Malang, East Java
*Lindsay Cleland B.A., Adelaide – 1955–57 – Faculty of Education, Tondano, Sulawesi
Merle Day B.Sc., Melbourne – 1955–57 – Botanist with Botanical Gardens, Bogor, West Java
*Ian Doig B.Sc., Melbourne – 1954–55 – Eijkman Institute, Jakarta, and Chemical Research Institute, Bogor, West Java
*Lou Eakins B.Civil Eng., Melbourne – 1962–63 – Civil Engineer with Indonesian Government Construction Firm "Indah Karja", Bandung
*Betty Feith (née Evans) B.A., Dip.Ed., Melbourne – 1954–56 – English teacher, English Language Inspectorate, Ministry of Education, Jakarta
*Herb Feith M.A., Melbourne – 1951–53 – Ministry of Information, Jakarta, 1954–56 – Ministry of Information, Jakarta
Alison Frankel, Pharmacist Melbourne – 1953–54 – Central Public Hospital, Jakarta
*John Gare B.Eng. (Aer.), Sydney – 1957–60 – Aeronautical engineer, Ministry of Communications, Jakarta
*Sylvia Graham (m. L. Cleland 1957) B.A., Dip.Ed., Melbourne – 1955–57 – Faculty of Education, Tondano, Sulawesi
*George Hicks B.Comm., M.Sc., (Econ.) Melbourne – 1963–65 – National Planning Council, Jakarta
John Janes B.Sc., (Agric.) Western Australia – 1963–65 – Department of Agriculture, Palembang, South Sumatra
*Mary Johnston B.A., Dip.Soc.Stud., Melbourne – 1963–65 (and successive terms) – Social Research Institute, Yogyakarta, Central Java
Adele Kerridge Dip.Occ.Ther. – 1962–64 – Occupational therapist, Bogor (placed with husband)
Peter Kerridge B.Agric.Sci., Queensland – 1961–64 – Faculty of Agriculture, Bogor, West Java
Keith Lethlean M.B., B.S., Melbourne – 1955–56 – Government doctor, General Hospital, Siau Island, Sulawesi
*Bernard Lionnet B.Comm., Melbourne – 1963–65 – Economist, Department of Basic Industries, Jakarta

Stuart Lipscombe B.Eng. (Elec.), B.Sc., Queensland – 1962–64 – Electrical engineer, Planning Department, State Electrical Authority, Jakarta
*Ann McDonald (m. Suyono Pryosusilo 1957) B.A., Dip.Ed., Armidale – 1955–56 – English Language Inspectorate, Ministry of Education, Jakarta
*Ollie McMichael (died 1978) Dip.Radio Eng. Technology, University of New South Wales – 1952–54 – Teacher, Air Training School, Jakarta Airport Complex
Jeff Miles B.A., LLB., Sydney – 1959–60 – English teacher, Air-training School, Curug, West Java
*Joan Minogue (m. Hardjono) B.A., Dip.Ed., Sydney – 1957–58 – English Language Teachers' Training Course, Semarang, Central Java
*Ray Mylius M.B., B.S., Melbourne – 1957–59 – Government doctor, General Hospital Ende, Flores
*Beth Mylius Dip.Social Studies, Melbourne – 1957–59 – accompanied husband
*Noela Motum (died 1984) B.A., Dip.Ed., Sydney – 1957–58 – English Language Teachers' Training Course, Semarang, Central Java
*Hugh O'Neill B.Arch., Melbourne – 1958–60 – Architecture lecturer, Bandung Technical Faculty, West Java
Hugh Reeves B.Sc., Tasmania – 1956–58 – Physics lecturer, University of Indonesia, Bandung
Janet Richardson B.Sc., Tasmania – 1957 – Taught briefly Botanical Gardens, Bogor before returning to Tasmania
*Gwenda Rodda B.Sc., Melbourne – 1952–54 – Eijkman Institute, Jakarta; 1956–57 Health Department, Banjarmasin, Kalimantan
*Ken Thomas B.A., Adelaide – 1955–57, 1958–60 – Research Assistant, Faculty of Economics, University of Indonesia
*Ailsa Thomson (m. Zainu'ddin 1954) M.A., Melbourne – 1954–55 – English Language Inspectorate, Ministry of Education, Jakarta
*Harry Whitfield M.Sc., Melbourne – 1954–57 – Lecturer in Physical Chemistry, Gadjah Mada University, Yogyakarta
*Elaine Wills B.A., Dip.Ed., Melbourne – 1958–60 – Teacher Training Course, Medan and Darussalem, Aceh, North Sumatra
*Carmyl Winkler B.Sc., Melbourne – 1961–63 – Teacher, University of North Sumatra, Darussalem, Aceh
Don Winkler (with Carmyl, placed as a married couple) B.A., Dip.Ed., Melbourne – 1961–63 – Teacher at same university

From 1957 to 1963 seven New Zealanders served under a parallel scheme administered by the New Zealand and Indonesian Governments. They were in close contact with the Jakarta Volunteers from Australia and with the Melbourne Committee, and contributed regularly to *Djembatan*.

Appendix B – Early Letters from Committee Files (Transcripts)

Appendix B (i)

(The original has here in ink:

Sorry this so badly typed. April 1951
Better next time (I hope)
Good luck! Bett.) 33 Range St.
  Camberwell

<u>PROGRESS REPORT 1</u>

GROUP SCHEME FOR INDONESIA.

Dear Olly,

The committee in Melbourne investigating the possibility of graduate employment in Indonesia, thought you might like to know what has been happening up to date.

<u>Student groups</u>
S.C.M. As you know, 7 members of National Conference gave us their names to be forwarded to the Government as graduates prepared to work in Indonesia. Inter-Varsity Fellowship (EU) and the United Catholic Federation (UCFA) are being approached for volunteers.

NUAUS Council are fully behind the scheme, and have appointed Ken Long as SE Asian Relations Officer. But John Bayly, who put forward the scheme to the Council at the recent NUAUS Congress, reports that little can be done in the way of getting groups of volunteers together before 1st term.

<u>Australian Government</u>
Before Xmas, we wrote to the following:
  External Affairs Dept:
  Mr T. K. Critchley, [Recently?] the Australian representative on the UN Commission for Indonesia (No reply yet.)
  Mr. Spender   Minister for External Affairs.
  Mr. Watt   Secretary of the dept. His reply we passed on to you at Conference, and we forwarded your name to him.

Mr. John Hood   we wrote also but no reply yet
Mr. Menzies   we wrote also but no reply yet

Dr. Evatt we contacted, and he is very interested. We also wrote Mr. K Beazley, member for Freemante [Fremantle], and Prof. McMahon Ball, who is very enthusiastic, and who has promised to help us in every way he can.

The Govt attitude as shown by the Dept. of External Affairs, is enthusiastic, but non-committal so-far. At the moment it does look as if some of those whose names have been sent on, could get across this year.

Indonesian Government:

We have written to:

Dr. M. Roem, Foreign Affairs minister.

Mr. A. Loebis, a delegate to the recent Bombay Conference, [who] asked there for outside help. He is in the Foreign Affairs Dept. too.

Mr. Bondan, a member of the new Interdepartmental Committee for foreign and technical aid, set up by the Indonesian Govt.

The Indonesian Student Union.

The Indonesian Student Christian Movement.

Dr Oetoyo, Indonesian Ambassador in Australia.

No official replies have yet been received, but private contacts with responsible members of the Indonesian Govt. Service are showing signs of keen interest on the Indonesian side.

In the meantime: we will try and move the Powers as fast as possible.

We have written to the Indonesian Dept. of Information for bulletins and publicity, and will forward them on to you when they reach us. If you want details about officials and others over there, and points on settling in, write to Herb Feith, of the Melbourne SCM. (75 Alma Rd Caulfield) He is preparing to leave in a couple of months.

All the best till more news

Betty Evans

John Bailey

John J. Bayly.

Appendix B (ii)
National Union of Australian University Students

Union House,
University of Melbourne,
Carlton Vic.
19th September, 1951

Dear Mr McMichael

Enclosed, at last, is a copy of a report from Herb Feith about conditions in Indonesia. We apologise that we have not been able to give you such information before this but it has taken some to get it together.

To date, the Ministry of Health in Indonesia has offered to employ four of the volunteers for the scheme – 3 Science graduates and one engineer. Mr. Feith and supporters of the scheme are investigating the possibilities of employing others in other Government departments.

We have not as yet had news of whether the Government or UNESCO through the Commonwealth Office of Education have considered our proposition to help the scheme by paying fares etc, but they are known to be sympathetic and we are proceeding hopefully.

In view of the fact that up till now you have had very little information on conditions in Indonesia, we feel that we cannot consider you as definitely wishing to participate in the scheme. And as we do not wish to obtain jobs and then have to cancel them because people do not want them, we would now be very grateful if you would complete the enclosed form and return it to us if you wish to participate in the scheme. Anyone whose name we now have as being interested in the scheme will continue to receive any information which comes to hand. In short, we will still send you material whether you return the form or not.

With best wishes,

Yours sincerely,

VALERIE WADSWORTH

General Secretary

Appendix B (iii)

Embassy of Indonesia
Canberra, A.C.T.

No.: C2/1944

11th June 1952

Dear Sir,

Further to my letter of June 5th No. C2/1917, I wish to inform you that I have received confirmation on your employment with the Ministry of Communication in Djakarta.

Herewith I enclose your passport in which an official visa has been inserted for an indefinite stay in Indonesia.

Yours faithfully,

Iljas Hamzah

FIRST SECRETARY

Mr. O. C. McMichael,

46 Holt Avenue,

Cremorne,

SYDNEY N.S.W.

Appendix B (iv)

KEMENTERIAN PERHUBUNGAN

DJAKARTA 8th December, 1953

SURAT KETERANGAN / REFERENCE

No. 3122/KPS/53

Dengan ini diterangkan bahwa

Tuan OLIVER CLEMENTS MCMICHAEL
telah bekerdja pada Penerbangan Sipil dari Kementerian Perhubungan Republik Indonesia sebagai Ahli Teknik Radio mulai tanggal 2 Djuli 1952 sampai achir bulan Nopember 1953.

Selama bekerdja pada Penerbangan Sipil ia menunaikan kewadjibannja sebagai pegawai Pemerintah Indonesia dengan penuh tanggung-djawab dan kegiatan dan ia menjelesaikan segala pekerdjaan jang diserahkan kepadanja dengan memuaskan.

Maka dengan ini pula dinjatakan penghargaan atas tenaga jang telah ditjurahkan oleh Tn.McMichael tersebut kepada Pemerintah Republik Indonesia.

This is to certify that

Mr. OLIVER CLEMENTS MCMICHAEL
worked in the Directorate of Civil Aviation of the Ministry of Transport and Communications of the Republic of Indonesia from 2nd July 1952 until the end of November 1953.

Whilst employed in Civil Aviation he carried out his duties as an employee of the Government of Indonesia in an active and responsible manner, and he has satisfactorily completed all tasks allocated to him.

With this we wish to declare our appreciation of the service which has been rendered by Mr. McMichael to the Government of the Republic of Indonesia.

KEPALA PENERBANGAN SIPIL

THE DIRECTOR OF CIVIL AVIATION

(Dr. R. SUGOTO)

Appendix B (v)

No. E7/5094

Embassy of Indonesia
Canberra, A.C.T.
1st November, 1954

Dear Miss Rodda.

Early last month the Warracknabeal Herald, in its editorial, referred to a Warracknabeal girl which I presume [is] none other than you. Our Melbourne office has been, every now and then, reported to us your constant interest and sympathy for Indonesia.

    I take this opportunity to thank you personally and on behalf of the Embassy and to convey to you our highest appreciation.

    It is my sincerest hope that the Volunteer Graduate Scheme will always serve as an ambassador of Good Will to both of our Countries.

Yours sincerely,
(B. A. UBANI)
Charge d'Affaires a.i.

Miss Gwenda Rodda,

C/- Public Health Laboratory,

School of [Bacteriology],

University of Melbourne,

Carlton.

VICTORIA.

Appendix B (vi)

In reply quote No. 707/1/5

AUSTRALIAN EMBASSY.
DJAKARTA
18th May, 1956

Dear Volunteer Graduate,

You will be pleased to know that the Australian Government has agreed to increase its contribution towards the scheme.

The following points may be of interest to you.

4. On your return journey to Australia you will be paid a travelling allowance of 12/6d per day.
5. Certain <u>major</u> bicycle repairs may be paid by the Embassy. A puncture would necessitate a minor repair.
6. Insurance premiums may be paid on clothing, personal effects including bicycles, typewriters, books etc. You should arrange your own insurance of these articles.
7. Re orientation allowance. This allowance is at the rate of £6 for every month of completed service in Indonesia subject to a maximum of £144 (2 years service) in any one case and subject to the condition that no payment be made in respect of a tour of duty lasting less than 12 months.

I hope to give you further information at a later stage.

Yours very sincerely,
(S. M. Dimmick)
<u>ATTACHÉ</u>

Miss Gwenda Margaret Rodda,

C/– Inspector Kesehatan Uman,

<u>BONDJURNAAIN</u>.

Appendix B (vii)

In reply quote No. 2004/5/10/33 and 35

DEPARTMENT OF EXTERNAL AFFAIRS
CANBERRA.
14th February, 1957.

Dear Miss Rodda,

The Minister for External Affairs has agreed to the appointment of Miss Joan Margaret Minogue and Miss Kathleen Noela Motum as Volunteer Graduates.

Some concern has been felt over their appointment because of their youth. Miss Motum became 21 this month and Miss Minogue will not be 21 until November. However, Miss Minogue's parents have agreed to her going to Indonesia and the Indonesian Government has agreed, at the request of the girls and the Department, that they should be posted together.

We have been informed that both girls will be posted to Banjarmasin, where they will be English teachers. Any guidance and assistance which you could give them would be greatly appreciated.

They sail for Djakarta on the "Nieuw Holland" from Sydney 27th February.

Yours faithfully,

(D. Dexter)

for the Secretary

Appendix C – NUAUS Material (Transcripts)

Appendix C (i)

<u>A PILOT PROJECT IN SOUTHEAST ASIA
THE AUSTRALIAN VOLUNTEER GRADUATE SCHEME
FOR INDONESIA</u>

- Since 1952 28 Australians, college and university graduates, have worked in Indonesia as public servants of the Indonesian government.
- This work is under the auspices of the Volunteer Graduate Scheme, which was initiated by the National Union of Australian University Students at the invitation of the National Union of Indonesian Students (PPMI).
- The basis of the scheme is salary equality with Indonesians. All participants receive standard Indonesian government salaries.
- Participants live with Indonesian families or in government hostels. They learn Indonesian and share as fully as possible in local activities.
- Volunteers are selected by the Indonesian government and are employed for periods of approximately two years. The Australian government provides the selected persons with return fares, an initial clothing allowance, a bicycle, and, upon return home, a small rehabilitation allowance.
- There is room for a wide range of occupational categories under the scheme. Among the ten volunteers currently in Indonesia are three English language teachers, two medical doctors, an architect, an aeronautical engineer, an industrial chemist, a botanist, a social worker and a graduate in economics. All are men and women in their twenties and the group includes two married couples.
- The Volunteer Graduate Scheme is primarily a venture in international friendship and understanding, an attempt at a practical demonstration of racial equality. In addition the aim is to provide technical assistance in a small way.

- Those who have participated in the scheme have been delighted by the warmth of hospitality with which they have been received in Indonesia and by the many Indonesian friendships which they have made. Most of them feel that the human experience of living in the new Republic has involved them much more in receiving than in giving. Already six volunteers have returned to Indonesia for a second term.
- February 1959 saw the inauguration of a New Zealand-Indonesia scheme on the same lines as the Australian–Indonesian one. Two young New Zealanders, an accountant and a college instructor in English, have begun work in the Indonesian government service.
- Americans interested in further information on these schemes may write to Herbert Feith, 912 North Cayuga Street, Ithaca, N.Y.

"The fact that, for the first time in our experience – and our experience, I remind you, includes many long years of European rule – white people have been ready and eager to live among us on our own standards of salary and living, to share family life with us, to become in truth real members of our community, is indeed striking. Such a contribution is worth immeasurably more to us than the rupiahs which it saves our Treasury. It is a demonstration of goodwill and understanding which has moved our hearts greatly and which we feel can do more than all the speeches of people in high places to cement friendly relations between our two nations".

H. E. Dr. R. H. Tirtawinata,
Indonesian Ambassador to Australia,
August 1956.

Appendix C (ii)
[Transcription of "What is a PEGAWAI?", Volunteer Graduate Association flyer]

The Republic of Indonesia
On 17th August, 1945, national independence was proclaimed in the name of the Indonesian people.

After 350 years of colonial rule, this independence was finally established with the transfer of sovereignty on 27th December, 1949.

Problems
This new Republic, with a population of over 80 million, faces tremendous problems of economic, social and political development.

The rate of progress and development naturally depends on the Indonesian peoples themselves, but others can help through their active interest and sympathetic understanding of the situation.

Education
One of the basic problems facing Indonesia is the severe shortage of trained personnel at all levels. This new nation not only lacks qualified people to carry out immediate plans, but also must create rapidly an adequate system of education.

In 1940, about 15% of the Indonesian adult population was literate. Only a small proportion received even the basic elementary education in village schools. A handful of primary pupils passed on to secondary schools and there were only a few hundred Indonesians at University level institutions.

Progress
Today there is a passion for education throughout the Republic. A strenuous effort is being made to expand the school system, to train large numbers of teachers and to establish adequate centres of higher education. New Universities have been created and undergraduate enrolments have increased from 1,700 in 1940 to nearly 20,000 today. By 1955, there were some 7 million children in schools compared with only 2 million in 1940.

Indonesia needs 7,500 engineers by 1960, but there are only a few hundred available at present. The Republic has only one doctor for every 80,000 people. Similar shortages exist in almost every field.

The extreme shortage of trained people gives us an opportunity to make some contribution to the modern Indonesia and also show our goodwill and respect.

The Volunteer Graduate Association seeks your support to enable many more young Australians to live and work among our Asian neighbours.

PEGAWAI is the Indonesian word for "Government Servant". It is also an abbreviation for "Plan for the Employment of Graduates from Australia to Work As Indonesians"!

This word, unknown in Australia a few years ago, is rapidly taking on a meaning for more and more Australians. To mid-1957, twenty-one professionally qualified Australians have worked as pegawais with a variety of Indonesian departments.

An Invitation from Indonesia

The history of these developments goes back to 1950 when two Australian student representatives met some Indonesians at a conference in Bombay. There the Indonesian delegates suggested that perhaps some young Australians would care to visit Indonesia and contribute their interest and skill towards the reconstruction and development of the country.

This suggestion was made known at Melbourne University and a small independent committee was formed to promote the idea. The idea became a reality when in July, 1951, Herbert Feith of Melbourne paid his own way to Indonesia and gained employment with the Ministry of Information.

Pioneers

The next year, two more pioneer graduates, Ollie McMichael, a radio engineer of Sydney, and Gwenda Rodda, a bacteriologist of Melbourne, also provided their own fares and gained employment in Djakarta.

As a result of the experiences of these three pegawais, the Indonesian and Australian Governments by the end of 1952 were prepared to arrange an official Volunteer Graduate Scheme.

Under this programme, approved Volunteers are employed by the Indonesian Government under standard conditions and rates of pay, and the Australian Government pays the fares and other minor allowances

Partners

From the start, a key idea in this plan has been that of "identification". Volunteers share Indonesian life as fully as possible. They live with families or in government hostels. They learn the national language and eat rice meals. Indonesian Public Service rates of pay are very low by Australian standards. Volunteers find they are able to live quite reasonably at the same standard as their Indonesian colleagues, but are unable to save.

Living thus in partnership with Indonesians, these young people have gained far more than they can ever give. Life in Indonesia for them has meant rewarding friendships, new and exciting experiences, interesting travel and valuable insight into the modern Asia.

The Volunteer Graduate Association, with the sponsorship of the National Union of University Students, desires to extend this venture in international and inter-racial friendship.

Past and Present Volunteers

The first Australian graduate was employed by the Indonesian Information Ministry in Djakarta. Later volunteers have not only been employed in a number of different Ministries, but have also worked in various parts of Indonesia.

Teachers: The Indonesian Education Ministry has employed seven Australian volunteers – three in the English Language Inspectorate, Djakarta, two at the Teacher-Training Faculty, Tondano, North Sulawesi, and two at an English course for teachers at Semarang, Central Java.

University Staff: Universities at Jogjakarta, Djakarta and Bandung have employed Australian graduates in physical chemistry, economics and theoretical physics.

Health Workers: The Indonesian Ministry of Health has employed two Australian girls – a pharmacist at the Central Hospital, Djakarta, and a bacteriologist in laboratories in Java and Kalimantan. The first two doctors under this plan were in charge of hospitals on an island off North Sulawesi and at Subang, West Java.

Engineers: A radio engineer and an aeronautical engineer have been employed by the Indonesian Communications Ministry.

Librarian: A girl from New South Wales was employed by the Libraries Bureau, Ministry of Education, Djakarta.

Scientists: Two botanists and an industrial chemist have been attached to research institutes at Bogor, West Java.

The Future

Opportunities exist for many more young Australian men and women to work as volunteer graduates. Two to three years is regarded as the usual term of service, but shorter periods are possible. The term "graduate" is interpreted widely to cover non-university personnel holding diplomas and other tertiary qualifications.

There are vacancies in all the fields listed above, but also required are accountants, civil and other engineers, social workers, marine biologists, architects, agricultural and veterinary scientists and many others.

Volunteer Graduate Association

The aim of the Volunteer Graduate Association for Indonesia is to promote understanding and good relations by sending to Indonesia trained Australians to work on a basis of equality with Indonesians.

The Association maintains a liaison with the Australian and Indonesian Governments, keeps abreast of developments in Indonesia, publicises Indonesia's needs and the opportunities which exist through the Volunteer Graduate Scheme and operates an information service covering all aspects of life in Indonesia for Volunteer Graduates.

The Volunteer Graduate Association, which is sponsored by the National Union of Australian University Students, needs financial help in order to intensify this work and desires the support and encouragement of interested people.

Membership

The membership of the Volunteer Graduate Association includes not only the Volunteer Graduates themselves, but also Friends who support this programme by their interest and financial contributions. The minimum subscription in order to become a Friend of the Association is £1/1/– per annum, or 10/6 in the case of students.

All members of the Association receive a quarterly newsletter containing news and views about Indonesia and the activities of volunteer graduates. From time to time, returned volunteers are available to address organisations.

Enquiries about membership of the Association and about employment in Indonesia may be directed to the Secretary, C/– Union House, University of Melbourne, Carlton, N.3, Victoria.

> "The fact that, for the first time, in our experience – and our experience I remind you, includes many years of European rule – white people have been ready and eager to live among us on our own standards of salary and living, to share family life with us, to become in truth real members of our community, is indeed striking. Such a contribution is worth immeasurably more to us than the rupiahs which it saves our Treasury. It is a demonstration of goodwill and understanding which has moved our hearts greatly and which we feel can do more than all the speeches of people in high positions to cement friendly relations between our two nations."
>
> H. E. Dr. R. H. TIRTAWINATA,
> INDONESIAN AMBASSADOR TO AUSTRALIA, 1956

Appendix C (iii)

Review of the Volunteer Graduate Scheme, 1960

"Some fundamental criticisms of the Scheme have been made recently, so this seems to be a suitable time for our policy to be reviewed." Such criticisms are not new – they have been made by outsiders for as long as there has been even an idea of the Scheme; they were made from within at the National Conference in 1956 by an Adelaide committee member who suggested that we were perhaps sending the wrong people under the wrong conditions. The general consensus of opinion then, reinforced by independently made comments from the Indonesian Ambassador and an External Affairs representative, was that any widening of the basis of the Scheme by added financial inducement might bring in people with an even greater mixture of motives than we have at present.

Eric, Joan and Noela, when they returned, all had some pretty trenchant criticisms of the fact that V.G.s tend to fall between two stools, being treated as foreigners in that they do not always get their dues (e.g. in matters of special payment, transport of luggage) without getting the other compensations which fall to the lot of foreigners in Indonesia. Eric felt that the Scheme should become something more closely resembling a Contract with some sort of foreign currency payment at home. (This had been the initial E.A. suggestion.) All three of them asked whether we were really wanted or whether it was simply policy to accept us, although we were perhaps more trouble than we were worth.

When the medicos returned, the Baileys carried this a stage further by suggesting that it was time for the Scheme to withdraw gracefully, that it had served its purpose, and that the doors were now closing. At the Committee's request, Vern prepared some "Comments on the V.G.S." and on the basis of this a questionnaire was drawn up listing the requirements for continued existence of the Scheme and questions designed to elucidate whether those requirements are still being met. These were sent to all past and present V.G.s, including the New Zealanders. Thirteen replies to the questionnaire were received, representing the opinions of 15 V.G.s and including all present V.G.s in Indonesia. Some of these have been amplified by letters sent at much the same time, but not specifically in reply to the questionnaire. "Comments on the V.G.S." has been taken as representing the Bailey view on the issues raised; Ken's opinions were expressed in comment on the "Comments". Eric's views have been taken from an article which he prepared before leaving for Europe, while Joan-and-Noela's views have been taken from points they raised just after they returned (as it is not clear from the correspondence how far these views were joint ones I hope they will excuse me for holding them jointly responsible). When you consider the various comments made please remember then that some are pre-questionnaire.

Unfortunately it was not physically possible for everyone to read everyone else's replies and comments. The substitute for this is the following screed. I arranged the answers received under the question headings and then various willing and semi-willing conscripts took a question apiece to "answer" from the documentation provided. I take editorial responsibility for the final form of this so – hurl your brickbats at me, see, hurl your brickbats at me.

AILSA ZAINU'DDIN

Appendix D – Overseas Service Bureau Hand-Out (Transcript)

Phone: 63 5857

Overseas Service Bureau
MAJORCA BUILDING 260 FLINDERS LANE.
MELBOURNE C.1. VICTORIA. AUSTRALIA

AN AUSTRALIAN PEACE CORPS?

The Director-General of the British Council, Sir Paul Sinker, regards Melbourne as the birth-place of the "peace corps" idea. He recalls meeting in Java seven or eight years ago a small group of Australian graduates who, equipped with bicycles as a simple means of transport, were contributing their skills to the new Republic of Indonesia. They belonged to the Melbourne-based Volunteer Graduate Scheme.

Later, with the support of the British Council, Voluntary Service Overseas was launched in London to enable matriculants and apprentices to spend a year working in the developing countries. Later still, in 1960, President Kennedy formed the U.S. Peace Corps.

Since 1962 the United Kingdom Government has provided half of the cost incurred by community organisations sending British Volunteers abroad. Next year this official support will be increased to seventy-five per cent. The British effort this year involves about 800 volunteers, including graduates.

Sir Paul is surprised that the pioneering efforts of Australians in this field haven't received more support and interest here. He hopes that the Overseas Service Bureau, which now administers the Volunteer Graduate Scheme and has launched Australian Volunteers Abroad, will receive substantial backing.

The above is an approved summary of views expressed by Sir Paul Sinker during his Melbourne visit last week.

The British Government is contributing £E. 270,000 this year towards service overseas by United Kingdom volunteers. Next year this support will be increased to about £E. 650,000.

At present 20 Australian volunteers are serving overseas under the auspices of this Bureau. This number will be expanded considerably within the next twelve months, provided financial support is available.

J.B.Webb

Director

4.3.64

AIM – To encourage Australians to serve in the developing societies of Asia, Africa and the Pacific

OPINION PIECE

AN INDONESIAN OPINION ON THE VGS

Jo Kurnianingrat

[This essay first appeared in *Djembatan*, Vol 2, No 4, Special Issue, September 1959.]

The following is an extract from a letter written to the Editor by Miss Kurnianingrat, the present head of the English Language Teaching Organisation. As a staff member of its predecessor, the English Language Inspectorate, she worked with several of the Volunteer Graduates. Possibly the fact that she herself had been one of the first Indonesians to study in Australia in the post-war period enabled her to make these newcomers feel at home very quickly. Perhaps, on the other hand, it is simply her power of inspiring devotion in her colleagues.

* * *

You asked me to restrict myself this time to my opinion of the Volunteer Graduate Scheme. I can understand that you are curious to know what the official, or maybe, the general opinion in Indonesia is, but unfortunately I cannot give you either. I am not in the position to give official statements, and to take my opinion for the public one would be very risky, because you know how diverse opinions in Indonesia are. So if you are content with just a personal opinion I can certainly give it to you, although you must keep in mind that my contact with the Volunteer Graduate Scheme has been rather limited. On the other hand, don't we all mostly form our opinions from our personal experiences? Having had one disagreeable experience with a foreigner, are we not inclined to be wary of all people of his country, although we know it's wrong; and having met one intelligent UNESCO expert, don't we say, "UNESCO has really picked out the best brains!" At least my experience with the Volunteer Graduate Scheme has not been limited to one person, and I have had the opportunity of working with some of you for several years.

My first contact with the Volunteer Graduate Scheme was through Gwenda Rodda. I did not learn to know her in her work at all, but I saw her in her room at the back of "Apotheek Nitra" (a city pharmacy), and she seemed perfectly content with her accommodation, although it must have been quite different from what she was used to at home. She took as much pains to speak good Indonesian as I do to speak English. When I invited her to my place, she ate the Indonesian dinner I gave her with gusto, which was more of a compliment than all exclamations like, "delicious, wonderful, etc" rolled into one. In short, it did not take long before I felt quite at home with her, and knowing me you must admit that that was quite an achievement on Gwenda's part. It was Gwenda too who applied for Betty and you at IPBI. To be frank, we were very hesitant about taking in two foreigners without knowing much about them, and after your stay in Indonesia I'm sure you understand why: there is often so much misunderstanding between Indonesians and foreign "experts" that foreign aid, which I'm convinced is offered with the best of intentions, can become quite a burden, especially when people have the bad taste of trying to impress upon us how valuable this aid is, whether in man-power or in money. It is often forgotten that we certainly cannot have fought for our independence to be dictated to again in building up the country, no matter how well meant this dictatorship may be. It would also be nice if clever people tried to remember that we are not entirely bereft of common sense and experience, and that we at least know the conditions and the needs of our own country, though the majority of us have not got the proper training for our jobs.

Do I sound very bitter and aggressive? It is not meant that way at all. I do welcome all people who want to help us build up the country; there is still so much to be done and there is a job for everybody – however, the cooperation should be based on mutual appreciation. Of course I do realise that the agencies who give us support want to see their money and staff used as efficiently as possible, which may account for their tendency to "guide" us. I am sure that everything could be settled in a much more satisfactory way if both parties could arrive at a better understanding. We certainly need to learn quite a lot yet, but learning from other people is quite a different thing from being told to do things.

Now don't get suspicious because I need such a long explanation for our hesitance in accepting you. I only want to point out that so much is involved in the giving and accepting of foreign aid.

Anyhow, to come back to our topic, you were one of the luckiest finds of IPBI. Though you did not claim to be experts, I can assure you that you did at least as good a job as many of those who are called thus. In fact, some foreign people have been honest enough to admit that with a few exceptions real experts cannot be spared from their country, and that most of the people who are sent to countries like Indonesia lack experience. We certainly would not appreciate them less for it if they could be honest about it; on the contrary, it would be a much sounder basis for a close cooperation, where there would be mutual appreciation and the sincere wish to learn from one another. This was certainly so in Betty's and your case, you came to us with an open mind, accepted the fact that we were the responsible persons, but tried to cooperate and assist us in every way possible. You did not think yourselves too important to do clerical work when it was necessary, but you also joined us in planning new schemes, setting final papers, running courses and all other responsibilities of our office.

I know that sometimes you disagreed with us, that you felt frustrated because we changed your suggestions – or did not accept them at all. Very often we had heated discussions and a tense atmosphere at the office. But I hope you have not forgotten how much you have contributed in our work, that in spite of all friction we really formed a team. You did not go about telling people how much you "loved" Indonesia and the Indonesians, implying that we ourselves did not care a bit about our own country and did not understand our own people. I don't know whether you love Indonesia or not – in fact, I am not particularly interested in it – but I know that you gave us your sincere friendship, and got friendship in return. You learned quite a lot about us and about what is being done in Indonesia, and came to appreciate the country.

Through you we learned to know other members of the Volunteer Graduate Scheme; Ann [Ann McDonald (BA New England), who worked in Indonesia from February 1955 to August 1956] joined us in the same spirit as you did, and Thelma [Thelma Ashton (BA New England), a librarian who worked with the VGS from March 1955 to February 1957] did a wonderful job for IPBI though she did not exactly belong to it. The others we did not know in their work, but all of them seemed genuinely interested in their jobs and seemed to enjoy their responsibility in spite of many frustrations.

Summing up, I can only say that I have a deep appreciation for the Volunteer Graduate Scheme and the way it tries to establish friendly relations with Indonesia. No matter how important knowledge, experience, and money are in establishing good relationships, it is the attitude of the people which counts most, and the Volunteer Graduate Scheme has been very wise in making this a point of consideration in their selection of people. On the basis of mutual appreciation and close cooperation so much can be achieved, and so much has to be done yet in Indonesia, that I am sure all of you who have been here have felt the satisfaction of being needed.

Sometimes I have heard people say that you – I mean the members of the Volunteer Graduate Scheme in general – are closer to us because you are living under the same financial conditions as we are. I personally wish you were financially better off here in Indonesia; it is hard enough to leave one's country without having to give up a reasonable and sufficient salary. I am sure that, with the same attitude, you would make as many friends as you have done so far, even if you had been in a better position financially.

In order not to give a false impression, I must add that at present more requirements are needed for jobs in Indonesia than was the case some 4 or 5 years ago. To stay in our own field, for instance [English language teaching], it is now required for people to have made a study of English as such – which aspect does not matter – if they want to teach English. It is not considered sufficient to be a native speaker only.

PART TWO

INTRODUCTION

> During the Dutch rule we, the native population, had not had much contact with the outside world; now, all of a sudden, it was as if the doors to the outside world were thrown open. ... What I remember of this time, right up to the time I left for Australia, was the general atmosphere of real friendship. We were all equals, only some got more important tasks to perform than others, but we appreciated each other. Nobody, no matter how high in rank, felt superior – Chapter 7, "The Early Years of the Republic", reproduced below.

"Other Worlds in the Past" is the unfinished memoir of Kurnianingrat Ali Sastroamijoyo, written during her retirement in Jakarta in the early 1990s. Over nine chapters, Kurnianingrat recounts her life from her childhood through to her 30s, by which time her teaching career was well established. A natural focus of the memoir is the Revolution and the political and social upheaval associated with it: it is front and centre in Kurnianingrat's account of daily life in occupied Yogyakarta during the 1940s, and it also surfaces in many other ways through the text. Another focus of "Other Worlds in the Past" is Kurnianingrat's family life and schooling as a girl. Kurnianingrat was the eldest daughter of R. A. A. Sastrawinata, the Bupati of Ciamis, and in her memoir she records her experience of growing up in the *kabupaten* (the residence and office of the Bupati). From the age of four through to around 15 years old, Kurnianingrat attended Dutch schools in Tasikmalaya and Bandung, and boarded with a number of Dutch and Indo-European families. Comparing the educational opportunities she enjoyed to those which had been available to R. A. Kartini a generation earlier, Kurnianingrat wrote that "whereas Kartini craved the opportunity to get Western schooling, we were encouraged to learn as much as possible about Western culture".[1] Her comment conveys the environment of change and transformation salient to her youth. In a similar vein, historian Jean Gelman Taylor describes Kurnianingrat's personal and professional life as having been "intimately connected with the creation of Indonesia".[2]

---

1   Kurnianingrat Ali Sastroamijoyo, "A Personal View from Indonesia [The Role of the Indonesian Woman]" [1980], Papers of Ailsa Thomson Zainuddin, privately held.
2   Introduction by Jean Gelman Taylor, *Women Creating Indonesia: The First Fifty Years*, Jean Gelman Taylor (ed.) (Clayton, Vic.: Monash Asia Institute, 1997), vii.

Introduction

Kurnianingrat begins the memoir with recollections of growing up with her extended family in the *kabupaten* at Ciamis. She records her father's three marriages: after the death of R. A. A. Sastrawinata's first wife, he married Kurnianingrat's mother, and then, shortly after Kurnianingrat's birth, he married one of the daughters of an aristocratic family from Sumedang. Kurnianingrat knew her birth mother simply as Ibu, and she addressed the Raden Ayu (the Javanese title for a married woman of noble birth) as Ibu Gedong. Other elders in the household included Kurnianingrat's paternal and maternal grandmothers, an aunt (Ibu Patih) and a sister of the first Raden Ayu. Also living in the *kabupaten* were at least 12 cousins, with whom Kurnianingrat "learned to give and take" as a girl, and whom she likens to brothers and sisters (two of her cousins, Kang Pelen and Ceuk Mustika, were her adopted siblings from her father's first marriage). Kurnianingrat was five years old when her brother Dicky was born, by which time she herself was attending the European Primary School in Tasikmalaya and boarding with a local family. Her sisters, Bibib and Yetty, were, respectively, 13 and 15 years younger than her (by comparison, her eldest cousin was about 14 years her senior). Additionally, Kurnianingrat refers to an "army of servants" who carried out cooking and other domestic tasks, and were domiciled in separate quarters on the grounds of the *kabupaten*.

"Other Worlds in the Past" conveys the supportive, stimulating atmosphere characteristic of Kurnianingrat's childhood, centred on her personal ties with her family and the variety of experiences and traditions she knew growing up in the *kabupaten*. Until her high school years, during school holidays when Kurnianingrat was staying with her family, she lived with Ibu at a residence located near the *kabupaten*; later on, the *kabupaten* itself became Kurnianingrat's base, a place where she "learned to cope with the outside world". Its spacious grounds "formed a continuous source of exploration". Kurnianingrat recalls the stories and games she enjoyed as a girl on the *pendopo* – a verandah in front of the house, where she also observed *kampong* heads sitting during *sebas* or gatherings of officials – as well as listening to Ibu Gedong tell *wayang* stories. Other recollections are of the feast, prayers and other activities undertaken as part of the annual Lebaran celebrations (the "greatest event of the year"), and visits with her mother to her home town of Gadog in the mountains near Garut. (She describes how she and Ibu would be welcomed by locals bearing gifts of food, and recalls the poverty endured by many of her mother's relatives.) Kurnianingrat's account of her childhood also includes signs of the political turbulence that was to come: in particular, she recounts a riot in 1926 involving the mass nationalist movement, Sarikat Rakyat, during which the quick-thinking actions of Kurnianingrat's father prevented the conflict escalating after villagers entered the *kabupaten* at Ciamis. This incident speaks to the animosity felt among parts of the community towards the *bupati* class, as Jean Gelman Taylor has observed.[3]

Kurnianingrat's Dutch skills were sufficiently established by age five for her to enter the European Primary School in Tasikmalaya. She advanced directly to the second form – a reflection of the skills she had acquired at the village school two years earlier. After moving to a primary school in Bandung when she was seven, at 12 she entered the three-year High School at the Zusters Ursulinin. Among the families she boarded with in Bandung were the Hoedts, whose simple living evidently appealed to Kurnianingrat. From the children, a daughter and a niece, Kurnianingrat acquired English words, and at that time she also experienced her first Protestant church service: she was amazed to observe that the congregation would "weep during a sermon". Other boarding arrangements proved less congenial. She recalls an encounter in Bandung in which her host mother took exception to Kurnianingrat's decline of an invitation to watch her son participate in a swimming competition. The mother suggested that Kurnianingrat was awaiting a visit by Kang Pelen: as Kurnianingrat puts it, "She suspected me of having a love affair with my own brother!" At Kurnianingrat's request, her father moved her to another family, whose attitudes were more inclusive and respectful.

After completing high school, Kurnianingrat graduated with teaching diplomas, specialising in psychology, from the Teacher Training School of the Indo-European Society (I. E. V. Kweekschool). Her first full-time teaching role was at the Dutch-Chinese Primary School in Jakarta. Following the Japanese invasion in 1942, the European Primary School in Purwakarta where Kurnianingrat was teaching closed down. She moved to Jakarta for work, carrying out administrative and translation tasks at the Municipal Office: she recalls how the latter called on the slender English language skills she had acquired at school. She describes the worsening of relations between Indonesians and Chinese which resulted from the Japanese Occupation, a development that would have unexpected and tragic consequences for Kurnianingrat herself. In 1943, Kurnianingrat took up a teaching role at the Teacher Training School for Girls (SGP) in Yogyakarta. While living and working in Yogyakarta, she began teaching English language and literature.

---

3   Introduction by Jean Gelman Taylor, *Women Creating Indonesia*, xxiii.

Introduction

In the period following national independence, Kurnianingrat was one of three Indonesians who travelled to Australia under Australian Government scholarships.[4] For a year from November 1949, she studied the Australian educational system and continued her study of psychology. Not long after returning to Indonesia, she joined Frits Wachendorff and Harumani Rudolph at the English Language Inspectorate (IPBI). Kurnianingrat was later to report that her positive experiences in Australia predisposed her to the idea of Australian volunteer graduates joining the team at IPBI;[5] this served, perhaps, to help counter-balance reservations among the staff at the Inspectorate about employing foreigners. The final chapter of "Other Worlds in the Past", entitled "Building the Future", closes with an account of Kurnianingrat's time at IPBI, which came to an end in 1956. That chapter comprises a first draft of a planned second part to the memoir, which was never completed.

Of her account of her childhood in "Other Worlds in the Past", Kurnianingrat describes having shown her readers "glimpses of the Sundanese *priyayi* world three quarters of a century ago, and of the Netherlands East Indies world, where we had to prepare ourselves for the future". Kurnianingrat's schooling was a crucial part of that preparation for the future. R. A. A. Sastrawinata's decision to educate his eldest daughter away from home, Kurnianingrat writes, reflected an assumption that Sundanese and Indonesian customs and values had sufficiently deep roots to be safe from "foreign fashions". Kurnianingrat also observes that her father was evidently "not entirely satisfied" with the "Western-oriented education" which she and Dicky received: he decided that their younger sisters Bibib and Yetty were to "stay with Ibu and have an education like every other Indonesian child did". With this final phrase, Kurnianingrat probably has

---

4   For more on the scholarships in question, see Jemma Purdey, *Scholarships and Connections: Australia, Indonesia and Papua New Guinea* (Working Papers, Series Two, No 46). Geelong: Alfred Deakin Research Institute, Deakin University, 2014.

5   See Ailsa Thomson Zainu'ddin, "Building the Future: The Life and Work of Kurnianingrat Ali Sastroamijoyo" in *Women Creating Indonesia*, p. 191. Another senior Indonesian public servant whose employment of volunteer graduates was preceded by a stay in Australia, Dr R. Sugoto, is referred to (though not named) in a footnote pertaining to Ollie McMichael's pro-Republican views which is located in Part I of "Putting In A Stitch Or Two". In that footnote, Betty Feith writes that Ollie's views were influenced by the head of the section of Civil Aviation where he worked (i.e. Dr R. Sugoto). There are also two other references to Dr Sugoto contained in this volume: his name appears as the signature of a reference for Ollie McMichael (in Appendix B (iv) to "Putting In A Stitch Or Two"), while Kurnianingrat refers to Sugoto in her account of a gathering of Asian students in Sydney in 1950, in which both of them participated (in Chapter 8, "Australian Experience" below).

in mind Indonesian children of the *priyayi* class, rather than children from non-elite backgrounds. Later in the memoir there are further references to her younger sisters' education, including to junior high schools (SMP) and senior high schools (SMA) they attended in Yogyakarta, Bandung and Jakarta. Kurnianingrat describes her delight when Bibib was entrusted to her care in Yogyakarta during the latter's junior high school years, and Yetty likewise stayed with her eldest sister for periods of her schooling.

It was Kurnianingrat's experience of an underlying social division among her classmates at school and also certain attitudes she met among her host families that first revealed to her the "great gap that existed between Indonesians and people of the ruling race". She describes a mutual disinterest and absence of contact between Dutch and other pupils, something which contributed to the isolation of her own school years.

Kurnianingrat records when she first learned of the nationalist movement. This occurred through her conversations with a colleague, Dahlan Abdullah, in her first teaching role, at the Dutch-Chinese Primary School in Jakarta.[6] It was also during the early 1940s that she became aware of the hierarchies and injustices of colonial Dutch East Indies society, including the barriers to a good education faced by most Indonesian children. For Kurnianingrat at that time, however, these new impressions were overshadowed by virtue of having recently fallen in love.

> These were hard times for the Republic: not only the troops fighting outside Yogya but the people in town too, tried to uphold the Republic, everyone to the utmost of his or her ability. – Chapter 7, "The Early Years of the Republic".

"Other Worlds in the Past" features a descriptive, moving account of the Proclamation of Independence and subsequent events through to the

---

6   Dahlan Abdullah's name reappears later in Kurnianingrat's memoir; during the years of the Japanese Occupation, he was instrumental in finding Kurnianingrat work in the Municipal Office, where he had become a senior official, and he assisted with housing for her cousin, Kang Sanusi, who was then assistant *wedana* (district head) at Jatinegara and whose household included Kurnianingrat. The colleague whom Kurnianingrat refers to here may have been H. Baginda Dahlan Abdullah, head of the municipal administration in Jakarta for a number of months during the Japanese Occupation. See Mien Soedarpo, *Reminiscences of the Past* (Jakarta: Sejati Foundation, 1994), p. 45, and Susan Abeyasekere, *Jakarta: A History* (Singapore: Oxford University Press, 1987), p. 136. Readers may also be interested to learn that Mien Soedarpo was the daughter of R. A. A. Wiranatakusumah, former Bupati of Bandung, whom Kurnianingrat refers to a number of times in "Other Worlds in the Past", including in relation to her weekend visits to the *kabupaten* at Bandung when she was attending school there.

ceasefire in 1949, during which time the author was living in Yogyakarta. As well as drawing upon her own experiences and memories, Kurnianingrat also includes in her narrative information provided by men aged in their 50s who had participated in political developments as students, identifying in particular her brother-in-law, Achmad Jayusman. She refers to some of the individuals, organisations and developments salient to the Indonesian Revolution, including, for instance, GASEMA, the youth organisation that acquired a combatant role at that time. She observes the importance of the role played by youth, in particular young men, in the Revolution. During a discussion of the continued campaign of guerrilla fighting against the Dutch, she writes simply "[i]n Yogya the boys disappeared from the classroom again". She recalls the mix of grief and renewed determination among the parents and teachers who, on one sad day, received a wagon-load of bodies of boys, many of them only young teenagers, who had lost their lives fighting in the Tentara Pelajar, or Student Army. Kurnianingrat notes that despite the protective efforts of many parents to try to stop their children from leaving to join the fight – one of her friends blocked her son's ears with cotton wool in an attempt to prevent him hearing news of the conflict – most of the boys and young men chose to defend the Republic.

As well as the fight against the Dutch, Kurnianingrat also recounts events surrounding the establishment of Yogyakarta as the base of the Republican Government. Among its early activities, the Republican Government established a national broadcasting station for overseas, the Voice of Free Indonesia. Kurnianingrat read out articles for the new broadcaster written by her friend and colleague Utami Suryadarma – part of the task of "contacting the outside world to inform them about the situation in our Republic". This was one of many ways in which Kurnianingrat put her skills to use in the cause of the Republic, as referred to earlier. Another was her work as a member of a team carrying out translation and secretarial tasks during the Renville negotiations. She recalls her astonishment and elation at being chosen for this task (despite gaps in her skills as a typist), and she also records the experience of travelling to Jakarta, staying at the hotel pavilion where the secretariat was based, and details of the work itself, carried out on board the USS *Renville*. She describes, for instance, puzzling over the etiquette around personal greetings, together with her friend Cing Sukonto, another of the secretaries. They knew to respond in kind to the greetings "good morning" and "good afternoon", but managed only a sheepish laugh when asked "how are you?", until they thought to be the first to pose the question; thus, the two women "learned how to react to the phrase

'How are you?'" That Kurnianingrat grounds her account of the prevailing political upheaval in the context of everyday realities, the sustaining of the means of existence and of human ties, is characteristic of her recollections as a whole.

During the period of Dutch occupation of Yogyakarta, Kurnianingrat's home at Gondokusuman evidently formed a hub of activity, its population periodically expanded by various visitors, friends, family members and refugees of the crisis. They included her sister Bibib, until she found herself unable to return home following a visit to Dutch-occupied Purwakarta. They also included Zena Algradi, wife of Hamid Algradi, who would go on to be celebrated nationally and internationally for his part in the fight for Indonesian independence, and who was then in Wirogunan prison. Like many other teachers, Kurnianingrat provided underground classes from her home so that students could continue their lessons in the wake of school closures. Kurnianingrat invites us to understand these and other acts by her as no more, and, in some cases, considerably less, than what others around her were doing to contribute to the cause of national independence, a natural expression of the shared ideals and resolve characteristic of the time. Elsewhere, she wrote of this time that "[s]ocial differences fell away; all of us, from all strata of society, did the little we could to help win the war".[7]

"Other Worlds in the Past" remained incomplete at the time of Kurnianingrat's death in 1993. Part Two was also to include an account of her time at Cornell University in Ithaca, New York, where she gained an MA in English language and literature. Other aspects of her life not covered in "Other Worlds in the Past" include her role as head of the English Language Department, University of Indonesia and her marriage to former Prime Minister Ali Sastroamijoyo. Further details about her life can be found in an extended biographical essay about Kurnianingrat written by Ailsa Zainuddin and published in Jean Gelman Taylor's *Women Creating Indonesia: The First Fifty Years*.[8] In that essay, which draws on

---

7   Kurnianingrat Ali Sastroamijoyo, "A Personal View from Indonesia", p. 3.
8   Other sources of biographical information about Kurnianingrat include two interviews with her, the first by Ailsa and the second by Betty and Herb Feith. The first of these interviews took place on 3 February 1992, and mainly covers Kurnianingrat's time in Australia in 1950, her experiences following her return to Indonesia, her work at IPBI, and her friendships with Harumani and Chris Rudolph. The second interview was carried out on 12 June 1993, which turned out to be the day before Kurnianingrat's final stroke. In this case, the conversation focused mainly on the latter's stay in the United States. Transcripts of both these interviews can be found in a file entitled "Building the Future: The Life and Work of Kurnianingrat Ali Sastroamijoyo" (1992–1996), Papers of Ailsa Thomson Zainuddin, privately held.

Introduction

"Other Worlds in the Past" as well as correspondence and other writing, Ailsa describes Kurnianingrat as "one of many 'ordinary women' living in extraordinary times and building the future independent Republic of Indonesia which their grandchildren have inherited".[9] The publication of "Other Worlds in the Past" in the present volume enables readers to enjoy Kurnianingrat's carefully observed and understated narrative in its entirety.

Editorial additions were made by Ailsa to the text of Kurnianingrat's "Other Worlds in the Past" prior to the start of the current project. These additions appear in the text as footnotes enclosed within square brackets. Also, two bracketed references to the year Kurnianingrat was writing appear in the main text where the narrative is in the present tense. Further minor editorial revisions made by Ann McCarthy in 2015–16 included ensuring consistent spelling (see also "Note on Spelling" in the Introduction to this volume), italicising non-English terms, and completing the footnotes. The reader will notice some variations of personal names among Kurnianingrat's friends and relations. For example, Utami Suryadarma's name is sometimes shortened to "Tami", while Samsudarso, husband of Tine Samsudarso, is also referred to as "Samsudarsono".

---

9   Ailsa Zainu'ddin, "Building the Future: The Life and Work of Kurnianingrat Ali Sastroamijoyo", *Women Creating Indonesia*, p. 200. This passage is similar to a statement made in relation to Harumani Rudolph-Sudirdjo by her friend and colleague Gillian Belben from the British Council. Belben describes Harumani as "[e]xtraordinary because she has lived through times of great upheaval and had to adapt to new social and political situations; ordinary because her experiences are no more than the shared history of many thousands of educationalists born before Independence, being educated and becoming teachers themselves while the Republic was still young". See Belben, "Harumani Rudolph-Sudirdjo: 'Learning and Teaching through Changing Times'", p. 71.

REMINISCENCES

OTHER WORLDS IN THE PAST

Kurnianingrat Ali Sastroamijoyo

To Rini and Ruli,
who used to ask me for a story at any time of the day when they were little.
This is my last story to them, trying to show them the different worlds in the past.

Written 1991–1993.

Contents

Contents 105
1. Early Childhood 106
2. Life in the *Kabupaten* 108
3. Primary School Days 114
4. High School and Teacher Training 122
5. Schoolmarm 127
6. The Japanese Occupation 131
7. The Early Years of the Republic 138
8. Australian Experience 152
9. Building the Future 164

1. Early Childhood

Ciamis at the beginning of the twentieth century was a friendly prosperous little town, the capital of a regency in the southeast of Priangan near the Ciandur river, which formed one of the natural borders between West and Central Java. Ciamis means literally "sweet waters"; it lies in an area with many big rivers which then had crystal clear, unpolluted water and big rocks in the river beds. I was born in Ciamis in 1919, the year after World War I ended. I mention this especially because your generation usually associates the words "World War" with World War II. World War I seems to lie too far back for you.

These were indeed very different times from the one you live in. For one thing we lived in a feudal society where social position was sharply defined. There was a great social gap between the aristocracy and the non-aristocrats. Imagine, when you happened to be born in aristocratic circles, you had many advantages without having to do anything for them although, no matter how high an Indonesian's social rank, he was always subservient to the Netherlands East Indies Government, then the rulers of our country. Consequently, the Dutch felt far superior to the Indonesians and having a white skin made a person feel himself far above the brown-skinned natives.

How I came to be born in Ciamis is rather a long story. My father, R. A. A. Sastrawinata, then Bupati of Ciamis, was a member of the *bupati* family in Krawang/Purwakarta. He received his training for the Civil Service in the School ter Opleiding van Zonen van Inlandse Hoofden, or the School for the Education of Sons of Native Heads. There the Dutch trained their future Indonesian civil servants. There was one such school in Bandung; the Sundanese referred to it by the shorter name of Sekolah Menak, or School for the Aristocracy. After having finished his training, my father became an apprentice with the Hoofd Djaksa in Purwakarta. He did not even receive a salary; he only got a little money to buy cigarettes. It amounted to f2.50.[1]

After some time he became apprenticed to a Dutch official for Cultuur Zaken. This Dutchman had to travel a lot to inspect the plantations the Dutch thought necessary to cultivate. In that way my father saw a lot of Central and East Java and even Madura and Bali. In 1892, after four years of apprenticeship, he obtained his first appointment as *mantri oeloe-oeloe* in the Residency of Banten. He gained rather quick promotion. During this time he made the acquaintance of the family of the Bupati of

---

1   [2.5 Dutch guilders.]

Rangkasbitung. Eventually my father became engaged to and later married one of his daughters. When my father became Bupati of Ciamis in 1916, she came there as his *raden ayu*. Unfortunately they had no children so they adopted a niece of Purwakarta, Ceuk Mustika, as their daughter and a nephew, Kang Pelen, as their son but, besides these two, there were always a lot of nephews and nieces in the *kabupaten*.

Ibu Moja, as the nephews and nieces called her, became ill. She had dysentery and this disease seemed difficult to cure at that time. My father took her to the Garut area where she received treatment from the best Dutch doctors but no-one could help her. She died of the disease. Before she died, Ibu Moja became acquainted with the daughter of a well-to-do landowner, a fifteen year old girl who taught at a girls' school in Garut. She came to like the girl so much that, before her death, she asked my father to marry the girl. A few months after her death, my father married the girl and took her to the *kabupaten* in Ciamis although she could not become the *raden ayu*, because she was not of noble birth.

My father was very happy when I was born. He had waited so long for a child. He called me "Kurnia" meaning "gift" but, ten days after my birth, he married one of the daughters of the Pangeran of Sumedang, a widow.[2] When she came into the *kabupaten*, Ibu and I moved to a house near the *kabupaten*. I don't remember much of this house but I remember Kaum very well, the second house where Ibu lived, in the area near the mosque.

Kaum was a simple but comfortable house. The wooden floor, covered with bamboo matting, was a few metres off the ground and under the house we kept the chickens. We also had doves; the cooing woke me up early in the morning. In front was a small yard where my swing stood. Often my friends and I sat, in turns, on the sheath of a palm branch to be pulled by the others with loud shouts of encouragement from bystanders. There were always lots of friends to play with. I also remember the front porch where we used to sit when it was full moon. Ibu and the other adults sat up till late at night then and I was allowed to join them until I fell asleep. I remember vividly the smell of the white flowers which the Sundanese call "Sundal malam", meaning "the prostitute", because their perfume could be smelled only by night.

This was my home and my base because every day I was taken to the *kabupaten* for a few hours. When my father went on a tour of inspection he

---

2 [For more information on the history of the Regent families in Sumedang and elsewhere in the Priangan region of Java, see Heather Sutherland, "Notes on Java's Regent Families: Part 1", *Indonesia*, No. 16 (Oct. 1973), pp. 125–131.]

usually took me with him. He told me all kinds of things and taught me songs. We became real friends that way but the *kabupaten* itself had many attractions too. There was the big *pendopo* with the huge pillars which easily hid a small child; it was our favourite hide-and-seek place. Behind the *kabupaten* there was a fish pond with big *ikan mas*. Ibu Gedong, as my cousins called the Raden Ayu, knew each fish by name and it was fun to feed them with her.

Then there were the heavy velvet curtains, which separated the sitting room from the dining room and which served us as curtains for our theatrical performances. At that time the popular theatre was the Stambul, which performed stories of *The Arabian Nights*. We children were allowed from time to time to see such a performance and we imitated everything at home. Ibu Gedong made a special *bandeau* for me of glittering beads and I imitated the prima donna. I don't remember having many bought toys like the children nowadays do. A giant cucumber served as a doll that we carried in a *selendang*. The dried pods of plants were used as boats that we raced on the small stream that ran through the *kabupaten* grounds. There was so much to play with and there were so many games and songs that we were never bored. As I grew older, about seven or eight years old, I sometimes slept at the *kabupaten* and finally, when I was in high school I had my own room there and then the *kabupaten* became my base. I spent several hours a day in Kaum [with my mother] but only slept there once in a while. That was still far off.

At that time there were no kindergartens so, when I was three or four years old, my father sent me to the village school. It stood on the left of the *kabupaten* and was separated only by a small street from it. I loved going to school because Ibu always put some drops of *eau de cologne* in the water with which I cleaned my slate. It was fun to learn all kinds of new things but I doubt whether it was fun for the teachers to have me with them because, when the spoiled brat started crying, it was easily heard in the *kabupaten* and they were afraid of the consequences.

After a year, when the pupils were promoted, we rode in carts around the *alun-alun*. That was the end of my happy time at the village school.

2. Life in the *Kabupaten*

The *kabupaten* contained a small but varied and busy world of its own, with well-defined rules for itself. My home at Kaum with Ibu was my warm nest, in which I fitted safe and secure but the *kabupaten* was where I learned to cope with the outside world. Never was I forced to go there but, as I grew older, it took more and more of a hold on me.

The spacious *kabupaten* grounds formed a continuous source of exploration. One of my father's hobbies was fruit trees and he had them planted all over the grounds. The shady *ketapang* trees offered the smaller children a place where they could sit for hours, playing at cooking and buying and selling, using the big rounded leaves as containers, folded in all kinds of shapes. We learned to beat the nuts patiently with a stone, until we got at the white, wonderful tasting kernel. The big *kedongdong* fruits were very popular among the youngsters who especially cared for the near-ripe ones, which they smashed to the floor so that they broke into big pieces, which they then started munching happily, apparently a much more enjoyable way of eating *kedongdong* than peeling and cutting it with a knife.

We learned that the flowerlike patterning at the bottom on the outside of a *manggistan* gave the exact number of parts within the hard purple shell; we learned to distinguish the different kinds of *jambu*: the *jambu kaget* with its mottled surface, which maybe resembled the colours of a face of someone in shock; the *jambu mawar*, so called because its taste had a delicate perfume; the *jambu bol* with its pimply leaves, and many others. We enjoyed the variety of *jeruk* and mangoes, we learned to climb trees and could pick everything we wanted, except for a few trees that were fenced off for my father's use and that of the other elders in the family.

We spent the greater part of the day in the open air, luxuriating in our freedom, because there were very few "don'ts" and no adults to watch us.

Then there were the animals. There were two big horses that were used to draw the *bendi* Ibu Gedong used to pay her visits. I loved to join her on these visits, especially when she went to Eyang Gunung, the widow of the previous Bupati of Ciamis, who lived on a hill and had wild strawberries planted all along the path leading up to the house. She had two monkeys which always started to shriek violently when they saw strangers. She also had a very interesting *batik* place where I could watch the women drawing patterns on cloth or patiently covering the patterns with wax or dipping the cloth in a steaming liquid to give it the brown or black base colour.

We also had some cows because Father wanted to have fresh milk every morning. I don't think they were beautiful cows but they gave one of my cousins the opportunity to play matador. One day he waved a red cloth in front of them and shouted *"Ayo, berani?* [Come on, I dare you.]" but when they came slowly after him, he ran for his life and shouted for help. The cows seemed to enjoy the running and quickened their pace. Fortunately old Pa Nayin, who used to herd and milk the cows, appeared and the cows docilely stopped and followed him. There was a goat as well. I don't remember to what use he was put. We also had a *kijang*, a small deer that had access to the back verandah, where we gave him banana skins and bread to eat. He seemed to be an intellectual animal, for he loved chewing printed matter and we had to be careful not to leave papers and booklets lying about.

Then there were the hens to feed and the cocks to be admired and there were the big *ikan mas* in the fishpond but more interesting than all this were the many people who lived in the *kabupaten*. When Ibu Moja came to live in Ciamis, her mother came with her and also a younger sister by another father. This sister, Bi Eni, was deaf and dumb but she was very intelligent and full of humour. She was like a caricaturist, who emphasised the weaknesses in a person. For instance, someone with a big nose was indicated by putting a big rice scoop to her nose and everybody knew immediately whom she meant; a thin person was pictured by sucking in her cheeks and dangling her hands limply in front of her breast. When you were dark-skinned, she would make a gesture of disgust, point to something black and say something that sounded like "*po-ek*" meaning "dark". In spite of the fact that she liked to ridicule people, nobody felt offended and she was popular with everybody because she was one of those rare persons who dared to speak her mind bluntly and to manage to make herself understood. Nenek, Ibu Moja's mother, I remember vaguely as a small, white-haired old lady. She died when I was still little.

The central figure in the *kabupaten*, of course, was Father. Everything was geared to his needs: the day started when we were awoken by his loud morning sneezes and ended when he went to bed. He was referred to by my cousins as Ama Kangjeng, Kangjeng being the appellation for a *bupati*. Even his mother, Ibu Bintang, called him formally "Kangjeng" but in her mouth it sounded like a term of endearment. She was called Eyang Bintang because her husband had received a decoration from the Dutch Government. She lived in Purwakarta but used to stay for long periods in Ciamis. She liked to treat her grandchildren and, from under her bed, came the most delicious cookies. Her eyesight had been impaired by trachoma and she always wore dark glasses. I do not think she was totally blind; she must have been able to see something because she never tired of letting me demonstrate how the pupils of the Roman Catholic school I attended first crossed themselves, then folded their hands, closed their eyes and said their prayers before class began. At the end of such a demonstration she used to chuckle, shake her head and mutter something like "Those foreign fashions!" Never did it enter her mind that those foreign fashions might change the grandchildren. She was so convinced that they were too firmly rooted in their own customs and ways to change much. That was my father's attitude too, so he had no qualms about sending me and my brother from home to live with foreigners at a very young age.

Ibu Gedong (meaning, literally, Mother of the Big House) of course was the second person in importance. She assisted my father in every way and was in charge of the whole *kabupaten*. Only now do I realise what a good administrator she must have been to be able to make both ends meet with so many people to take care of. She had a good friend in Ibu Patih, Eyang Bintang's youngest daughter and my father's favourite sister, who came to live with us when her husband, Ama Patih, retired. At first she and her family occupied the whole east wing of the *kabupaten* but, after Ama Patih died, she moved, with her two daughters and three of her four sons, to the main building. Her eldest son, Kang Basarah, was already married and worked as a civil servant but he and his wife often came to visit us. Ibu Patih's five other children grew up together with me. She was another mother to me and also a friend. When I grew older we used to tease one another.

These were the elders of the family and we learned to behave to them with respect. We really looked up to them and even when we became adults and they had grown old, we never felt protective towards them. Rini sometimes calls me "my baby" when she wants to console me, and I love her for that, but we would never have dared to say something like that to our elders, whom we considered with such respect that we always felt small in comparison to them. We loved and cherished them, yet it would never have entered our minds to tell them our secrets as young people nowadays do to their parents.

You must have noticed that I am not referring to the older generation by their names; this was seldom done. They were referred to by the position they held – like Ama Kanjung, Ama Patih – or the place where they lived or had worked – like Ibu Gedong, Ibu Gunung – and my father, when he had retired, was sometimes called Ama Ciamis. So we never associated them with a proper name but I noticed that the women, when they signed something, used their own name as their signature and not Mr and Mrs So-and-So. For instance, Ibu Gedong's signature was Kancaningrat and not Mrs Sastrawinata: Ibu Patih always signed with Soehaerandiningrat.

The younger generation consisted of Ceuk Mustika and Kang Len, my father's adopted children; Ibu Patih's children; and five cousins from Purwakarta, who also went to school in Ciamis. When they grew older they went to the high school in Tasikimalaya. They left with the first train and only came home in the afternoon. There was a wide range of ages in our group. Ceuk Mus and Ceuk Endeh, who did not differ much in years, must have been about eighteen when I was four. Kang Sadeli, one of my favourite cousins, was already in training to become a civil servant at Mosvia, a modern version of the old Sekolah Menak. He came home only for the holidays. Kang Sanusi, my other favourite, was already at junior high school. I really looked up to them – Kang Sadeli because he always taught us funny songs and had all kinds of interesting things to tell; Kang Sanusi because he was kind hearted and sensitive. Ceuk Entus, Ibu Patih's youngest daughter, was only a few years my senior. In spite of the variety in age we were very close together and grew up as sisters and brothers. In the twilight on the steps of the big *pendopo* we used to tell each other ghost stories, ready to run away if the story became too frightening. The older ones did not mind playing games with the younger ones. In the evening we read magazines Father was sent in a *leestrommel* – a collection of magazines to which one could subscribe – or kept talking under the bright gaslight, which made a cosy humming sound. We learned to give and take, and quarrels never lasted long enough to become disagreeable. Most members of this group have died now; there are only four of us left. [1992]

Then there was the army of servants. I do not remember them all; the ones that are still in my mind are the two cooks, Ma Hati and Ma Karti; Ma Ito, Ibu Gedong's special maid servant and Pa Nayip, who functioned as a kind of major-domo, a strong, healthy-looking man with a big moustache. As I told you, in that feudal society rank and position were clearly defined. We knew that the servants were lower in rank but we were taught to be polite to them. As a child you were not allowed to call servants by their names. We always called them "Ema" or "Ma", meaning "mother", or "Pa" meaning "father". We learned to appreciate them and they became friends and, if they stayed very long with us, they became part of the family. They were housed in a special building, with a row of rooms next to each other and a front verandah connecting all the rooms. We sometimes visited them in their quarters. We also liked to make use of their bathing place, a *pancuran* with very clear, cool water at the back of the *kabupaten*, which we thought much more attractive than the big, dark bathroom we ordinarily used.

Breakfast was served at eight o'clock. After breakfast Father usually disappeared into his office or went on a tour of inspection on which I often accompanied him. At regular intervals he used to go to a *seba*, a meeting of heads of *kampong*, at the house of a district head, *wedana*, on which occasions Ibu Gedong always went with him to visit the district head's family. During such a meeting the heads of the *kampong* sat on mats on the floor and the *wedana* sat with Father behind a table on chairs. They discussed problems in their regions and so Father was kept informed of what went on in the regency. After the *seba* there was always a nice lunch because the women of each district prepared the nicest food they could make and Ibu Gedong in this way kept in contact with the women.

At home lunch was served after Father returned from his duties. The elders sat at table and I was allowed to join them but I often preferred to eat together with my cousins, who had their meals sitting on mats on the floor, after the elders had finished. They, of course, did not eat the leftovers from the table. They had the same food, served to them afterwards, and it was nice to eat together with so many people. I learned to sit on the floor properly, with my head bent over my plate and to eat without fork or spoon in a neat way. That is why, to this day, I still prefer to eat rice with my hand.

After dinner Father usually talked to the women of the family, or sometimes to one of the cousins, when they needed a talking-to. He often played the gramophone; he liked light classical music and I often fell asleep with the soft music in my ears. Sometimes there was a special disk, for instance "Hallo, Hallo Bandung", the story of a Dutch mother who had a son working in Indonesia. She longed for him but he did not have the money to visit her with his wife and child and, while she was listening to their voices, she died. Ibu Gedong and Ibu Patih used to listen raptly and discussed the story afterwards. It did not matter that it happened to a foreign woman in a foreign country but, as mothers, they could perfectly understand the mother's longing for her son until her heart broke.

In the evening Father disappeared into his office again. After Ibu Gedong had said her prayers, the children used to gather on the big bench on the back verandah and Ibu Gedong started telling us her *wayang* stories in instalments but at seven o'clock the children, especially the boys, had to learn their lessons in such a way that Father could hear their voices in his office. I sometimes kept him company, sitting in a big chair near his desk, reading or watching him go through his files. I smelled the perfume of the same flowers Ibu had planted in front of the house at Kaum, and that also grew in the garden to the left of his office; I felt happy and secure.

I realise that life in Ciamis must have been quiet for adults. The men could go to a *societiet*, a gathering place where they could play billiards or cards. To bring some variety, a *tayuban* was held monthly at the *kabupaten*. On these occasions the civil servants danced to the music of the *gamelan* with a professional dance maid, the *ronggeng* as their partner. Sometimes the Bupati of Tasikmalaya attended these *tayuban* too as father sometimes went to his *tayuban* but Father cared more for other kinds of relaxation like hunting, playing billiards or a game of whist with his friends. Another break in the monotony was when there was a big *seba* when the *kampong* heads came to meet in the *kabupaten*. The large *pendopo* was full of people sitting on mats. The *wedana* came too with their ladies, who helped Ibu Gedong prepare the food for the big gathering of people.

The greatest event of the year was celebration of Lebaran. Very early in the morning the *priyayi* women were already gathered in the *kabupaten*, where they busied themselves with the preparation of the Lebaran food. Before sunrise the people of Ciamis came to fetch Father for the Lebaran prayer at the mosque. It was an impressive sight to see the procession approach in the dark, with gaily flickering torches in their hands. When the collective prayer was finished the men returned to the *kabupaten*, where they were welcomed by a loud burst of firecrackers. The women and children stood ready to greet Father and their respective husbands and ask each other for forgiveness. I learned to approach Father on my haunches and press my forehead against his knee before greeting him in Sundanese fashion. Father always rewarded my clumsy efforts with a warm kiss. The greatest fun for the children consisted in receiving money from the adults as a special Lebaran gift. We had no idea of the value of the money we gathered that way but we felt very rich.

Everyone wore new clothes on Lebaran Day. Later I learned that people gave each other clothes or material for clothes at Lebaran, that this period was the time to make each other happy and, much later, I understood that the cleaning and whitewashing of the houses and the new clothes were symbolic of the new life that was started on Lebaran Day.

So much about the varied life at the *kabupaten*. I am sure you would have liked to spend your childhood there because we all have kept happy memories of that time.

3. Primary School Days

The persons who influenced me most during those early times and maybe long after, were Ibu, warm-hearted, emotional, full of humour and with a great capacity for endurance, which I only understood at a later age. The second was my father, big-hearted, trying to do what was best for those he was responsible for and protecting us with his position, his name and his love. The third person was proud and wise Ibu Gedong, who treated me like her own child.

Thinking of my father, I am reminded of a film I once saw about horses. A baby horse sought the protection of its mother but the mare did not want it near her. She forced her child to stand on its own feet.

I told you that the Dutch then ruled our country. In order to get a good education or a good job it was necessary to master the Dutch language, so, when I was four years old, my father thought it necessary to send me to Tasikmalaya, half an hour's drive from Ciamis, to stay with an Indo-European family to learn Dutch. He and Ibu Gedong took me there and, sensing there was something afoot, I clung to them. Somehow they succeeded in lulling me half asleep and left me. I was inconsolable and refused to eat or drink anything. They put me in a playroom full of toys but I didn't touch any of them. Just as they were debating whether it would not be better to take me home to Ciamis, I asked for something to eat after one day's fasting. Then I was taken up in the family.

It was a nice family with daughters, one a bit younger and the other a bit older than I. The mother always wore a white *kabaya* and a coloured flowered *sarong* at home. The father we only met when he was leaving for his work or coming home from work. The girls used to creep into their parents' big four-poster bed early in the morning and generously invited me to join them. I doubt whether the parents liked me there but there we were, every morning at five o'clock, nestling ourselves between the father and the mother.

Only one thing impressed me during my stay with them: the installation of a shower. For me, who knew only the shower of real rain in which we were permitted to bathe once in a while, this new gadget was amazing. For the rest I have not many memories of that time, save one, when Lisette, the youngest daughter, won the first prize at a fancy dress ball, as a doll. She was strapped into a box and had to stay there all the time unmoving. Furthermore I lived for the times when they drove me to Ciamis for an evening or when my father came to fetch me home.

Life in Ciamis went on as usual. Ibu once took me to the market to see a baby crocodile but I was so fascinated by the first gramophone that appeared in Ciamis that I thought that was the baby crocodile about which she was so excited.

We had a car, our first car. We, the children, were all very proud of it. None of us knew what make it was but on the engine was clearly printed "De La Haye" and we called it our "De La Haye". Often on an afternoon father loaded us all into the car and off we went to one of the big rivers near Ciamis to have a bathe. For long trips Ibu Gedong had knitted black woollen caps for each of us except for my father, who always wore an *uding* (a *batik* head cover). On those trips we always brought spittoons with us for invariably one of us would be car sick.

A romantic event was Ceuk Mustika's wedding to a cousin, Kang Pen Atmanegara. Sometime before the wedding they were not allowed to see each other but Kang Pen used to sneak up to the window of the room where Ceuk Mustika was finishing her trousseau. In these days I often kept her company and I saw her whole face light up when she saw Kang Pen. The wedding was a big party because it was combined with the celebration of the occasion when my father received his Adipati title. I don't remember much of the party but only how lovely Ceuk Mustika looked in her bridal clothes. They became the grandparents of Cintami, Asih and Fra, and many others.

In the meantime I kept learning Dutch in Tasikmalaya. One day one of the girls asked me what I called my father and I said "Ma-ma" from the word "Rama", meaning "father". She started laughing and said "Only women are called that". From that time on I used the prosaic Dutch word "Pa" for my father.

When I was five years old I was considered to know Dutch sufficiently to enter the European Primary School, where Dutch was the medium of teaching. I was put in the first form but, after a few days, I was moved to another classroom. At that time I did not understand why but later I was told that I already knew the material of the first form and was promoted to the second form. Apparently the village school had taught me a lot. I hope my father had complimented the teachers on their teaching.

In the same year something exciting happened. I got a baby brother. I remember that, on the day Ibu had to give birth, my father was very nervous. He took me to his favourite resting place, Panjalu. Panjalu is famous for its lake. In the middle of the lake is an island with a mysterious atmosphere. It was fully grown with trees and the ground was covered with moss. There were a few graves but I don't remember whose. Bats hung like fruits on the trees. You could not tell they were bats until they were startled by a noise and flew up so that the sky became black with bats. From the lake steep steps led up to the *pasanggrahan* which stood on the hill overlooking the lake. The place had a peaceful atmosphere. It was here that we awaited the arrival of the baby. Again and again the telephone rang to keep my father informed of Ibu's condition. At last, in the late afternoon, the message came through: a son had been born. When we came back to Ciamis early the next morning, we could still hear the explosion of the fireworks that celebrated the birth of my brother.

My father was elated to have a son. The baby was put in the special care of Nini, my Ibu's mother, who had come to live with her after my grandfather's death. Nini was a healthy, robust country woman, who remained herself in spite of the different environments. She preferred to walk barefoot and refused any privileges she was entitled to as a member of the Bupati family. She was easy to laugh with and we all loved her very much but she favoured my brother, who was nicknamed "Dicky" because he was a plump little boy and the Dutch word "*dik*" means "fat".

When I was seven, I was sent to Bandung for further schooling. Bandung had better schools than Tasikmalaya. I stayed with an Indo-European family by the name of Hoedt. They lived in a very nice part of the town: opposite their house was St. Pieter's Park, a little further away was a girls' primary school and, across the street from there, was the big Zusters Ursulinen School compound.

The Hoedts were a very simple living family. I liked them all. Mr Hoedt had a small chemist shop attached to the house and, when I sometimes dropped in to look at the interesting variety of things he had there, he always gave me some sweets. Mrs Hoedt, like Mrs van Leeuwen in Tasikmalaya, wore a white *kabaya* and a flowered *sarong* at home. She used to make her own bread; her fresh bread was delicious. There were a daughter and a niece, both high school students. I admired them for their knowledge. They even taught me some English words. They sometimes took me to the Protestant Church at the corner and I saw with amazement how they used to weep during a sermon. There were so many new things: the girls' school; the new surroundings; the new people I met; that I had no time to feel homesick.

I think Father did not want me to lose touch with my own environment so he arranged with the Bupati of Bandung, the well-known R. A. A. Wiranatakusumah that I should spend the weekends at the *kabupaten*. The *kabupaten* in Bandung was much, much more luxurious than ours in Ciamis. The Bupati had just returned from a pilgrimage to Mekkah and he had installed an Arabian room in the *kabupaten*. It had very large windows, shaped like the windows in the beautiful pictures of *The Arabian Nights*. All along the walls there were low, cushioned divans and the floor was covered with thick carpets. In the middle of the room was a pond and a fountain dropped its water into it with a clear tinkling sound. This Arabian room was separated from the other rooms with curtains of gaily coloured glass beads.

There were lots of children in the *kabupaten*. I did not see much of the boys but the girls were very good company. I liked the eldest daughter best, for she always mothered me. I stood in awe of the second daughter, a real beauty who had many admirers. The third daughter, who was about my age, was a merry, vivacious girl. The girls used to treat me to such delicacies as *es putar*, or *gulali*, a sticky substance of melted brown sugar with lots of peanuts in it, wound around a stick so that you could lick it like a lollypop. I enjoyed all this the more because I was never allowed to buy food off the streets.

The girls were well-versed in Sundanese manners. For instance, when they handed something to their father or to an older person, they always made a *sembah*, which we in Ciamis never did. They were very clever at serving visitors. I think my Father hoped I would be like them but, though I admired them greatly, I never came to doing things their way. Later, when I had seen more *kabupaten*, I realised that ours was one of the simplest.

Remembering what I told you about the names by which we knew our elders, you won't be surprised that, at the age of seven, I still did not know my Father's name. Nowadays, very small children are taught to answer three questions: "What is your name?", "Who is your father?" and "Where do you live?" I had heard Dutch people call my Father "Regent" and I thought that was his name. So, when I moved from the Girls' School to the Zusters Ursulinen Primary School and I was asked my name, I answered "Jootje Regent".[3] They heard "Agent" and, for some time, I was registered under the name "Jootje Agent".

Especially during the holidays the house [at Ciamis] was full of young people, relatives from everywhere. There were no luxuries but there was plenty of fruit on the trees to make *rujak*. Together we visited places like Karangunggal, an ancient wood with moss covering the ground and tall, old trees. You could easily imagine Lutung Kasarung living in such surroundings. We went to Cipatujah on the south coast, where there was a cave which was said to lead to Mekkah and many other places. Even if we stayed at home we were never bored. Kang Sadeli, the most sophisticated

---

3 ["Jootje" is the diminutive form of "Jo".]

of us, taught us to dance the Charleston and I remember us forming a long queue, hands upon the shoulders of the person in front of us, Charlestoning through the house. I remember an old photograph of the boys in *kimonos* and shawls around their heads and the girls in boys' clothes, complete with *udeng*.

In order to relate the events which follow, I have to tell you a little about the layout of the *kabupaten*. In front of it was an iron fence; on the left and on the right the driveway led to a space between the *pendopo* and the main house. A flight of steps led to a spacious verandah with three sets of chairs for visitors who came on business or for those who did not have the time to be entertained in the sitting room. Behind that verandah on the left was Father's study and, in front of it, a flight of steps led to the offices of the *kabupaten*. On these steps there usually sat an *oppas*, a man who had to run errands for Father and who guarded the security at night. Behind my Father's office was Ibu Patih's bedroom, which she shared with Eyang Bintang and her two daughters. These two rooms opened out to the large sitting room and, opposite those rooms were a guest room and my parents' bedroom. These rooms were the only ones that were rather protected because doors that could be locked separated them from the front verandah and from the dining space at the back.

Then followed a large open space where we had our meals, with my cousins' room on the left and, on the right, what was to be my room. Further back there was a set of chairs where my father used to drink his morning coffee, with a salvo of loud sneezes which made everyone know that he had begun the day. Still further back was the huge wooden sitting place, covered with a carpet, which one usually sees in Sundanese houses. Here Eyang Bintang used to sit. Ibu Gedong received her women visitors there and, in the evening, we all gathered there to listen to Ibu Gedong's series of *wayang* stories. Still further back there were other rooms but what I want to emphasise is that all this space was open; there were no walls to protect it from the outside. There was only a wooden balustrade all around it. The servants' quarters stood apart at the back of the premises and an old rickety gate allowed everyone to leave the premises or to enter them.

In Father's diary he mentions all through the year 1925 that the Sarikat Rakyat became active. I have been told since that the Sarikat Rakyat was originally a section of the Sarikat Islam but was influenced by the Partai Komunis Indonesia. In 1923 it separated itself from the Sarikat Islam and formed a new party, the Sarikat Rakyat. This party had nationalistic ideals. It wanted a free Indonesia and therefore opposed the Dutch Government. It wanted equal rights for everybody and therefore opposed the feudal society. It wanted to improve the lot of the mass of the people and therefore was against big landowners. At that time they thought this only possible under the protection of the Union of Soviet Socialist Republics.

Not only in Ciamis but in other areas too, for example, in the Residency of Banten, the Sarikat Rakyat became active. In Father's diary it is mentioned how they started harassing the people and tried to attack the village school so that it had to be closed because the people were afraid to send their children to school. They burnt houses and molested people until it culminated in the riot of 1926.

One evening a mob of people entered the *kabupaten* from the front side. They entered the verandah, where they molested the *oppas* who was on guard. Ibu Gedong, who heard the strange noises, was on the point of unlocking the sitting room, when she heard a shot. She then returned to her room. The shot had been fired by a man who saw his own face in the mirror of the umbrella-stand and, in his nervousness, mistook it for another person's face. The people then left and went to the *alun-alun*, where they murdered the Head of the Chinese.

If I am not mistaken, Father was in Kaum at that time. When he heard the uproar he returned quickly to the *kabupaten*. There he found the wounded *oppas*. There is no mention in the diary of my father's role that night but, as he told it to us, his first idea was to stop the chaos, come what may. He had a hunting gun with three cartridges in it. Armed thus, accompanied by the police commissioner, who had a gun, and an old *oppas* armed with a *klewang*, he went to the *alun-alun* and faced the mob. As if by a miracle, after three shots – I don't know who fired them – the people withdrew and dispersed. The next day the rioters were rounded up, imprisoned and later tried. Some were sentenced to death by hanging and about a hundred were deported to Digul.[4] I think my father was sorry for them, he did not feel they were his personal enemies for, during their exile, he regularly visited their families to see if they were in need of something; I sometimes accompanied him. In the same way, the exiles did not seem to consider my father their personal enemy for, when they returned, they brought small gifts from Digul. I remember a gaily coloured parrot-like bird that father was given by one of them. We called him "Si Digul" and taught him to talk. He died at a very old age in Purwakarta where he had moved with Father.

---

4 [This estimate of deportations to Digul (Irian Jaya) internment camps is probably too high.]

1: 'Just arrived! Outside our new home – 31 July 1954', Jalan Halimun 9, Jakarta:
(l-r) Gwenda Rodda (Australian volunteer graduate), Ailsa Thomson, Herb Feith and Betty Feith.
Image courtesy of Betty Feith.

2: English Language Inspectorate (IPBI), Jakarta c. 1955: (l-r) Mahomed, Betty and Ailsa.

3: The IPBI team, Jakarta c. 1955: (l-r) Betty Feith, Kurnianingrat Ali Sastroamijoyo, Frits Wachendorff, Harumani Rudolph-Sudirdjo and Ailsa Zainu'ddin.

4: IPBI in action, Jakarta c. 1955: (l-r) Betty, Ailsa, Harumani, [unidentified woman,] Frits Wachendorff and Kurnianingrat.

5: Harumani Rudolph-Sudirdjo and Kurnianingrat Ali Sastroamijoyo.
Image courtesy of Hadayanti Jayusman.

6: Kurnianingrat's mother (whom she refers to in her memoir simply as Ibu) and her father,
R. A. A. Sastrawinata. Image courtesy of Hadayanti Jayusman.

7: Visiting friends, Canberra, 1961.
Back row (l-r): Herb Feith, Ibu Saodah (Ailsa's mother-in-law), Ailsa Zainu'ddin, Zainu'ddin (Ailsa's husband).
Front row (l-r): David Feith, Betty Feith holding Lisa Zainu'ddin, Nila Zainu'ddin, Annie Feith.

8: Harumani and Chris Rudolph, Jakarta 1974.

9: Betty and Ailsa, Melbourne, June 2016. Image courtesy of Suyin Lim.

During the trials the people were asked why they had not entered the *kabupaten* from the back. The answer was that the rear side was strongly guarded by soldiers. Now I must tell you about a popular belief in Ciamis. The people there believed in *onom*, spirits that can materialise and often mingle with people, especially at parties. It was said that the *onom* protected the Indonesian local rulers. Be that as it may, my family had been saved as if by a miracle. If people had entered from the back, the whole family could have been massacred, as happened in other places. Even now, thinking back on all the events, it seems a miracle how Father, Ibu Gedong and all the family escaped death. Only a month later the Dutch Government sent some troops to guard Ciamis. In the following year Father received a decoration. The Susuhunan of Solo, who seemed to like my father – he had visited Ciamis in 1923 and had presented my father with a *kris* at that opportunity – now sent him two small reproductions of that decoration.

In Bandung, in the meantime, the family Hoedt had moved to another part of the town and, as it was too far away from school, I moved to another family. This family lived more luxuriously than the Hoedts but there was a loveless atmosphere. More children boarded there but we were treated differently from the children of the family. Why I did not tell my parents that I was not happy there I do not know; they would certainly have listened to me. Every day I looked forward to the holidays when I would be home again but I stuck it out there for five years.

My heart really bled when Dicky came to join me there when he was four years old and I did not know how to protect him. All his homesickness he expressed when one day he had a stomach ache and he said "Ibu always makes me some *nasi goreng* when I have a stomach ache". Now I know that I should have cuddled him and shown my feelings for him but we had not learnt to do that.

I finished the seventh year of primary school uneventfully. I liked the nuns and the other teachers but I had no friends among the classmates. We were friendly enough with each other and I don't think they looked down on me. They could not very well do so because I easily equalled them in class but they lived their own lives and I lived mine. There was just no contact.

With no school friends and the loveless atmosphere at "home" I did not know what to do with my leisure time. On Sundays I went to the cinema, it was the time of the silent film. The adventures of Tom Mix and Rin Tin Tin held me in suspense, especially when, during a chase, the piano played exciting music. It was at that time that I began to become a film fan.

After seven years of primary school I passed the final exam and it was decided that I would enter the three-year High School at the Zusters Ursulinen.

4. High School and Teacher Training

In the previous chapters I have shown you glimpses of the Sundanese *priyayi* world three quarters of a century ago, and of the Netherlands East Indies world, where we had to prepare ourselves for the future. Now I am going to tell you a bit about the environment from which Ibu came.

Once in a while Ibu visited her home town, Gadog, a small village on the slope of one of the mountains near Garut. As Dicky was too small at that time, I was the only one to accompany her. Such holidays in Gadog were a special treat. The long train trip itself was very interesting. At the station we got into a *sado*, from the French *dos-à-dos*, a cart where two people at the back sat back to back with two people in front. So we drove up to the house which stood on a steep slope.

It was the only brick house in the environment and quite spacious. I do not think it was suited to the climate because we always felt cold. As soon as we were awake, we assembled in the bamboo kitchen, where there was always a fire. You have never seen the house; it was burnt down when the Darul Islam terrorised this area. The small bamboo house that you know was built in its place.

After my grandfather's death only Yuyu, my great-grandmother, lived in the house. She was a small woman, bent with age and rheumatism. She was always very happy to see us and always welcomed us with her typical greeting, *"Amboi, amboi*! [Surprise, surprise!]". Immediately all kinds of snacks appeared, quite different from those we got in town. Lots of people came to welcome us, not only relatives but also the people who worked on the land and each of them brought a gift: some eggs, potatoes, vegetables and sometimes even a chicken. We could not possibly go hungry there.

The big garden was planted with the famous *jeruk Garut* trees which we do not see very much nowadays. Rosy-cheeked children with protruding bellies and perpetually running noses ran about on the premises. Then I thought them a picture of health but later I was told that the protruding bellies did not always signify that they had plenty of food; sometimes it was a sign of worms, because they walked about barefoot. For a bath I preferred to go to Nini Lurah, who had a roofless bathroom with seven or eight *pancuran*, bamboo pipes spouting fresh, clear water. Another attraction was

Nini Lurah's mulberry bush; the black berries picked fresh from the bush tasted wonderful.

Ibu was mostly busy with her relatives. Many were not very well-off. Some of the younger boys came to us at Ciamis, where they were prepared for a job, and some girls came to help in the Ciamis household. While Ibu was busy with the relatives, I went with the women who worked on the *sawah*. There I learned to walk quickly on the *galangan*, the narrow dykes between the *sawah*, and I learned to make all kinds of things from the rice straw. The days went by too fast and too soon the time came to leave. I always went home sunburnt and healthy.

During the long vacation after I had finished primary school, a big box was delivered in Ciamis. It contained a bicycle, which my father had thoughtfully ordered for me. It was easy to learn to ride the bicycle with so many hands to help. Of course my cousins wanted to use the bicycle too, and we spent hours trying not to fall off it. There were many quiet lanes in Ciamis so we learnt quickly. When I went back to Bandung I took the bike with me.

In Bandung it was different; there were far more people and other vehicles in the street. So, the first time I ventured out, everybody advised me "Careful, stay to the side of the road as much as you can". That was exactly what I did and consequently bumped into every unsuspecting pedestrian's shoulder from the back with my handlebar, especially when I went downhill.

When, on the first school day I went to school in a new dress, with a new school bag big enough to contain the *Atlas of the World* which was on our book list, and on my bicycle, I felt very important. I liked the lessons, especially the foreign languages. At that time German films were very popular. The sound film had been introduced and we learnt the popular songs of *Der Kongress Tanzt* and other such films that were exciting for teenagers. So we learnt German the easy way. Therefore, when in my third year some girls were asked to entertain the guests of an international conference at the *kabupaten* in Bandung, I was not surprised to find that I could easily converse in German.

In High School I found some friends, though not among the Dutch girls. There was Ida Wazar, a Sumatran girl, who was a very intimate friend of mine. There was Emmy Kakisina, an Ambonese girl, who lived with her big family in a small house; there was the quiet Indo-European, Els van Paas, who lived close to Ida Wazar. The Dutch girls formed their own clique. There was Mimi van Essen, daughter of the manager of Hotel Homann, who invited the whole class to Hotel Homann on her birthdays. That was the only contact we had.

Through Ida I was introduced to the world of tennis. We were enthusiastic beginners and spent hours on the tennis courts. We also made a whole set of new friends. I was never at a loss any more what to do with my leisure time; I went to the tennis court.

It was at that time that I announced I did not want to stay in the same boarding house any more. Another boarding house was found for Dick and me. This time we stayed with Dutch people. The man was nice enough but his wife did not understand our ways, and the son, Martin, was a nice fellow. I got on well with him until he told me one day he had seen the driver of a *delman*, a four-seat cart, whip his horse. Martin had somehow stopped the cart, taken the whip out of the hands of the driver and had whipped him. Of course in his mind it was a noble gesture but I felt sick. That was the end of our friendship.

One Sunday morning his mother asked me to join her to see Martin in a swimming competition. I had a lot of homework to do for the next day and said I would rather stay at home. The woman immediately suspected me of wanting to stay at home for Kang Pelen, who sometimes came along for a chat and who was never invited in; we talked over the fence with each other. She suspected me of having a love affair with my own brother! I refused the more to go with her – then she pulled my hair. That was the end; I asked my father to move me from there.

This time a nice family was found, the André Wiltens. Mr André Wiltens had been a planter but, for reasons of health, had to quit the job though he still held an important position in the Plantersbond. His wife was a well-educated woman, who stimulated my study by giving me all kinds of articles and books to read. They had two daughters; the elder, about my age, was a dark-haired beauty who was very good at making dresses and sewing in general. The younger daughter was a clever little blonde girl, the apple of her mother's eye. I felt really at home with them but now I realise that, for Dicky, the woman-dominated household must have been less congenial.

Dick, in the meantime, had entered primary school. I remember my father going to the headmaster of the so-called best primary school in Bandung. They did not even admit my father to the headmaster's office but kept him sitting on a hard wooden bench on the gallery in front of the classroom. That was the first time that I saw him being treated impolitely but my father did not budge; he waited for hours on that bench until it pleased the headmaster to see him. Dicky was accepted.

The André Wiltens definitely did not feel superior. We were really friends, but it was there that I came to realise the great gap that existed between Indonesians and people of the ruling race. The girls' friends just did not acknowledge Dicky's and my existence. You could say Dicky was too small for them but I was their age and had an education similar to theirs. It did not hurt because by then I had my own Indonesian friends – but it registered.

When I was thirteen an unexpected thing happened: a younger sister was born. Again my father took off to Panjalu; again I accompanied him and, after a long wait, the message came over the telephone: a daughter safely born. My father rather doted on her; he thought her the most beautiful baby. Because it was so funny to hear many people older than she call her aunty, "*bibi*" in Sundanese, she was nicknamed "Bibib". She became a chubby little child and was pampered by all of us.

By that time father decided to retire. He had wanted to do so for some time but the population of Ciamis had asked him to stay for some time more; now he decided to do it. Ibu Gedong was to live in Bandung and Ibu was to live in Purwakarta. Father had rented a villa a little outside Bandung, in Andir, which has now become just a part of Bandung. I was to stay with her, Dicky would stay a bit longer with the André Wiltens. Ibu moved to Purwakarta, where a new house had been built for her and we helped her settle there. Her mother, Nini, went with her. The cousins also moved back to Purwakarta to their respective parents. The day Father and Ibu Gedong moved to Bandung, many of the civil service officials and their wives travelled with them to Bandung and helped them settle into the villa.

In the meantime I had finished the three-year High School and had the choice between continuing my study at the five-year High School from where I could continue studying at university, and a vocational training to prepare me for a job. Seeing that my parents were growing old, I decided to earn a living as soon as possible. So I registered at the Teacher Training School of the Indo-European Society, I. E. V. Kweekschool. I liked the school. The director was a big man with a goatee; his name was Greeven. He used to stand on a spot where everybody entering the school had to pass, so he knew who was late. He had a good memory, because he knew each of us by name. He always greeted me with "Hi, Jootje with a 't'". (Joodje with a "d" meant "little Jew".) He seemed to dislike Jews, because he often imitated their way of speech and made jokes about them but he was a good administrator and a good teacher too. In fact, most of the teachers were very good and I learnt with pleasure.

There was the sad-faced, grey-haired maths teacher. At that time I was very bad at maths. When he returned our work he said "Excellent, excellent! Not bad," and ended invariably with "Jootje, sad." I say I was bad at maths at that time because, in the third year a few months before the final exam, we had a new maths teacher with dark hair and blue eyes, very good looking. He must have been a very good teacher because I suddenly understood everything and could do the most complicated problems. It can't have been only because of his black hair and blue eyes that that happened.

There was the drawing teacher, who was really a friend to us. He saw that I really had no aptitude for drawing and, to let me pass the final exam, he taught me to draw chickens. They could be used for everything, for decorative drawing; for nature drawing; and so on. And there was Sybesma, the psychology teacher from whom I have learned a lot and who instilled in me my interest in psychology. There were too many teachers to mention them all.

The classmates were also very nice, Indonesians as well as Indo-Europeans. There was Annie Natakusuma, now Annie Hidajat, who introduced me to her party-going set of friends; I came to like dancing. By the way, at that time the girls danced in *kain* and *kabaya*. For me dancing was more a sport like tennis and that was what made the parties attractive to me, not the flirtation. There was Henny Eykemans, who owned a two-seater, and sometimes loaded her friends into her small car to drive us to one of the swimming pools in the neighbourhood.

I enjoyed staying with Ibu Gedong in Andir. It was a quiet household but, when Father was there, he often brought Bibib from Purwakarta with him. Then the household became livelier. Early in the morning I cycled to school, for it was quite a distance and, after lessons, I cycled the same way back in the hot sun. I did not mind that; I thought it good sport for, at that time, I was very weight conscious. I must have looked a sight, being so much in the sun, for the tennis games also exposed me for hours in the sun – and you must remember, at that time girls had not learned to improve their looks. We knew only two kinds of powder, the medicinal Purol powder for when we had pimples and the Marck's powder – no other cosmetics, no lipstick, let alone eye shadow – but my looks did not worry me over much. I had early discovered that people in general, as well as boys, did not only value good looks; companionship, the capacity to share things, were equally important. What *did* worry me was that I could not fall in love. Left and right I saw my friends fall in love, finding a partner. I started wondering if there was something wrong with me. In those days Ceuk

Patih, Ibu Gedong's daughter, came often to stay with us. She was a real sister to me, a very good companion, in spite of the fact that she was older than Ibu. We went shopping together, saw a lot of films and took snacks in little restaurants.

When I was fifteen, the last of our foursome, Yetty, was born in Purwakarta. I was not there when she was born but she was received with as much joy and love as her elder sisters and brother before her. Father used to say jokingly that he loved her most because she was the youngest, me because I was the first born, Dicky because he was the only son and Bibib because she was nothing in particular in the row and he had to make up for that. We all felt the love of our parents and it gave us a feeling of security which stood us in good stead when in later years life played havoc with us. I have tried to give you both that feeling of security but I am afraid I did not succeed.

After I had passed the final exams of the Teacher Training Course, I took a two-year course of more advanced teacher training, the Hoofdacte in Dutch. This course did not take up as much time as the former one. I started teaching part-time at a girls' school where they emphasised the teaching of skills the girls would need as future housewives. The head of the school was Suhaermani, now Mrs Parjono, who became a very good friend of mine. We played tennis together, went to the same parties and did many things together. I was very proud that I could earn money; but, thoughtless that I was, I did not spend any of it on the persons I loved most: Father, Ibu and Ibu Gedong. They would have been so proud and pleased to get a small something from my first earned money but I was so used to receiving things from them that it did not enter my head to do something for them. It is only while I am writing this that I realise how thoughtless I was.

So, after two years, equipped with good diplomas, I started my career as a teacher.

5. Schoolmarm

In the meantime Dicky had entered the five-year High School. He was a big boy then; the difference in age between us had fallen away. We debated endlessly about all kinds of problems and neither of us ever gave in. Yet we were very close, maybe like Bibib and Yetty were to each other. Father was not entirely satisfied with the result of the Western-oriented education he had given his two eldest children. He decided to give his two youngest ones quite a different education. They were to stay with Ibu and have an education like every other Indonesian child did.

Ibu Gedong, after a few years in Andir, had moved to a house in Bandung, near my school. Now she moved to Purwakarta, where she stayed in the house that Eyang Bintang had left us. Ibu Patih was to stay with her. It was a friendly, comfortable house and I think we all have good memories of it.

When I had finished the Hoofdacte, Father took me to the Ministry of Education in Jakarta and, as my first job, I became a teacher in the Dutch-Chinese Primary School in Glodok, downtown Jakarta. I taught the third form and worked from half past seven to eleven o'clock. For that I earned a salary of f100.00, with which I could easily pay my monthly needs. Through Ceuk Patih I was introduced into the household of the Patih of Weltevreden. The household was well-known for the six beautiful and charming daughters. The eldest daughter had married Kang Djugi, Ibu Gedong's only son. Another had married Kang Sanusi, who had become an official with the police in Jakarta. The two youngest daughters were still at home and the one before the youngest was engaged to Sule, Ceuk Patih's only son. Besides there was also a cousin, Toos Prawira Adiningrat, who was to become one of my most intimate friends. She had finished the five-year High School and was doing one year at the Secondary School for the Education of Housewives, or Middelbare Vakschool, which she did not enjoy very much.

It is true that I had had a good teacher training and that I had passed it with satisfactory marks but I was very inexperienced. All the way in the tram, when I rode from Laan Trivelli to Glodok, I rehearsed what I was going to teach. Fortunately we had a very good headmaster, by the name of Geleynse. He told me later that for the first three days I did not touch the blackboard but he did not say anything about it because he saw how nervous I was and how anxious to do things well.

I admired my colleagues, who were all much more experienced and handled their classes with ease. There was An Latuassan in the first form, an Ambonese with a lovely voice; next to my classroom there was Loes Djajadiningrat, who taught the second form and seemed so sure of herself. In the fourth form there was Mrs Tjindarbumi, who seemed to be very popular with her class. In the fifth year there was a very pleasant Chinese colleague by the name of The. In the sixth form there was Mr Dahlan Abdullah, an elderly Sumatran. The headmaster himself took the seventh form. I felt so small and insignificant compared to all of them. I was not used to Chinese faces and, in the first weeks, they seemed all alike; only after some time did I manage to distinguish one from the other. Those poor little pupils must have had a terrible time with me.

Mr Abdullah told me a lot about the national movement for independence. He was very upset when Husni Thamrin, the famous nationalist leader, died. He suspected foul play.[5]

So far my life had been so protected that I did not notice the injustices around me. I did not know that there were certain swimming pools with the notice "Dogs and natives not allowed entrance". I had no idea that it was difficult for Indonesians to be accepted at the European Primary School, which paved the way for further good schooling. I did not realise that, for most Indonesian children, it was made difficult to get a good education and I was oblivious of the fact that the masses were kept ignorant and poor. However, all these new impressions were overshadowed by the fact that I fell in love.

I learned to know Jusuf Prawira Adiningrat through his sister, Toos. It was not long after that we both fell in love with each other. So I did not have to worry any more that there was something wrong with me. The sky was literally bluer, the grass greener and the people kinder than ever but Jus and I were so wrapped up in each other that we did not pay much attention to our surroundings. In the evenings we used to take long walks, along the Jakarta canal, even to Glodok and back. We did not have much money; once in a while, when we were in clover, we treated each other. He was still a law student but sometimes he earned a little by giving people advice.

We did not notice how we inconvenienced and shocked others by coming home late every evening. Finally the Patih told me that he did not want to take the responsibility for me anymore, so he asked me to find another boarding house. It was a shock to feel unwanted. Fortunately Kang Sanusi, who had become assistant *wedana* in Jatinegara – then called Mr Cornelis – and his wife, Ceuk Iyoh, took me into their house.

Jus had a brother and a cousin working in Purwakarta, so he sometimes accompanied me on my weekends home. On one of these occasions we got the idea that he should officially ask Father for my hand. Now that is not done that way in our society. A marriage is not an affair between two people, it is an alliance between two families but, with our new-fangled ideas, we did it in the Western way. Jus asked for and got an audience with Father – but when he left he had neither said nor asked anything; he had only talked about me. Father said to Ibu "The poor girl is imagining things; the boy did not ask at all to marry her."

So I asked Jus to do it and, this time, he did it. Later everything was done in the correct way. The Bupati and Raden Ayu of Cianjur, cousins of Jus, came to propose officially for Jus and we were properly engaged.

---

5   [Mohammad Husni Thamrin died on 11 January 1941.]

Father was not very happy with the idea that Jus and I would be in Jakarta, not properly chaperoned. He went to the Ministry of Education again and asked them to transfer me to Purwakarta. After a few weeks I received a letter stating that I was appointed teacher at the European Primary School in Purwakarta. The letter stated "transferred on request".

After the outbreak of World War II the Netherlands East Indies Government seemed to transfer a little more authority to Indonesians in the higher echelons. At that time Mr Lukman Djajadiningrat was in charge of the Ministry of Education. I came to see him and protested that I had not requested a transfer to Purwakarta. Mr Lukman seemed to understand the situation; he was very understanding and promised to call me to Jakarta from time to time.

So I moved to Purwakarta. The people in Purwakarta were very happy that an Indonesian was appointed at the European school and I taught many nephews and nieces and even my own little sister Bibib. Jus came to Purwakarta every weekend. We were always heavily chaperoned; poor Bibib and Yetty did not move from my side when Jus was there; we went to the cinema with lots of cousins and took walks only when others came with us. So when I was called to Jakarta – for Mr Lukman Djajadiningrat kept his word – we enjoyed the privacy.

In the meantime the threat of a Japanese invasion became more and more real. The headmaster of our school had to join the Landwacht and I was left in charge of the school. The other teachers, mostly older Indo-Europeans, did not like it, nor did the assistant Resident but, as I had the best diplomas, as the most highly qualified staff member I had to become head of the school. It did not last long though, for the Dutch parents became restless. They moved to other places and soon the school had to be closed. It was only later that I understood that the Netherlands East Indies Government had evacuated to Australia and had left Indonesia practically without defences.

Jus and I had arranged that, when the Japanese came, he would join me in Purwakarta and, as he would then be in possession of an emergency diploma, he could get a job and we would ask to be married. Purwakarta became very quiet; many people left and stayed in the country. Father had also decided to evacuate to the country with Ibu Gedong, Ibu and the children. I stayed in Purwakarta as long as possible because of my arrangement with Jus.

Ibu's house was near the Arab quarters. Across the street from us were Arab families. We got on very well with them; they respected my father highly and Bibib and Yetty played with the children. The head of those families we called Abah Salim and I still remember how he came to see me when the family had evacuated and I was left with one male servant in the house. He had an Arab sword in his hand; I think it is called a *scimitar*. He said "You need not be afraid. Abah Salim is there to protect you." I felt really touched and grateful but when, after some time, Jus still did not turn up, I decided, though with a heavy heart, to join the others in the country.

At that time the antagonism between the Chinese and the Indonesians had flared up again and in the place of evacuation this was discussed as an added threat. In March 1942 the Japanese came, occupying Purwakarta and the neighbouring areas.

When after some further time Jus still had not arrived, I told Father that I could not stand it any longer and that I wanted to make enquiries in Purwakarta. Accompanied by the same male servant who had stayed on with me, I walked to Purwakarta. I mention this servant especially because, in fact, he was in mortal fear of the Japanese and I remember with gratitude that, in spite of everything, he was willing to accompany me.

We went to the *kabupaten* where the Bupati and his wife welcomed me like their own child. They made the necessary enquiries and it was soon found out that Jus had safely arrived at his brother-in-law's house in Barangdan and, from there, had set out to Purwakarta on foot. He had been intercepted by some village people who took him for a Chinese. Whatever he said or did to convince them that he was a Sundanese and a Muslim, they refused to believe him – and killed him.

I shall never forget how kind people were in their efforts to console me. I especially remember Dicky's friendship and warmth. I felt very responsible to the family for the death of Jus but they were very nice to me and, to this day, I am still considered one of the family, which I accept with humble gratitude.

From that time I also remember how Kang Sadeli came to fetch me. He had become assistant *wedana* in Cianjur and he took me there on foot to avoid the Japanese. We walked through woods where not many people came. It was peaceful and quiet where we walked on moss-covered soil and heard a solitary bird singing now and then. We crossed a big river and so arrived in Cianjur. Kang Sadeli and his wife, Ceuk Ida, did everything they could to divert me but, after some time, I went home with the same heavy heart.

6. The Japanese Occupation

The Japanese Occupation had been predicted centuries before. In the eleventh century Joyoboyo, King of Kediri whom the Javanese considered to be a reincarnation of Wishnu, prophesied that "a yellow race of short people would come and reign over Java for as long as the maize plant lives. After they left, the country would be independent (*merdeka*). Justice (Ratu Adil) would then reign." This prediction was inserted in a Javanese adaptation of the *Bharatayudha*, made by Empu Sedah, a poet at the court of King Joyoboyo.

At the end of the nineteenth century, Ronggowarsito, a poet at the court of Sunan Paku Buwono IX of Solo revived this prediction by translating it into modern Javanese and drawing people's attention to it. So when the Japanese came in 1942, the people were reminded of the prophecy. Now the life span of a maize plant is about three and a half months and most people took the prediction literally. A friend of mine even planted a maize plant in front of his window on the day the Japanese invaded Java. Unfortunately a few weeks later a goat nibbled at the young plant – and that was the end of the experiment. The Japanese did not stay for three and a half months but three and a half years. Maybe Empu Sedah wanted to say that the Japanese would only stay for a short time and expressed this poetically by comparing it to the life span of the maize plant.

Three and a half years may have been a relatively short time but it was a devastating period. I am not thinking of the crash troops because crash troops, no matter what nationality, seem to be cruel everywhere but their Kempeitai, a kind of Japanese Politbureau, was notorious for its cruelty. The wealth of Indonesia was scooped up and used for Japanese war purposes, leaving the people poor and hungry. The Dutch and the Indo-European men and women were put in separate camps and often the men were transported to other countries to do forced labour. This happened to a lot of Indonesians as well. If they did come home, they were emaciated and not capable of much.

Yet, in spite of all the hardships, several good things came out of this period. For one thing, the suffering made nationalism stronger among the Indonesians. We did not want to be under foreign domination any more. Second, the Japanese-trained troops became the kernel of the future Indonesian army. Third, the Japanese set up hundreds of primary schools so that many more people had the chance of formal education. At first the quality of these schools was rather low because of the explosion of the number of pupils and a shortage of teachers but it was a good beginning. Fourth, in all schools at all levels Indonesian was the medium of teaching. The aristocracy had no special privileges any more. They were poor and hungry like all the others. The feudal society ceased to exist.

Father had been able to live easily on his pension as a former *bupati*. With the arrival of the Japanese this pension stopped and he was left without any income. This was the time when we had to live from the sale of anything we had. Tablecloths and bed sheets were cut up for underwear; curtains for dresses. Yet many people came to stay with us, some for a short time, others more permanently. There were many who had to leave their homes when the Japanese invaded the country.

I had been unemployed for several months and I decided to try to find a job in Jakarta. Again Kang Sanusi and Ceuk Iyoh took me up in their home. At the municipality I met my former colleague Mr Dahlan Abdullah. He had become an important person because he had always opposed the Dutch Government. He offered me a job at the Municipal Office. At first I had to weigh and dole out sugar to lists of persons; later they gave me translation work to do, mostly from Dutch into English. As my experience in English was confined to the English I had learned at school, my translations must have been rather poor but my superiors were satisfied.

Mr Dahlan Abdullah was very nice. He gave Kang Sanusi a better and bigger house to live in. More people came to stay with us. Dicky, who had meanwhile entered the first Indonesian High School under the able leadership of Mr Adam Bachtiar, came to live with us. The students were proud of their school because it was known for its high quality and its real Indonesian atmosphere. Kang Penen and Kang Kachpi, also in search of work, joined the household. Kang Sanusi's salary at that time must have been small but the couple shared everything generously with us. Ceuk Iyoh must have found it difficult to make ends meet. In spite of the hardships it was a happy household. We teased each other and made jokes about each other's difficulties.

At the Municipal Office I met some interesting people. One of them was Ceuk Sukesih, who held a high position at the municipality and who may have been the first Indonesian woman who had been able to make a trip to Europe on her own earnings.

The Japanese thought their physical exercises, called *taiso*, very important. At all schools and offices, every day, some time was made free specially for *taiso*. We all gathered in the open air and did the exercises for half an hour or so. It must have been good for us, for I noticed that the children, in spite of the food shortage, became taller. Now you are all used to regular physical exercises and, combined with better food, it has made your generation much taller than mine.

My salary at the Municipal Office was very small. I remember the time when Dicky needed a pair of shoes. We went all along Pasar Baru, in and out of shop after shop, but there was not one pair of shoes that I could afford. So, when I learned that a Teacher Training School for Girls, or Sekolah Guru Puteri, in Yogya needed a psychology teacher, I went to the Japanese Ministry of Education to apply for the job. The Indonesian official who received me told me that this was *not* the time to walk about with one's chin in the air; you had to bow a lot, especially women. My haughty demeanour must have irritated him: I was really sorry, for I did not mean to appear haughty and did not feel superior at all.

Fortunately the Japanese official in charge of the applications was an elderly, fatherly man, who did not stand on formality. I got the job and was to leave in a few weeks' time. Before I left, he told me that if there were any difficulties at school I could always report to him and count on his help. I took it to mean that he would help the school if there were anything we needed but, when I conveyed this message to my new colleagues in Yogya, they thought I was to report on them and at first took me for a spy for the Japanese. It took some time before they learnt to trust me.

Father was rather happy that I got this job, although it meant I would be far from the family. He had been in Yogya several times and had made several friends there. Among these were K. R. T. Mangunjaya and his family. K. R. T. Mangunjaya himself had died in the meantime but his family still lived in the same house. I knew the son, Soemarsono, from his school days in Jakarta. It was arranged that Soemarsono would meet me at the station in Yogya, where the train was to arrive at midnight. He would take me to his family in Mangunjayan and, from there, I could go to the school where I was to work.

Everything went according to plan. Soemarsono was at the station to meet me. He took me to Mangunjayan and delivered me at his sister's quarters. Mustinah, his younger sister, had a big, comfortable bedroom with two beds in it. The annex was an old-fashioned big bathroom with toilet. In front of the bedroom there was a small sitting room with two wooden sitting places, half the width of the Sundanese ones. In reality it was a Javanese-style self-contained apartment. I never had the opportunity to look at all parts of the house; I saw the big, open front verandah and was admitted to a small dining room but I guess that for each member of the family there was such a self-contained apartment.

I was tired after the train trip and soon fell asleep. It did not seem long after that that I was woken up. I was told that Mustinah's mother wanted to see me. I hastily took a bath, dressed and went to the sitting room. On the wooden sitting place sat a thin, wiry woman with sharp features. She was cross-legged and bolt upright. She was an aunt of Hamengkubuwono

IX, Sultan of Yogyakarta. She asked me all kinds of questions about my family and, after about an hour, she left. There was something in her that reminded me of Ibu Gedong and, really, when she knew me better, she soon treated me like a close relative.

When Mustinah came home from school – at that time she was a student of the first Indonesian High School in Yogya where the medium of learning was Indonesian – we sat on the front verandah and I could see the beautiful white sand all around the house, so lovely that on moonlit nights it gave everything a romantic atmosphere. The whole place was so peaceful that one tended to forget the Japanese Occupation – but not entirely, because one of the cousins had arrived with her baby after her husband had been killed shortly after the Japanese invasion.

After two days I went in search of the Sekolah Guru Puteri (SGP), which was in the northern part of Yogya, while Mangunjayan lay in the southern part. All along the road young men were stationed at regular intervals to urge the passers-by not to speak a foreign language but to use Bahasa Indonesia. This was very necessary for people like me, who spoke Dutch all the time.

The Sekolah Guru Puteri was a large, friendly-looking building. I was taken to the director, Ibu Sri Umijati, a petite, charming woman with big eyes who, for all her petiteness, had an iron will, as I was soon to discover. The SGP was a teacher training school at secondary level, training girls who had finished primary school. The girls boarded at school. There were big dorms with rows of beds in them. The teachers were mostly accommodated in houses around the school; only a few lived further away. This was necessary because, beside their teaching duties, they had also to look after the girls after lessons. In turns they had to watch the girls doing their homework after early dinner until they went to bed at ten o'clock. It made teachers and students know each other better. The girls got three meals a day and a snack in the afternoon. The food was simple but healthy. The matron, Ibu Sunyoto, saw to that. Of course it was Ibu Sri Umijati who ultimately had to see to it that the girls had sufficient food, which was not an easy task at that time.

For that matter it was not an easy task to be responsible for hundreds of girls in their teens, especially not during this period of Japanese rule. Ibu Sri Umijati always seemed calm and controlled but, when I roomed with her before I had my own accommodation, I heard her, night after night, having nightmares. It helped her when we could laugh about it and we became real friends.

The girls had enough variety in their lives. They could take *serimpi* lessons if they wanted to; twice a week, early in the morning before lessons started, they had compulsory swimming lessons and, accompanying them, I learned swimming too. Then there were excursions on weekends; we went to the Borobudur, to Kaliurang and many more places in the neighbourhood. We had to be very economical with these excursions and we walked most of the time or went by train to the places further away. Once in a while the girls had to learn cooking – special dishes from material that we had never used before in our diet – for instance, they were taught to cook the snails (*bekicot*) that were becoming a plague in the gardens. These cookery lessons took place in the homes of Japanese men. It was on these occasions that the girls had to be guarded with extra care and several teachers always accompanied them.

After some time I got a big house next to Ibu Sri Umijati. Only the pavilion and one room of the main building were occupied by two colleagues, the rest was to be my domain. I had not one piece of furniture and no money to buy any. Fortunately Soemarsono, who worked with the police, got me enough furniture for me to fill the rooms. He obtained this from Dutch people who were leaving Indonesia. My parents sent me a cousin, Bi Oele, to do the housework for me. I was all set.

It was during this time that Father, Ibu and Nini undertook the long trip to Yogya by train to see how I lived. Travelling at that time was not comfortable and I saw Father, who was used to comfort, sitting outside the coupé near the railing, on some suitcases, when the train arrived.[6] Thanks to Ibu Sri Umijati, who thoughtfully sent them extra dishes every day and took us into the cool climate of Kaliurang for two nights, they enjoyed their stay.

I knew practically no Indonesian and I had to teach psychology in Indonesian. Fortunately one of my colleagues, Ibu Nurseha, translated everything that I wanted to say into Indonesian and I learned it by heart. I was always in mortal fear that the students would ask me questions but it seemed a good way to master Indonesian. After some time things became easier and I even learned to answer questions unprepared.

At first everything in Yogya seemed very cheap compared to Jakarta and Purwakarta and I enjoyed the typical Javanese dishes but in the course of time the Japanese money lost its value and it was no longer possible to live

---

6 [The term "coupé" probably refers to the end compartment of a train carriage containing seats on one side only.]

on the salary of a teacher but, at that time, we could barter a *batik kain* for a hundred kilos of rice. With the bartering of my *batik kain*s and the sale of my jewellery I managed to keep the household going. That was very fortunate because I had young people to stay with me – Hapid, Jus's youngest brother and Boy, son of Ceuk Mus and Kang Pen, both stayed there. They were high school students.

Later, to my great joy, Bibib was entrusted to me. She was so trusting and innocent and always told me stories about the school, her friends and everything that happened to her. She gained entrance to a good junior high school and had a nice set of friends. At least I could give her that because there were so many things I wanted to give her but could not in the circumstances then. I would have liked to give her good clothes and pleasant outings and I wished I could give all the young people in the house better food – but it was impossible.

The hardships and the cruel Japanese regime made the people restless. In Aceh the people rebelled under the leadership of a young teacher of religion. Twice they succeeded in driving back the Japanese troops sent to quell the rebellion. The second time Aceh troops under the command of Teuku Hamid went into the forest and from there started attacking the Japanese but, when the Japanese threatened to kill the rebels' families, Teuku Hamid and his men surrendered. The third time the Japanese burnt down the mosque in which the people were praying and shot everyone nearby on the spot.

In Singaparna, West Java, an influential Muslim leader saw how the people were sucked dry by the Japanese. They were forced to work for them without pay. The Muslim leader taught them to defend themselves through *pencak silat* and instigated them not to give their harvest to the Japanese. A Japanese messenger was sent to talk to the people but he was attacked and only barely escaped. Then the Japanese attacked and quenched the rebellion forcibly. In Indramayu there were several rebellions too but the greatest rebellion was that of the PETA in Blitar.

Dicky, who had enrolled at the medical school set up by the Japanese in Jakarta, told me that the students refused to be shaven bald. Fortunately the students were left unmolested. Only the leaders of the resistance, amongst whom was Soedjatmoko, were expelled.[7]

Then we heard about the fall of the Japanese Empire.

---

7   [Another account of the outcome of the rebellion against the Japanese by students of the medical school features in Mien Soedarpo's *Reminiscences of the Past*, p. 49.]

It was during one of the vacations, when we were all in Purwakarta, that I heard something that shook me awake. At that time I was still numbed by Jus's death. Then I heard about the kidnapping of Bung Karno and Bung Hatta, when they were taken to Rangasdenklok by a group of young people who urged Bung Karno and Bung Hatta to proclaim Indonesia's independence then – before the arrival of the Allied forces.

Back in Yogyakarta we witnessed the end of the Japanese rule. The Japanese were to surrender their arms to the Allied forces but our young people, armed with bamboo spears (*bambu runcing*) tried, with or without the help of the PETA, to get hold of those arms before the arrival of the Allied forces. Some Japanese troops voluntarily handed over their arms to Indonesians whereas others were afraid that, if they did so, the Indonesians would take revenge on them.

Then we heard about the Proclamation of Independence by Bung Karno and Bung Hatta on 17 August 1945.

7. The Early Years of the Republic

Much of what I am going to tell you in this chapter I have gathered from men in their fifties, like Oom Achmad [Achmad Jayusman, Kurnianingrat's brother-in-law], who at that time were adolescents, junior or senior high school students or first or second year university students. The Indonesian youth has played an important role in our revolution.

In Yogya we did not hear about the Proclamation of Independence until a few days later, because of the bad communications. During the Japanese time our radios were sealed, so that we could only tune in to Japanese-sponsored broadcasting stations. Listening to overseas broadcasts was punished with death. Yet quite a few among the young people managed to manipulate their radios in such a way that they could catch the ABC [Australian Broadcasting Commission] or the Voice of America. In this way we learned about the total surrender of the Japanese and, in the same way, heard mostly from the ABC about the Proclamation of Independence.

When Bung Karno read the Proclamation of Independence, signed by him and Bung Hatta, there was only a very limited audience present at his residence in Pegangsaan where the ceremony took place. This residence was later called Gedung Proklamasi and is now known as Gedung Pola. The broadcasting station was still under Japanese control and heavily guarded but, in the evening, some Indonesian young men who worked at that station had to read the evening broadcast and it was then that they broadcast the

Proclamation of Independence several times. The young men were beaten up by the Japanese and put in prison but, fortunately, after a few days the Japanese retreated and the young men were freed.

In Yogyakarta our spirits were high too. People felt the need to voice their support of the Republic, Bung Karno and Bung Hatta, often gathering in Malioboro, Yogya's main street, to do so. We yelled "Merdeka" when we met; we shouted "Merdeka" when we parted; we called "Merdeka" before starting a speech. "Merdeka" became our national greeting.

The schools were not exactly closed but the students and also the teachers were more intent upon following the political developments than upon regular lessons in the classroom. The students made posters in English and, in spite of the little English they knew, they produced hundreds of posters, which were pasted on trains arriving in Yogya. When the trains left they looked very picturesque with the brightly painted posters covering them. Next to slogans like "Long live our Republic" and "Never more under foreign domination" one could read "Free, free like a bird in a tree".

The Allied forces started landing in September 1945. When part of them arrived in the harbour of Jakarta the people wanted to meet Bung Karno and Bung Hatta to receive some directives from them. A public meeting was sponsored by the youth at Ikada Square, now Lapangan Merdeka. Thousands of people came to the square but it was guarded by heavily armed Japanese troops. In order to avoid bloodshed Bung Karno and Bung Hatta were dissuaded by their advisers from fanning public enthusiasm so Bung Karno only said "We are *merdeka*; we are now *merdeka*. Go home now." The people had expected to hear more but even those few words strengthened them in their determination to defend their independence.

In Surabaya the Dutch troops made the grave mistake of hoisting the Dutch flag. The people were wild with rage. In a moment the Dutch flag was pulled down and the Republican flag hoisted in its place. The British troops, who were clearly in favour of the Dutch, ordered the people to surrender their arms. Surabaya was fired on from land, from the air and from the sea. The whole population threw themselves into battle with bamboo spears or whatever arms they could get hold of. The battle raged for nearly one month. Bung Tomo, with his fiery speeches over the radio, fanned the people's fighting spirit. At last Bung Karno was called in to calm the people down but Surabaya remained in Republican hands.

In Ambarawa the English troops were driven back to Semarang. In Bandung the Allies met with resistance too. All these events made the

English change their opinion. They were convinced that the Dutch-Republican dispute should be solved by negotiation.

It was not long thereafter that the Republican Government decided to move to Yogyakarta. Only Premier Sutan Syahrir would stay in Jakarta for foreign relations. The people in Yogyakarta were wild with enthusiasm and Sultan Hamengkubuwono IX, who was a staunch supporter of the Republic, prepared everything. It is said that the head of the Railroad Service prepared a special train that stopped behind Bung Karno's residence at Pegangsaan so that Bung Karno, Bung Hatta and their families could move unobtrusively to Yogyakarta.

The residence of the former Dutch governor of Yogyakarta was used as the Presidential Palace. It was a simple but spacious building where Bung Karno could easily receive hundreds of guests. We were very proud when we saw our "Red and White" hoisted in front of the building and we were elated when we heard the official band playing the national songs, most of which were still in the making. It was not long before Yogyakarta became full of new arrivals. The top command of the Republican armed forces was in Yogya. Other departments moved too but the town was so full that it could not accommodate all of them. For instance the Department of Education was temporarily placed in Solo and the Department of Industry in Magelang.

At home we had another family to house, one of Jus's sisters, Tine, with her husband, Samsudarsono, an army officer. Lots of foreigners arrived too, not only state visitors but also American, English and Indian journalists and others. During the Dutch rule we, the native population, had not had much contact with the outside world; now, all of a sudden, it was as if the doors to the outside world were thrown open. Yunus, India's representative for the Indonesian Republic, and his wife, Laj, became very good friends of the Indonesians. Their house was hospitably opened to their friends.

All kinds of things started happening. The Japanese money was replaced by Republican money; we had a broadcasting station for overseas, the Voice of Free Indonesia. The first Indonesian university, Gadjah Mada, was opened. It was temporarily located in a front part of the Kraton, called Setinggil. Many teachers were eager to study again and many of us enrolled at the new university. For some time we managed to attend the lectures but soon most of us had to quit because our teaching took up too much of our time.

In 1946 I was moved from the SGP to the Senior High School where I had to teach English. It was here that I met Achmad Jayusman for the first time, as a third year high school student. Little did I know that he was to become my brother-in-law. The other English teachers were Utami Suryadarma, wife of our first Air Commodore and Endang Sulbi, one of the first students at Gadjah Mada University. Tami was a very beautiful woman, always elegantly dressed and many people idolised her. Yet she was very earthy too. When we received our first salary she treated Sulbi and me at the well-known restaurant "Toko Oen", and there I saw to my amazement what a healthy appetite she had.

At that time there were not many people who spoke English. Those who did were recruited to entertain foreign guests and visitors. I was one of them and so I came to attend many state dinners at the presidential palace. On these and many other occasions I met Tami and because we shared many experiences together we became close friends – and, as you know, we still are up to the present. [1992] Tami was given the task by KOWANI [Kongres Wanita Indonesia, a national women's organisation] of contacting the outside world to inform them about the situation in our Republic. She wrote the articles and I read them over the Voice of Free Indonesia.

What I remember of this time, right up to the time I left for Australia, was the general atmosphere of real friendship. We were all equals, only some got more important tasks to perform than others, but we appreciated each other. Nobody, no matter how high in rank, felt superior.

At first the high school students were loosely gathered into an organisation, GASEMA [Gabungan Sekolah Menengah Mataram], which had mostly on its program sports, cultural and social activities. Gradually GASEMA grew into a combatant organisation. They worked together with the professional and non-professional troops to defend the Republic and swarmed out to places where they were needed. Others were in Ambarawa to drive the English troops back to Semarang and others again went to West Java. At this time the Central and East Javanese youth thought the West Javanese young people were very inactive. So they sent them a mirror and face powder to challenge their fighting spirit. Maybe the West Javanese youth were slow at the outset but, in the course of the revolution, they too showed their mettle.

In Central Java parents were concerned about their over-active children. I remember a close friend of mine, Dinem Wongsodjojo, putting cotton wool into her son's ears to prevent him from hearing any news that could cause him to leave and endanger his life. Of course it did not work. Like so many others he left and risked his life to defend the Republic. Later the youth organisation was officially accepted by the Indonesian National Army (TNI) and was known as Tentara Pelajar, or Students' Army.

One of the first things the Allied forces occupied themselves with was freeing the prisoners in the Japanese internment camps. For that purpose a combination of Allied troops and the International Red Cross (RAPWI) were to evacuate the prisoners to certain harbours, from where they would be shipped to Holland. The Indonesian Republic did not want the Allied troops to come to the interior. So Mrs Maria Ulfah, then Minister of Social Affairs, offered the help of the Republic to bring the ex-prisoners safely to the harbours appointed. The offer was accepted and the Indonesian Army and troops of young people accomplished this task. Thus the Republic showed the outside world that it was capable of acquitting itself of its responsibilities.

The Chinese, who did not feel safe, left Yogyakarta and went, together with the ex-Japanese prisoners to Semarang. The Chinese shops on Malioboro were all closed and our young people occupied them. In their enthusiasm they declared that, from then on, Malioboro would be only for indigenous shopkeepers but later the Chinese returned and were allowed to occupy their shops again.

More and more people came to live in Yogya, amongst whom were Dr Suhardi and family. I had known them since Dr Suhardi became head of the hospital at Purwakarta. During the revolutionary years I came to know them even better and we became very close friends. Another person who arrived in Yogyakarta was Jo Abdurachman, then one of the leading figures in the Indonesian Red Cross (PMI).

The Military Academy was set up and Dicky, whose medical school had been closed when the Japanese surrendered, came to Yogya and enrolled at the Academy. Bibib and I were very happy to have him in Yogya but he did not feel very happy at the Academy. Bibib had, in the meantime, moved up to senior high school. In one of the vacations she, Boy Singgih, Dicky and Bi Oele went to Purwakata but, due to the first military attack of the Dutch, it was impossible for them to return to Yogyakarta.

The Dutch never expected the Republic to last long: they thought it would be easy to restore the former Netherlands East Indies. So, on 21 July 1947, they launched their first military attack. Everywhere they met with resistance. You know the song "Hallo, Hallo Bandung". It says "Sekarang menjadi lautan api". This sentence refers to the time when the Dutch occupied the northern part of Bandung. To prevent them from occupying the whole town the Indonesian military troops and the young people practised the scorched earth policy before they left and the whole southern part of Bandung became "a sea of fire". When the Dutch occupied Surabaya there were skirmishes in the town every night. Yet the Dutch succeeded in occupying practically the whole of West Java, certain places in Central Java and most of the coastal towns in East Java.

In Yogya the boys disappeared from the classrooms again. One sad day many parents and teachers were at the station of Yogya to receive a wagon-load full of dead bodies of our Tentara Pelajar. They were mostly *very* young boys from junior high schools; they had been killed near Purwokerto. Parents wept but the young people were more determined than ever to go on fighting.

After this Dutch aggression, more refugees came to Yogyakarta. My cousins, Tuti and her husband Samsuddin, who was with the Indonesian Police Force, came to stay with us in Gondokusuman with their children. Kang Pelen also joined us. Titi Sukonto, who is now sorting out and typing these reminiscences, happened to be on holiday in Malang, could not return to Jakarta, arrived in Yogya and stayed there. Tambu, a Sri Lankan from Singapore, who published an English newspaper, *The Indonesian Times*, was banned from Jakarta by the Dutch because his newspaper, which reported the true situation in the Republic, damaged the prestige of the Dutch in the eyes of the world.

Tambu was a tall, ugly man in his forties but, when he talked, we were so spellbound that we did not see his ugliness. He had a perfect command of the English language and his ideas were refreshing to us. He was engaged to Titi's younger sister, Cing Sukonto, who arrived in Yogya sometime after him. In Jakarta she had been his assistant for the newspaper. Cing and I became very good friends.

The Dutch did not want the issue between the Republic of Indonesia and the Netherlands to become international but it was discussed in the Security Council of the United Nations. The Security Council, concerned to avoid further bloodshed, ordered a truce between the parties and suggested that the problem should be solved by arbitration. The Dutch did not heed the resolution of the Security Council and went on with their attacks. They tried to isolate Indonesia from the outside world, politically and economically. They put a blockade around the country so that it became practically impossible to contact the outside world but, through smuggling, we managed to have some contact with India, for example. From the very beginning India had supported our cause and another staunch supporter was the Australian Labor Government. But it looked bad for the Republic.

Yet, looking back to that time, nobody felt poor in spite of the many deprivations. We were all in the same boat and shared whatever we had with each other. We did not have real tyres and cycled on what we called "*ban mati*", solid rubber bands, so that we felt every bump on the road. We had very little petrol or kerosene and in the evenings we cycled with "*upets*" in our hands, long wicks made of pleated coconut fibre, which we had to make sway all the time to keep the end glowing. Even cars had to use them, so you can imagine how slow the traffic was in the evening.

One day an Indian plane, with a representative of the International Red Cross on board, flew from Singapore to Yogyakarta to bring medicine for the Republic. We saw Dutch hunters chasing the plane and it was shot down above Maguwo, Yogya's airport. On that plane were also some important figures of our Indonesian Air Force. They all died on this sad occasion.

At that time a certain Mr Ratcliff was with us; he may have been from British Intelligence. He always wailed about the liquidation of the British Empire. When the incident with the plane happened, he wrote a plea to the outside world for us. I had the task of reading it over the Voice of Free Indonesia. After that, medicine was sent to us from everywhere. I was quoted in the foreign press as "the head of the Indonesian Red Cross", which I certainly was not. I was only a means to get the appeal across.

State dinners went on. As I had only two *kebaya*, Utami thought it very brave of me to appear in the same clothes every time. But in a very unfeminine fashion, I did not mind it at all. I kept attending these dinners in the hope that I would help dispel the image of Indonesians being ignorant half savages.

I don't know for what reasons and I forget exactly when but about this time I was allowed to go to Jakarta by plane. Kang Pelen, who at that time was a black marketeer, gave me a hundred guilders to buy things for him. As I had no idea of what he had in mind, I misunderstood him and thought it was meant as a present for me. Cing got the same opportunity and we left by the same plane. I remember that I was violently air-sick during the trip, maybe because I was not used to flying or maybe because the plane was very old and uncomfortable.

I was impressed by everything I saw in Jakarta – the white towels and the clean clothes of the people. In Yogya we had no good detergents; we could not get our towels white and our clothes were never pure white. At the best they were creamy or greyish. I had not seen good bath soap for a long time; I sometimes got samples of the soap our students in chemistry tried to concoct, and I was always very grateful for the nice smelling soap, although they never could make it hard. I enjoyed the films; in Yogya we had one cinema and for months it has shown the same film, *Gone with the Wind*. Yet when it became evident that it was difficult to return to Yogyakarta, I felt very unhappy. Every plane to Yogya was full; there were always more important people who had to return to Yogya. Cing was luckier and managed to get back to Yogya one day.

Fortunately I could stay with Kang Sadeli and Ceuk Ida. Kang Sadeli had joined the Dutch Police Force and was very well-off. So we were in opposite camps but it did not alter our relationship of sister and brother. I did not go home to Purwakarta because I was afraid that from there I could not go back to Yogyakarta at all; Purwakarta had become a Dutch occupied area. I heard that Father, who was then practically the head of the Purwakarta family and a very influential person, was sought out by the Dutch. He got his pension paid, starting from 1942; so he was very well-off. I could not help being glad for him; he had suffered enough in his old age.

Dicky and Bibib were convinced supporters of the Republic. Dicky, with a friend, hoisted the "Red and White" in Purwakata one day. They were thrown into prison but Father went to the Assistant Resident and said "No child of mine shall be in prison." The Dutch could not refuse him and so the two boys were set free. I doubt whether Dicky liked the course of events.

After a long wait, Jo Abdurachman came with the news that we could get a lift from an International Red Cross officer, who was to leave for Yogya. There were four of us in the jeep: the driver, the Red Cross officer and the two of us. It gave me an eerie feeling to drive through deserted areas; not a single person was to be seen in "no man's land". Every second a sniper might fire at us but we arrived in Yogya unscathed.

The Security Council of the United Nations had in the meantime passed a resolution that a Three Nations Committee would offer its good services to arbitrate between the Republic and the Dutch. The Committee consisted of a delegate from Australia, one from Belgium and one from America. They held the discussions in Kaliurang, the famous mountain resort near Yogyakarta.

In this connection many more people came to Yogyakarta. Among these was Adik Budiardjo, later Mrs Simatupang, who came from Jakarta to join the secretariat for the discussions in Kaliurang. The womenfolk of Yogya could not take their eyes off her modern "new look" dresses, which came right down to her ankles. In Yogyakarta, where there were no fashions, we still wore our dresses very short, barely covering the knees.

At last it was decided that the parties would confer on the deck of the American ship, USS *Renville*. I was flabbergasted, but elated, when I heard that I was chosen to be one of the secretaries for the Renville negotiations. I could be of some help with translation work but I had never done any secretarial work. I could barely type and Pak Isaq, head of the secretaries, would look, with a bewildered expression on his face, at my feats on the typewriter. I asked Cing, who was also one of the happy few to go to the Renville as a secretary, to train me but time was too short for that.

So we all left for Jakarta by plane. The secretariat was housed in a pavilion of the well-known Hotel des Indes, where Cing and I got a comfortable room together. The waiters and servants at the hotel were very nice to the people from Yogya, though they were not as chicly dressed as the other guests at the hotel. We always got first class service from them and, when there was a pork dish during the meals, they always warned us. I remember the time when one of the heels of my shoes flew off and I could not afford to buy another pair. Our room servant, Dudung, took the trouble to take my damaged shoes to the shoe-repair outside the hotel.

Sometimes we did translation work at the pavilion and went in shifts to the *Renville*. The trip there and back by motorboat was very enjoyable, especially at night time.

Of course we saw a lot of the Indonesian delegates but not much of the other delegates. We mostly saw them at meal times on board ship or at the hotel. We knew that if one said "Good morning" or "Good afternoon", we had to react with "Good morning" or "Good afternoon", too but what to say when they ask "How are you?" At first we only laughed sheepishly, until Cing and I decided to be the first to ask "How are you?" In that way we learned how to react to the phrase "How are you?"

The meals on board the ship were excellent, we always enjoyed them. We were served by American Negroes and, because I had heard about the racial discrimination in the USA, I was friendly with them. We were so used to being friendly with the opposite sex, especially during the days of the revolution, when we worked side by side in almost everything. So I was surprised to notice that my friendliness was taken as a sort of "come hither" signal. They became fresh, and I did not know what to do. Fortunately one of the officers on board seemed to notice the situation and I had no further problems with them.

One afternoon I was the only secretary on board. Pak Amir Sjarifuddin wanted to despatch a letter, so I was called. It was a short, simple letter but I was so tense that Pak Amir noticed it. He was a very kind person and told me to relax. When I had typed the letter and saw that I had made some typing errors, he said kindly "It does not matter. I shall ask someone else to retype it". I could have died with shame that I failed to carry out a simple task like that.

We secretaries did not see or hear much of the negotiations. Only at the final stages do I remember us looking down to where the delegates sat at the conference table. We noticed that the Indonesian delegate on the Dutch side was a mere puppet and were very proud of the Republican delegates. We listened with aversion to the Dutch representative.

After the Renville Agreement had been signed we went back to Yogya. I so much wanted to give Dudung a substantial tip but all I could give him was a bottle of perfumed coconut oil for his wife's hair. The planes which flew between Jakarta and Yogya were very old and rickety and each passenger always had to sign a statement that he was fully responsible for anything that might happen to him during the trip and could not claim anything.

The Renville Agreement was not favourably accepted by all political parties. Many people were disappointed at the result of the negotiations. It was too much to the advantage of the Dutch. The Siliwangi, the West Java division of our national army had to vacate West Java and withdraw to Republican occupied territory. The Dutch, who, according to the agreement, had to withdraw to where they had been before their aggression, did nothing of the kind. They remained in the territories they had occupied.

One day Samsudarso, Tine's husband, left on a tour of duty. He was to come back after a few days – but he did not come. Tine waited and waited, day after day, and we all waited with her. Then we heard about the PKI rebellion in Madiun. The communists had seized the whole residency of Madiun. People whom they considered their enemies were killed. Samsudarso was one of those who lost their lives then but the national army succeeded in reconquering the residency. Many of the rebels were killed too. It was a sad affair, especially as we were still facing the Dutch threat.

After the Renville Agreement the Dutch had started creating puppet states like Pasunden in West Java, with Wiranatakusumah as president, the state of East Indonesia with Sukowati as president, West Kalimantan with "their" Sultan Hamid Algadri as president and so on. I say "their" Hamid Algadri because we had ours. The two namesakes were of opposing characters and often met in opposing camps. The Dutch set up the puppet states because one of their concessions was that they would confer independence upon a Federal State of Indonesia, which would form a kind of union with the Netherlands. They also wanted to weaken the position of our Republic, which they tried to exclude from a Federal State of Indonesia. But everything went differently from what they had planned.

Their second military action made them very unpopular. Several important officials of the puppet states laid down their jobs in protest. I remember

Wiranatakusumah moving to Yogyakarta. He lived in a house in the same street as ours. Once he honoured me with a visit and I was very grateful, remembering the many weekends I had spent in his *kabupaten* in Bandung when I was a child. It was not long after this that the Siliwangi Division decided to return to West Java. They undertook what we still refer to as the "long march", during which songs like "Hallo, Hallo Bandung" came into being.

It was about this time that we learned to know George Kahin. At that time he was a young academic, doing research on nationalism and the Indonesian Revolution. He needed people to translate the material he collected and so we learned to know him well.

Another person who arrived in Yogyakarta about this time was our Hamid Algadri, who had been banned from Jakarta by the Dutch for political reasons. I knew him from his student days, when he and Jus had been studying at the Law School in former Batavia. It was good to see him back again after all those years. He had married in the meantime and his wife, Zena, was soon to follow him to Yogyakarta. He was still the same old Hamid, a good friend, interesting to talk with, very down to earth. I remember him one evening taking me somewhere on the back of my bicycle while I was swinging an *upet*. Because it was easy to lose my balance, he said "Grasp me around the waist." But that was not done during those times and, although both sexes were real friends and learned to appreciate each other in their work together as equals, we did not touch easily. So I remained precariously balanced on the back seat. You will be surprised to read this because nowadays you see people of my generation, men and women, kissing each other every time they meet or part. So you see how times change.

One evening there was a gathering at our house in Gondokusuman, I forget on what occasion. There were Simatupang, Broer and Bob Gond, brothers of Zus Nasution, the Siliwangi Commander's wife, all close friends of the Samsudarsonos. They all tried to cheer Tine up. We had games and laughed a lot. It must have been late by Yogya standards when the party broke up, for I was still sleeping at half past six when I was woken up by violent explosions. The Dutch had launched their second military attack on 19 December 1948 and were bombarding Maguwo airfield. I dressed quickly and went in search of Jo Abdurachman. I asked her to lend me a Red Cross band, so that I could see how my friends were. Jo at first refused. She said that she could not do that – but at last she gave in and I could do my rounds.

I heard a lot of stories then: how one of my colleagues had run out of the bathroom without any clothes on when she heard the bombing; how a doctor and his wife had taken shelter under the bed and the wife, when she felt something warm against her leg, told her husband to be careful with his cigarette. On closer inspection it turned out that it was not a cigarette that lay nestled close to her leg but a cartridge, still warm from its flight. But they were all safe. I went to Tami, to Cing, to the Yunuses. In the afternoon we saw Dutch soldiers walking about. The Dutch had occupied Yogya.

When I came to the Yunus's house the next morning, I found them all set to leave for Jakarta. They told me that George Kahin, who lived across the street from them, had been transported to Jakarta and that Hamid, who stayed in the same house with George, had been taken to Wirogunan prison, the place for political prisoners. Many of our friends were kept there. Samsudin eventually landed there too. The place became the centre of people's attention. The wives visited their husbands twice a week and many of us collected reading materials and food for the prisoners. Zena, who had arrived two days before, with her ten-month-old baby, was now left alone. I was glad to be able to offer her accommodation and so she stayed with us until she and Hamid were transported to Jakarta too.

Bung Karno and Bung Hatta decided to stay in Yogya. Bung Hatta happened to be in Kaliurang, where the Three Nations Committee held their discussions. Sultan Hamengkubuwono, who was at the president's residence with some Ministers of State, volunteered to go to fetch him, in spite of the incessant firing of the Dutch. After a long wait he returned with Bung Hatta and a cabinet meeting was held. An emergency government was established, with Sjarifuddin Prawiranegara as president. Sjarifuddin happened to be in Sumatra at that time; the government succeeded in contacting him by radio and he formed an emergency government in Sumatra.

When the Dutch troops arrived in the town they went immediately to the president's palace. Bung Karno, Bung Hatta and the ministers present were detained in the palace. The next day some of them were flown to Sumatra; the following day some more followed. Bung Karno, Haji Agus Salim and Sutan Syahrir were detained at Prapat on Lake Toba; Bung Hatta, Air Commodore Suryadarma, Ali Sastroamijoyo, Moh. Roem and A. K. Pringgodigdo were taken to Bangka. You should read your grandfather's account of their stay there in his book, *Milestones on my Journey*; I am sure you will be proud of our government in exile.[8]

---

8   [Ali Sastroamijoyo, *Milestones on my Journey: the Memoirs of Ali Sastroamijoyo, Indonesian Patriot and Political Leader*. St Lucia, Qld: University of Queensland Press, 1979.]

In Yogya the Republican money was changed; we had to use NICA money then. It was very difficult for us to make ends meet because many of us became unemployed. It became the fashion to open small restaurants or *warong*s, where we sold the snacks and food each excelled in and, because we wanted to help each other, we bought from each other. In these confused times looting took place nearly everywhere in the city. We agreed to warn each other when we were in danger by beating on a piece of rail or whatever else we had that made a noise.

We in Gondokusuman felt rather safe because we were about twenty in number but Tami, whose husband was in Bangka, was alone with her two small children. I sometimes stayed the night at her house to keep her company and fortunately nothing happened because I don't think I would have been of much help if looters came. It was only the feeling that you shared the danger with someone that gave one a little relief in such situations.

Schools were closed at that time; the Dutch tried to run a school but very few Indonesians wanted to make use of Dutch facilities. Most of the boys – and this time more of the girls than before – had gone to the front. For those who stayed, Mr Prijono and the senior high school teachers organised a regular timetable for every year of senior high school. The lessons were given at the homes of the teachers, and students had to go from one house to another and sometimes had to cover quite a distance, but they came regularly.

Once one of my former students, who had chosen to attend the Dutch school, came to my house to threaten us that he would tell the Dutch about our clandestine school. I think he did it just to justify himself. When I pointed out that if he did so, he stood in as much danger from his friends as they did from the Dutch and that it was better to leave everybody free to choose for himself, he left and I never saw him again.

When I had no lessons I did some administrative jobs at the PMI, the Indonesian Red Cross. In those days I had to compile lists of the casualties that were reported daily. One day George Kahin, who was allowed to return to Yogya, came to see me at the PMI office, escorted by NICA soldiers. I gave him some casualty lists. Some friends, who thought this a good opportunity to tell the outside world about what was happening inside the Republic, had put some more information among the lists, unnoticed by the soldiers. I saw George several times but always escorted by NICA soldiers, so that it was impossible to talk freely. He was very nice and gave me money to help people who really needed it.[9]

---

9   [George Kahin, *Nationalism and Revolution in Indonesia* (Ithaca, NY: Cornell University Press, 1952), pp. 338, 397.]

Our troops and the Pemuda had gone out of town to fight at the fronts and to harass the Dutch in Yogya by guerilla warfare. Nearly every night they invaded Yogya. On such occasions Kang Pelen used to open all the doors and windows, I don't know for what reasons. It irritated Zena terribly, as she was afraid that stray cartridges might hurt her baby daughter, so she and Kang Pelen always quarrelled about this.

These were hard times for the Republic: not only the troops fighting outside Yogya but the people in town too, tried to uphold the Republic, everyone to the utmost of his or her ability. Some people organised soup kitchens for the very needy; others collected news about the Republic from overseas broadcasting stations and distributed it. Others again maintained contact with the guerilla troops by messengers serving as couriers – not only young men but also young women disguised as village women, went on foot to the guerilla camps. My house was one of the places where parcels were sent to be forwarded to the guerilla troops.

I remember once that I had just received a lot of parcels for the guerilla troops when some NICA soldiers came to search my house. As if by a miracle they overlooked the cupboards where I had put the parcels. A second time I was sorting out the things to be sent to our troops when a loud knocking was heard at the front door. When I opened it I saw an Ambonese NICA soldier standing on the doorstep. Fortunately he sat down in the front room and did not see all the things spread out on the floor of my bedroom. He stayed for hours; fortunately only to vent his great love for Jo Abdurachman, who had been imprisoned by the Dutch.

It was about this time that we heard about my old friend Soemarsono. He had been caught by the Dutch and taken to Kaliurang. In order to have a reason for killing him, they staged a mock escape. They told him to run away and shot him in the back. Another version has it that Soemarsono was captured by the Dutch and, with some other prisoners, cold-bloodedly shot down for no reason at all. Poor old Soen had just married a few weeks before. You can imagine what this must have meant to his young wife.

In this chapter I have mentioned mostly the names of people you know. There are still many others who have their own stories to tell. You must remember that the Revolution has been won not only by the leaders but by the Indonesian people as a whole.

Once more I have to refer to your grandfather's book, *Milestones on my Journey*, to tell you how world opinion turned in favour of the Republic and against the Dutch. At last pressure was put upon the Dutch to return Bung Karno, Bung Hatta and the others who were detained in Sumatra, to

Yogyakarta. The streets were crowded with people to welcome the homecoming leaders. The Dutch were forced to agree to a ceasefire and, after several discussions, plans were made for the Round Table Conference in The Hague.

Then schools were re-opened and life became more normal. At that time Pak Ali Sastroamijoyo was Minister of Education. In that capacity he met me several times and one day I was offered a scholarship for one year of study in Australia.

8. Australian Experience

Not even in my wildest imagination had I ever dreamed of going to study abroad. During the Dutch regime there were no scholarships for Indonesians to do so. The few people I knew who had studied abroad had to pay for it themselves and this was totally beyond my reach. And here I had a scholarship thrown into my lap, without having to compete for it, without any special merits on my side. To me it seemed like a miracle![10]

The scholarship entitled me to one year's study in Australia in Sydney. I was allowed to decide for myself what I would study and the Australian Office of Education would provide the facilities. I chose to study the Australian educational system in practice – to see what we could learn from other systems from other countries – and to take a few courses in psychology, simply because I liked the subject.

By this time several of my friends had already left Yogya. Cing had married Tambu and had gone with him when he was posted to Manilla. Tine and Hapid had left for Jakarta, while Zena and Hamid had been returned to Jakarta by the Dutch. I left for Jakarta to prepare my departure.

I went to Purwakarta to see my parents. Ibu Gedong had died in 1947; she had had a bad fall and had been an invalid for some time. I told my parents about my good luck and they were happy for me. I saw Dicky once before I left for Australia. He told me that he had met the girl of his life. I was sorry not to be able to meet her then; we only met after they had married in Gadog, where her parents had evacuated after the second Dutch aggression. Father, as I told you in the previous chapter, had come into money and, first of all, he put a sum aside to let Dick finish his medical studies in Holland.

Bibib had been sent to Jakarta to continue her study at the SMA, or Senior High School. She stayed with an elder brother of Kang Sadeli, Kang

---

10   [Jo did acknowledge, when asked, that her experience in translating, broadcasting and teaching English may have had some relevance and influence.]

Djajusman, who worked for the Dutch and was Patih of the area that was called Meester Cornelis then, the present area of Jatinegara. I am pointing this out to show that, in our family, there were those who worked for the Dutch and others who were very anti-Dutch but family relations were maintained and, although we did not hold the same political views, we felt no hostility against each other; we left each other free to decide. I met Tom Praaning, Jus's eldest brother. Of course he was on the Dutch side and was mayor of Jatinegara. Yetty was to stay in Bandung with Ibu's younger brother after she had finished SMP, or Junior High School.

I had to choose my wardrobe carefully so that a few *kebaya*, *kain* and *selendang* would give quite a different impression in every combination. Fortunately Ibu Sri, Cing's and Titi's aunt, whom I was later to see more as Pak Ali's elder sister, helped me with my clothes. She was known for her good taste.

So I left for Australia on 17 November 1949. Father and Ibu came to Jakarta to see me off and, with them, a lot of relatives and friends came to Kemayoran airport to wave me goodbye. That was my first journey abroad and I felt rather tense. When I heard the words "on board" called, I took all my bags in one hand and, enthusiastically waving to the group of friends with the other hand, strode to the plane only to be called back by loud shouts; apparently the summons had been only for the crew.

We had a stop-over in Darwin. It looked just like any place in Indonesia and the climate was no different either. I had no company and did not know what to do. So I took a shower hastily because I was afraid of being left behind and, refreshed, boarded the plane again.

In Sydney I had to leave a box of *kemiri* nuts that I had brought with me for my hair with Customs. Not knowing that it was forbidden to bring in any plants, I was surprised that they made such a fuss about it. A reporter asked me all kinds of questions, maybe because of my different clothing. I felt very important to be interviewed and gave all kinds of wrong information. I told the reporter that English was the second language in Indonesia, whereas the term was "first foreign language", which I learned years later.

Someone from the Office of Education was there to meet me and I was taken to a hotel – if I am not mistaken, at King's Cross. After that we went to the Office of Education, where I was introduced to Mr Morrison and Mr Phillips, who were to look after me, and the two secretaries, Ruby Dyer and Bette Gray, who were to become close friends of mine. I had my first "morning tea" to be followed a few hours later with "afternoon tea" and I learned that people had an hour off for lunch. At that time of the year it was very hot in Sydney and yet the men were dressed in dark clothes and a tie. The office was rather cool compared with the heat outside because I remember that, coming out of the office, it was as if the heat slapped you in the face.

I was taken back to my hotel and, worn out by the plane trip and the new impressions, I soon tumbled into a deep sleep, to be woken by a loud knocking on the door. I jumped up and opened the door. Mr Morrison was standing in front of me with a telegram in his hand. I must have looked a sight to him, in my crumpled dressing gown, my hair hanging down my back, eyes swollen with sleep.

This telegram was from the Indonesian *Chargé d'affaires* for Australia, Pak Usman Sastroamijoyo. I had known him in Bandung during my school days there, when we were both tennis fans. It was thoughtful of him to send me a token of welcome. So far my impressions had been very pleasant; the only disappointing thing was that there were no windows in my room to let the sunshine through. I always had to switch on the electric light. I had seen so many advertisements like "Come to Sunny Australia" that I was very surprised to be walled in like that.

I don't know how I got myself a meal that evening but, in those days, I was resourceful enough to look after myself.

The next day was a Saturday and I remembered a British couple whom I met on the plane and who had given me their hotel address in Sydney. So I went off in search of them. I found them, barely awake, among their opened and unopened trunks and they seemed very surprised to see me. They were very nice though and took me to a beautiful park near the coast or, maybe, it was a lake. As the couple seemed to prefer to be by themselves, we did not stay there long. They told me that on Sunday afternoons there was usually a concert in that park. I decided to go there by myself the next day.

In the afternoon I ventured on a double-decker bus. It made me rather sick to be swayed left and right on the top of the bus but the view was interesting. I was so used to the leisurely pace of Yogyakarta that I got the impression that the people in Sydney were all running. "Where are you running to and why?" I thought. There was a nice young girl near me and she took me to a place where ferries carried people to the other side of the bay and told me that people played music on the ferry. Coming back to the hotel I felt nicely tired and had a fitful sleep.

In the morning I was woken by a loud knocking. This time I took care to look more presentable when I opened the door. There was a man who offered me a cup of hot tea with a biscuit and a newspaper. I thought it a very nice beginning to the day and gladly paid for everything.

In the afternoon I walked to the same park and there was a concert on. The people were sitting or lying on the grass enjoying the music. "This is wonderful," I thought happily. After some time a young man sat down next to me and started talking about himself; how rich he was; he had several planes, he boasted. He went on talking and talking and spoiled everything for me. When the concert was over, people strolled away. I did not know how to shake the young man off. Near the exit I met a young officer from the Office of Education. He looked at me with surprise, seeing that I had an escort. I wanted to ask him to help me but did not know how. Fortunately the young man left me in front of the hotel.

I did not stay long at the hotel. They found me a room in a house that was beautifully situated on a hill. The borders in the garden were full of beautiful hydrangeas. It all looked more like the posters about "Sunny Australia".

The landlady, Mrs Hill, was a pleasant, elderly woman. She told me after a few weeks that she had her alcoholic daughter and her grandson staying with her. The grandson looked unhealthily plump; I really pitied the boy because, in spite of his eight years, there was nothing childlike in him anymore. The daughter I saw very rarely; she seemed to be seldom sober. She had all kinds of treatments to cure her but so far, nothing had worked. I had never thought much about the problem of alcoholism but soon I realised that it was a problem in Australia. Sometimes I saw drunken men just lying on the streets, often on a Friday evening. People said it was because the pubs closed early on Friday evenings and so people tried to drink as much as possible before closing time. That argument did not make much sense to me.

At Mrs Hill's place there was a nice elderly man. He once came home with a small, withered mango for me. I was so touched by this thoughtful gesture that I did not want to think of the nice fresh mangoes at home. This man once took me for a bus ride. At one of the bus stops a young man got on to the bus. He was certainly not sober; how drunk he was I could not tell but he insisted that he wanted to kiss all the women on the bus. I was horrified and sought protection from the elderly man but he looked calmly at me and asked why I made all that fuss. The other women did not mind being kissed, he said. I was even more horrified but, fortunately, the young man got tired before it was my turn.

In the meantime the Office of Education had arranged with Sydney University that I was to take some psychology courses. I was introduced to Professor O'Neill, head of the Psychology Department, a very nice man, who gave me a list of the books I would need. The next day Mr Phillips and

I went to a bookshop to buy them. As I came home I eagerly opened the books and started to read. To my horror nothing really registered. I understood the words but nothing made sense. I understood that it was because of the tense time in Yogya, with all its emotions and stresses, that I could not think properly. I tried not to panic and kept reading a little every day. And one day it was as if something clicked in my brain and I could digest everything normally.

One morning I woke up when the sun was already shining brightly. I thought I was late and jumped out of bed but, when I looked at my watch, it was only four o'clock. That was my first discovery of summer time. Then I made another discovery. Small, black insects were hopping around in my bed. I had never seen such insects and, in the morning, I told Mrs Hill about them. She told me they were fleas and she would get rid of them. However, they had infested my clothes and were hopping in and out of my pockets and socks.

At the office when I told them about the fleas, they decided to move me to another house. On the one hand I was sorry to leave. I liked Mrs Hill and the elderly gentleman but, on the other hand, the fleas were a real plague. At that time I had the chance to visit a migrant hostel somewhere in the country, so they had time to look for other accommodation for me.

The wooden barracks where the migrants as well as the teachers were housed and where the classes were held, were simple but comfortable and clean. Maybe everything impressed me because in Java housing areas were always crowded. I did not have much contact with the migrants and saw them only when they were in class, being introduced to Australian life or taught English. I was more with the teachers, young people who seemed to enjoy their work and they struck me as being self-sufficient, capable and humane. They dressed much more informally than the officials at the Office of Education, much more suited to the hot climate. Christmas was celebrated with a hot Christmas dinner and a heavy plum pudding in the sweltering heat. One of the migrants gave a piano recital; everything had a friendly, cosy atmosphere.

In the meantime I had started my psychology courses. Sydney University was housed in an old building but it had atmosphere and I felt very much at home there. I had difficulty making notes but a young, friendly girl student, Heather, always generously lent me hers. The lectures were very interesting. When we got psychological tests I realised, for the first time, the difference in values between different societies. For instance, one of the questions was "What would you do if you stood in a line and someone came and shoved himself before you?" You were supposed to make a fuss about it, assert yourself; otherwise it would show a lack of self-confidence. Maybe in modern Indonesia the same is expected of you; in my time we learned to smile at such impoliteness, to shake our heads incredulously at such rudeness but let it go.

The Office of Education had found another address for me to stay at, in one of the many suburbs of Sydney. The landlady was an elderly woman with a hoard of lap dogs which followed her everywhere. When you came too near their idol, they bit you in the leg, as I was to experience one day. The landlady loved music and played the piano very well. Later she told me that she had often played at the Eisteddfod. My room was smaller but more comfortable than the one at Mrs Hill's. Her boarders only got breakfast from her but later she often gave us lunch on Sundays and other holidays.

At this address I had a new companion. Apparently Indonesia had been given two scholarships that year; one had been given to the Republic and the other to the Dutch. The Dutch candidate was an English teacher, Amisah Bakti. She was a very likeable person and, in spite of the fact that we were candidates from opposite camps, we had many acquaintances in common. She had quite a different program from mine and I forget who looked after her needs; it was not the Office of Education.

At Mrs Hill's place I had already met another student, a teacher from Burma, Tin E. He was not there under the same scholarship plan as we were because he was not invited to the activities staged for us. He was a convinced communist, a very soft-hearted man. If he was a prototype of the Burmese, the Burmese must be a simple, modest and very friendly nation. I have lost track of him but I hope he knows that I admired him for his gentleness, in comparison with which Indonesians looked rude and self-assertive.

One day our group assembled in a big house. We stayed there for several days, listening to talks, having discussions and learning about each other's countries. There was a pretty young student from Thailand; a dentist from Malaysia; two students from Pakistan; one from Brunei and a civil engineer from Indonesia, Sugoto, who was married to a younger sister of the Paku Alam. She was a wonderful *serimpi* dancer and once gave a solo performance in Sydney which was quite successful. I remember that Sugoto and I sang "Indonesia Raya" together and everybody thought that it sounded very belligerent. The two Pakistani students took us to the Pakistani Embassy, where we were introduced to Pakistani food.

At the Office of Education I learned to know Bernice Julius, one of the nicest persons I have ever met. One Saturday afternoon she invited me to her home for tea. She lived with her father in one of the suburbs. Her father tended roses and had won several prizes for "the most beautiful garden in the neighbourhood". His garden was indeed a pleasure to look at and I admired the competitive spirit in which the neighbours tended their gardens.

That afternoon we played lawn tennis; I had never played on a lawn before and had difficulty adapting my timing because, on a gravel court, the balls bounced up more quickly. We sipped tea in the shady garden and I really enjoyed everything but, when I prepared to go home, Bernice was astonished. "But I invited you to tea" she said and then I learned that it meant staying for a meal, not only drinking tea. I was only too glad to stay and ate heartily from Bernice's cooking. I did not care very much for the food they served in restaurants; all the restaurants smelled invariably of lamb. At that time there was no good coffee to be had in Sydney and I had resorted to drinking tea but the meal at Bernice's home and all the other home cooking I was invited to, was delicious.

Through Bernice I also saw the Australian countryside. One weekend Amisah and I were invited to Mr Julius's farm. One afternoon we walked through the bush and I gave a wild shriek when I saw how some leeches sucked themselves round on my legs. Mr Julius showed us how to get rid of them with tobacco. He also made us climb on horseback. I had never done this before and had the feeling that I would slide off the horse's neck again when the animal started to nibble at the grass. In the meantime Bernice made all kinds of nice things for us. For the first time we had hot scones, which since has remained my favourite English snack.

It happened to be full moon at that time and Bernice moved our couches on to the verandah. We fell asleep bathed in the clean, white light of the moon. It was a weekend I shall never forget.

Another time Bernice and her father took us to an agricultural festival, where they showed giant pumpkins, very big strawberries and many more wonderful countryside products. I became so used to seeing giant this and that, that I was not surprised when they showed me a lamb a big as a calf but then they had a good laugh at me because what they showed me was a calf and not a lamb.

Another time Bernice took me on a trip along the coast. I had heard Australia's beaches much advertised but, in Sydney, they were always overcrowded and one could not see anything of their natural beauty. Outside Sydney they were really marvellous. Bernice took me to her friends' house high on the top of a cliff. All day and all night you could hear the sound of the waves; it gave you a wonderful feeling of peace.

Bernice's friends were perfect hosts and I was impressed by the courteous way they treated their four-year-old son, who ate with us at table. Unlike other adults, who tend to treat little children condescendingly, though lovingly, this couple treated the little boy with courtesy and he responded to it by putting on his best behaviour.

The next day we continued our trip along the coast and we saw a dead whale that had been washed ashore. In fact we smelled it long before we saw it. Bernice took a photo of me standing on the top of the whale. It felt as if I was standing on a heap of rubber.

Thanks to Bernice I have a host of beautiful memories of Australia. Unfortunately I lost track of her. Six years later, when I was on my way to the States, where I was to study for two years, I stayed with Bernice somewhere outside Sydney. I don't remember if she lived there or was just staying for some time. Her father had died in the meantime. That was the last time I saw her. Meanwhile she must have married but I don't know the name of the lucky fellow who got her for his wife. I asked the Commonwealth Office of Education if they knew where she was, without result; I asked Bette Gray but she could not give me any information about Bernice either. I sometimes think how nice it would be if I could meet her at this age and we could tell each other our experiences.

You may get the impression that I was doing more sightseeing than study. This is partly true but I visited a lot of schools, in Sydney as well as in the country. Nowadays I hear from Indonesian parents who have their children in Australian schools that all kinds of new teaching methods are being applied and how they use the psychological approach to the students in Australian schools. In those days I did not see much difference from the Dutch schools in Indonesia and, at that time, psychology was still questioned as a science.

What struck me was that there were more single-sex boys' and girls' schools than in Indonesia, where this segregation was found among Roman Catholic schools. The segregation between the sexes seemed to continue in adult life. I found that men had their own recreations, where no women joined them, such as the race track. I wondered whether the two sexes were really so different that they had to live as if in two worlds.

I was very much interested in the implementation of compulsory education; I had never thought that it involved so many officials, like social workers. Unlike in Java, where students stopped their schooling at a certain level, for instance after finishing primary school or junior high school, here a student had to continue schooling up to the age of sixteen. I thought this school leaving age very sensible.

I must not forget to mention my visit to the Girl Guides. Before I left for Australia, the Indonesian Scout movement gave me a written message for the Australian Boy Scouts. One morning Mr Morrison and I went to the Boy Scouts' headquarters. One of the leaders came to meet me. Mr Morrison introduced me to him and I handed him the message from the Indonesian Boy Scouts. The man got red in the face; he hummed and hawed, stuttered and stammered. I thought his behaviour most peculiar. On the way back to the office I asked Mr Morrison why the man had behaved so strangely. Mr Morrison laughed and said that the man had not expected to see such a sophisticated woman from Indonesia. I was far from sophisticated – and felt even less so – but, compared to the poor man's image of the Indonesian savage, I must have looked sophisticated.

Sometime later I received an invitation to join a group of Girl Guides in their camp in the Blue Mountains. I had seen the Blue Mountains in the distance and had wondered what they looked like. The area where the Girl Guides had put up their camp was marvellous. It was very cold up there and it really stimulated the appetite. Especially because we were active all day, everybody wolfed down the tasty food. At the immigrant hostel I had learned to smoke and, because it was so cold here, I thought this a good opportunity to put it into practice but, when I did so, the girls shouted that smoking was forbidden.

The girls were friendly and one of them invited me to her house when the camping was over. She told me that they were poor because her father was a simple labourer. Their house was simple and small but quite comfortable. They had a refrigerator and the children had each their own bicycle. According to Indonesian standards they were very well-off. In the afternoon we went for a ride through the village. It all looked very friendly and I had a very pleasant stay with them.

Quite a different gathering was the United Nations anniversary to which I was invited. A lot of young people attended the celebration but there were no Asians except me. There were several talks about the political situation. Indonesia was discussed too. The speaker eyed me accusingly and asked why Indonesia had to resort to arms and could not settle things through arbitration. Most of the attendants looked at me accusingly too, at least it seemed so to me at that time and I failed to convince them that we were forced to take up arms. Not one of the younger people came up to talk to me; I was rather left alone. This was really unlike the spirit of a United Nations as I imagined it. Only some said, while passing me, that I should not take everything so much to heart.

At a gathering of women, where they also discussed the political world situation, I met Dr Lotte Fink. She was a physician, an active, warm-hearted woman. She introduced me to her husband, a psychiatrist, and to her daughter, Ruth, whom I was to meet often as she was studying psychology too at Sydney University at that time. I visited their home several times and thought their company very stimulating. Mr Fink always tried to shock me with his statements but, because I saw through him, he never succeeded. Ruth was much younger than me. I think she was eighteen, whereas I was twenty-six, but somehow we became friends.[11] She was much more mature than Indonesian girls at that age, a self-reliant, decisive person she seemed to me. She had a small car in which she drove to the university. One day, when there was a strike on and all buses and trams lay still, I suddenly saw Ruth, in a blue dress that suited her very well, behind the wheel of her small car. She had come all the way to the suburb where I lived to take me to the university.

There was a time when I started coughing badly. No matter what medicine I tried, the cough kept on. One morning I could not get out of bed; I had a temperature. I happened to have an appointment with Dr Lotte Fink. She came up to my bedroom and stated that I had the measles. I had had the measles as a child and now realised, with surprise, that it was possible to get a child's disease for a second time in one's life.

The landlady was very anxious to get rid of me. The Office of Education found me a small private nursing home. What I liked about the place was that they did not force me to eat; they coaxed me to try the food by giving small portions, tastefully served up – a small cup of soup or a very small pudding. After some time I ate everything they served me and it did not take long before I was cured. I was not sure if the landlady wanted to take me back but Mrs Morrison, and her husband too, assured me that I was welcome to stay in their guest room and of course there was Bernice, who offered to take me in but fortunately the landlady was willing to give me accommodation again; after I had been cured there was no danger of contagion.

I mustn't forget to tell you also about the wonderful weekend we spent at Bette Gray's house at Lithgow. It was such a lovely, sunny house and the garden was beautiful. The family was very hospitable and, on Sunday, they took Amisah and me to the Jenolan Caves. It was very interesting how they

---

11   [Born in 1919, Jo would in fact have been 30 or 31 years old at the time she met Ruth Fink.]

lighted the stalagmites and stalactites in such a way that you could see all kinds of figures in them; the figure of a woman, a castle, a horse and so on. The caves were a civilised version of the Indonesian stalagmite and stalactite caves, which were full of bats.

So you see I had all kinds of experiences in that one year but mostly good ones. On the whole people were friendly and hospitable. It is true, people were not always nice, but that happens everywhere. For instance, one day I bought a return ticket to Canberra and they wanted my name for it. I said "Kurnianingrat!" but they asked "Don't you have another name? Mary? Or Elsa? Or Topsy?" I was annoyed with the man but I couldn't help laughing at his impudence.

I had another experience of that kind when I was sitting in the National Library. I used to balance my shoes on top of my toes, when I suddenly heard a voice behind me saying "Put your shoes on immediately! I have never seen anything like that!" Whether he was shocked at the sight of my ugly feet or had never seen bare feet at all I don't know – but the man was really shocked. So I docilely obeyed him.

For some time I went to the Teachers' College every day. I could make use of the study of one of the lecturers who was on leave. There I sat studying and reading. The Teachers' College possessed a very well-equipped library and I found a lot of interesting material there. One of the lecturers helped me to improve my English. He also helped me write a talk on Indonesia that I had to deliver to the students. I had never had to speak in public before. I was so nervous that I felt nauseated but, once started, everything went all right.

One of the teachers invited me to have dinner at his home. Unfortunately I had no idea of the distances. I arrived two hours late at his house. The family, who was still waiting for me, was very nice about it and, as usual, the homemade cooking was delicious. The teacher's wife and children were very interested in Indonesia.

The scholarship also generously gave me the opportunity to travel. I went to Canberra, where I visited the Indonesian *Chargé d'affaires*. Pak Usman Sastroamijoyo presented me with a tennis racquet for old times' sake. He asked one of the officials to show me the city. I saw some parks and many government buildings. There was an atmosphere of formality in Canberra which was totally lacking in Sydney.

In the hotel where I stayed, I met a psychologist who had to apply tests at various schools and institutions. Of course I was very interested in his work and, when he offered to show me some of the tests in his room, I accepted readily. As soon as I had done so I started wondering whether it was all right to go up to a man's bedroom but he looked very dependable and the tests sounded attractive. So I went. Fortunately nothing dramatic happened and we had a lively discussion, he sitting on his bed and me sitting on a chair opposite. So you see, Rini, that your grandmother did not always know what was *comme il faut*.

My second journey was to Melbourne. I arrived in the evening and, from the air, the city, with its bright lights, looked very picturesque. I didn't know anybody in Melbourne but some Indonesian students showed me around. It was winter and, for the first time, I saw the roads in the parks covered with ice and frost on the leaves.

The third and last journey I made was to Tasmania. It was a long way from the airport to the town. We passed one apple orchard after another and it all looked very peaceful. I imagined the English countryside to be similar. The long ride made me hungry; a woman who sat next to me offered me a small shrivelled apple. I looked at it doubtfully but, when I set my teeth into it, it tasted nice and sweet. She told me it was a winter apple and gave me some more. She invited me to her home and told me that she had just lost her daughter. When I left, she gave me a parcel, containing two pairs of silk pyjamas that had belonged to her daughter.

The hotel where I stayed was very conveniently situated at walking distance from the Office of Education that arranged my program of the day. It was also close to a small theatre and a small shopping district. So when I read in the newspaper that the play, *Love From a Stranger* was on, I went to see it that evening. I had a very enjoyable evening and walked home contentedly. This is one of the things that I really enjoyed during that one year in Australia, the safe feeling that you could go out unescorted at any time of the day and night. Often I had come home from my outings rather late at night to walk leisurely back to my boarding house from the station. I wonder if it is still like that nowadays.

The next morning, when I wanted to take a bath, I landed in the men's bathroom. A kind man told me by gestures that I was in the wrong place and pointed out where I had to be. At breakfast he did not sit far from my table and, when he heard me talk in English, he became red faced; the savage turned out to be a little civilised.

I enjoyed the long trip that the Office of Education organised for me to visit some rural schools. The driver told me a lot of things about the area. He told me about the prisons, where the prisoners could work freely in the open air; we passed some and they looked just like any free men at work.

The schools were centres of activity in rather isolated areas. The children had to cover long distances to get to school and stayed there practically the whole day; it was quite a different sight from schools in over-populated Java.

It was also in Tasmania that I saw snow for the first time. It looked so clean, untouched, with a lovely blueish tint.

I must tell you a funny incident. One morning, walking through the park to the Office of Education, my *kain* somehow came loose. There was nowhere I could go to readjust it; I had to walk on until I could do it in the toilet of the Office of Education. But I thought, people here didn't know how an Indonesian dress should be worn; so I took the loose end of my *kain* over my arm and managed to walk with dignity, I hope, to where I could adjust my clothes.

This was my last journey in Australia before returning to Indonesia in December 1950. It had been a full year of study, visits and interesting contacts. I had been fortunate enough to meet all kinds of people and to learn what they were most concerned with: at that time the most popular topic of conversation was free medicine, which had just been introduced. I thought it wonderful to get free medical treatment but quite a few people didn't like it because they weren't free to choose their own physician. Another topic was the arrival of foreigners, European as well as Asian, who might change life in Australia.

I noticed the women were always busy, even when they were chatting together – and this could take hours as in any other country – the hands were never idle. They were always busy knitting or crocheting. Even on trams and buses they didn't stop knitting.

It had been a happy year for me, coming straight from the Revolution. I remember vividly how one day, when I was sitting at the station waiting for a train, I felt a deep joy and peace within my heart for no apparent reason. Never again did I experience the same feelings. I shall always remember the scholarship with gratitude because it gave me the opportunity to learn and to appreciate Indonesia's nearest neighbours.

9. Building the Future

In late December 1950 I returned to Indonesia. The plane trip back home was quite pleasant. The captain invited me into the cockpit and I could see the Lesser Sunda Islands far below. I tried to distinguish each of them by its shape but did not succeed very well. Then suddenly I saw little, dark brown figures working in the fields and I knew that I was home again.

Besides my relatives, Cing was waiting for me at Kemayoran Airport. I remember this vividly because she used to tell all our friends how awkwardly I had greeted her; no embrace, no friendly kiss after the long separation. The Purwakarta clan is indeed very undemonstrative; I had to learn how to hug and kiss people graciously from the Sastroamijoyo clan.

Cing had returned from Manila and was in the process of a divorce from Tambu. She worked at the Ministry of Foreign Affairs where her sister, Titi, also had a job. Most of my Yogya friends had moved to Jakarta with the central government. Amongst them were Titi and her husband, Samsudin, and they generously offered me a room in their house at Jl. Sultan Agung 60.

At first I was full of good intentions, willing to do everything myself as I had become used to doing in Australia. I washed my clothes, ironed them, kept my room tidy but, alas! it lasted only two weeks. After that I fell back again on the servants.

At the Ministry of Education I was warmly received. It was decided that I should give talks in Bandung, Surabaya and Semarang about my experiences in Australia and, in the meantime, it would be decided what job I was to get. But first I went home to Purwakarta to see my parents. Father had aged; he was now over eighty but he and Ibu were in good health. Father was rather annoyed that I did not get a job at once; he did not think much of my travelling and giving talks.

It was rather quiet at home without the younger children. Dicky had left for Holland and his wife, Ash, was to follow him soon. Bibib had entered the Medical Faculty and was rooming with Tine Samsudarso in Jakarta; Yetty was in Senior High School in Bandung, where she stayed with Ibu's younger brother and his wife. It was decided that the three sisters would stay together in one place as soon as I found a house but the Family Samsudin hospitably invited my two younger sisters to come and stay with them too, provided that we could share the one room. We were only too glad to be able to be together again and gratefully accepted their offer.

My talk in Bandung was a success. My audience consisted of senior high school students and they seemed to be genuinely interested in my stories about Australia. Some officials from the Ministry of Education, who were curious to know how the talk would be received, were surprised. They had not expected such a disciplined audience and I had not the faintest notion that it could be hell to talk to senior high school students.

My stay in Surabaya was rather annoying. It started with a man pestering me when he heard that I was travelling alone. In Australia I had got used to travelling alone and nobody had ever troubled me, maybe because of my foreignness, whereas in my own country a single woman was not supposed to travel all by herself. Fortunately the Inspectorate in Surabaya moved me to another hotel and the talk was a flop; my whole audience consisted of a former colleague from Yogyakarta and his wife.

In Semarang I had a full house. The audience consisted of adults of all kinds of social groups. At that time not many people had been abroad and a lively discussion followed my talk.

Back in Jakarta I received my appointment as head of a Teacher Training School, based on the same principles as the teacher training schools during the Dutch colonial period. The students were high school graduates. The director of the school to which I was appointed was a Dutchman and the teachers were mostly Dutch too. I had to take over and make it a Republican institution.

One day in June 1951 we got a telephone call to leave immediately for Bandung. We guessed that my father had fallen ill so my sisters and I boarded the train straight away. In Purwakarta, where the train stopped, we were told to get out of the train and there we saw Father in the car, sitting straight up fully dressed with Ibu beside him. He had had a stroke and was to be transported to Bandung but he wanted to wait for us in Purwakarta. That was the last time we saw him fully dressed. In Bandung he had to be in bed all the time and, after two days, he was taken to hospital. He died there on 21 June and was buried on the same day in Purwakarta where the heads of our family have a special burial place.

After the death of my father I concentrated on the school. This is one of the periods in my career that I think of with a feeling of failure. As an Indonesian who took over from the Dutch it was easy to be popular with the students. The Ministry of Education was always ready to help me and I knew many influential people in the Ministry personally from my Yogya days. I should have been able to make something of the school but I did not. I busied myself too much with small details and did not see the broad outlines. In short, I did not make anything of the opportunities given me. When, in 1953, I heard that an inspectorate for the teaching of English was to be set up, I applied and was accepted.

At that time it was very difficult to rent a house. I had the good fortune to teach English to some cadres of police officers and, through one of the police officers, I got the front part of a house at Jl. Salemba Tengah, consisting of two bedrooms and a big space which must have served as a kind of sitting room – part of which we now used as a dining and living room.

A part of it had to be kept free to let the occupants of the back part of the house get to their quarters. The three of us had a good time there. Bibib looked after the accounts, Yetty's responsibility was to make the house cosy and I had to see to it that we had sufficient money to keep the household going. Strangely enough at that time a teacher earned enough to live on. We could afford to go to the cinema regularly, as all three of us were film fans; from time to time we could treat ourselves to a meal in a restaurant; we could buy magazines and books and we could keep ourselves dressed to our liking. The Indonesian currency was stable. From time to time we bartered newspapers for a chicken but it was a golden age compared with the Japanese Occupation period.

The Inspectorate for English Teaching, known as IPBI, was a small but active inspectorate. The head was Frits Wachendorff, an Eurasian who had chosen the side of the Republic and had become an Indonesian citizen. He seemed to have made a thorough study of the problems attached to the teaching of English. He termed the language rightly "Indonesia's first foreign language". Unlike Wachendorff I had never thought about these problems but I was interested and eager to learn. The third person on the staff was Nini Rudolph. Nini was also a graduate of the I. E. V. Kweekschool, three years my junior. As an English teacher at Cikini Junior High School she had got a Fulbright scholarship and had been a special student at Barnard College and the Teacher Training College of Columbia in the United States. Her husband, Chris Rudolph, I had learned to know immediately after my return from Australia when he was head of a junior high school. In the meantime he had become an official at the Inspectorate for Junior High Schools. After their marriage the three of us became very close friends. Both of them knew the art of making people feel welcome at their home and, as both were very good listeners besides, their house was a haven for many people, amongst others the volunteer graduates from Australia.

We were very fortunate to get two volunteer graduates on the IPBI staff, Ailsa Thomson, later better known as Tommy Zainu'ddin, and Betty Feith. Not only were they a great help in IPBI but they became real friends. At that time we received help from other countries as well, in the form of young enthusiastic workers but they were salaried by the Foundations who sent them to Indonesia and were much better off than the Indonesians. For instance, the Ford Foundation sent some twelve people to help us with the teaching of English but we never learned to know them as well as the Australian volunteer graduates, who were salaried just like the Indonesians. In those years the financial situation in Indonesia had worsened. Now I realise how hard it must have been on the Australian volunteer graduates but at that time I just thought of them as people who belonged.

One of the first programs of IPBI was setting up a syllabus for the secondary schools. We had the help of two British Council officers, Professor Hill, who also taught at the Facultas Sastra Universitas Indonesia [Faculty of Arts/Letters, University of Indonesia] and Mr Baily. From the Ford Foundation, Mr Van Syoc, head of the group of teachers who came to help improve the teaching of English in Indonesia, also sat on the syllabus committee and the whole IPBI staff was on it too. We met at least once a week and, as far as I know, this syllabus is still used at present. After some time we tried the syllabus out with the help of some experienced teachers recruited from several areas in Indonesia.

Another activity was controlling the B 1 courses. These were two-year courses to train teachers for secondary school level. They trained teachers in one subject only; for instance there were B 1 courses for history, geography, mathematics and English. The English B 1 courses were mostly conducted by Dutch teachers. IPBI gradually had to take over the management of these courses from the Dutch teachers. Nini was already in possession of an English B 1 Diploma but I was not, so I had to sit for a B 1 examination before I could help control those courses. Gradually the Dutch teachers were convinced that the courses would be in good hands, especially after we had had several conferences where they were duly impressed by Professor Hill's ability and pure British accent and Mr Wachendorff's sound planning.

Another item on IPBI's program was setting up courses similar to that of the B 1 course for English but with a slightly different curriculum. They were called Standard Training courses. The Ford Foundation teachers were each given one such course to guide. We also had to see to it that they got comfortable accommodation and were introduced properly to the local government. For IPBI it meant a lot of travelling because these courses were widely spread. We had one in Makassar, one in Padang, one in Bukittinggi, one in Semarang and others in some other places. It also meant having conferences to guide the American teachers. We had one such conference in Puncak which seemed rather successful. Beside the technical side of the conference there were very animated gatherings in the evening. Tommy had translated several Indonesian folk songs and Betty spiritedly conducted a choir of enthusiastic singers.[12]

---

12 [The folk songs in question, collected and translated by Ailsa Zainu'ddin, and with the music transcription by Helen McMahon and illustrations by Jonathan Waud,

In the meantime Ann McDonald had joined IPBI. She didn't stay with us very long but, after a brief period in Australia, she returned to marry Suyono Pryosusilo and followed him to his first post in Sumatra. She was just in time to help us set up the English B 2 course. The B 2 courses were new two-year training courses to prepare teachers for senior high schools. There were not many B 2 courses, probably because we didn't have the required teaching staff for them. The English B 2 course we set up only lasted for one cycle. All of us taught at the English B 2 course but I really have no idea of the quality of the teachers we turned out because most of the IPBI staff left Indonesia before the end of the first cycle.

The IPBI was a very active body but, alas, didn't last for very long. Nini was the first to leave because she had to look after her first baby. Not long after that, Tommy, her husband and her first daughter returned to Australia; Betty and Herb following not long afterward. Mr Wachendorff decided to accept a teaching post at the Faculty of Letters at Universitas Indonesia and so I was left to hold the fort until, in September 1956, I left to study English literature and linguistics at Cornell University in the United States on a Ford Foundation scholarship.

At our home in Gang Tengah too, many changes took place. After having finished high school, Yetty decided to study dentistry in Surabaya where she was going to stay with Dicky and Asih, who had returned from Holland. She met Tonny Purwanto, a fellow student at the University, and in her third year they were married. Bibib had decided to give up her studies at the Medical Faculty and obtained a job at Pembangunan book store. There she met Achmad Jayusman, an ex-student of mine in Yogya. When he first came to our house at Gang Tengah on his scooter, I thought how nice of him to remember his old teacher but it turned out that he was not interested in his old teacher at all. Instead he concentrated all his attention on the younger sister. They were married on 1 April 1956 being the date for jokes, according to the Dutch. By the end of 1956 both IPBI and the Gang Tengah home had been dispersed.

---

were later published as *Lagu-Lagu Dari Indonesia: Songs of Indonesia*. South Yarra, Vic.: Heinemann Educational Australia, 1969].

PART THREE

INTRODUCTION

A Friendship in Writing

When Kurnianingrat began writing her memoir in May 1991, she did so in conjunction with many friends and family members, including Harumani and Ailsa. Harumani had written to Ailsa in January 1990 outlining her idea that Kurnianingrat could write something in the style of *Yesterday's Daughters*, a compilation of autobiographical writing by Australian women which Ailsa had sent across.[1] Ailsa was aware that Kurnianingrat had hesitated to open old wounds by writing about her past, especially the personal cost of events during the Japanese Occupation. Among her suggestions to Kurnianingrat at this time was that she keep in mind the person to whom she was telling her story, advice she herself had received from Manning Clark and which she put into practice in her book, *A Short History of Indonesia*.

It was common for Kurnianingrat and Ailsas' letters to encompass an exchange of ideas and writing in this way. One historical figure whose life and work is frequently a subject of discussion between them is R. A. Kartini. In 1980 the two friends communicated about a planned publication to do with women's roles and feminist developments in Indonesia. The idea for the volume stemmed from a public lecture series commemorating the centenary of Kartini's birth, held at Monash University's Centre for Southeast Asian Studies and involving Ailsa and four other female speakers. The book was to include an opinion piece by Kurnianingrat, together with her response to Marilyn French's *The Women's Room*, another book received from Ailsa. Kurnianingrat wrote to Ailsa of having greatly enjoyed French's novel, and of being very interested in its central feminist stance, though she found no correlation with her own experience as an Indonesian: "This makes the book so intriguing to me; the different emphases on things, the different approaches and solutions towards problems, and yet I can follow these characters entirely."[2] The planned book was never published. In 1981 Kurnianingrat wrote to Ailsa of having revised her broadly positive stance on the situation

---

1   *Yesterday's Daughters: Stories of Our Past by Women over 70*, Alma Bushell (ed.). Melbourne: Nelson, 1986.
2   Jo to Tommy, 19 December 1979. For the letters exchanged between Kurnianingrat, Ailsa and Harumani, as cited and reproduced in this part of the book, see "Jo – Correspondence and Autobiography/Biography" (1955-1993), Papers of Ailsa

of Indonesian women, as expressed in her opinion piece.³ She cites the official requirement that women applying for an exit permit from the country must first obtain consent from a male relative. Kurnianingrat learned of this rule when she set out to travel to Penang to consult retina specialists for a prognosis in relation to her eye problems. She had not left Indonesia for some thirty years at that point, and her letters to Ailsa record her surprise and dismay at what she described as the "great, great fall" evident in the position of Indonesian women over recent years.⁴

Additionally, it was from Kurnianingrat that Ailsa learned, in March 1987, of the discovery of unpublished letters of Kartini. Writing of the discovered letters, Kurnianingrat cites the view of Sumartini, then head of the National Archives in Jakarta, that they "would change the opinion of those who see Kartini as the product of Dutch thinking at that time. She really had quite an independent mind".⁵ Ailsa, who was then involved in teaching and writing about Kartini (in an essay published in 1979, Ailsa had said of Kartini that she was "greater than any of the moulds and frameworks within which different people have chosen to confine her"⁶), was intrigued to learn of the new Kartini letters. The letters would be translated into English a few years later by Joost Coté. Joost, a historian who has published four works of translated letters by Kartini and her sisters, knew both Ailsa and Betty through their work in Indonesian Studies; Ailsa taught Joost and supervised his postgraduate research on two occasions, while Betty and Joost shared an office at Deakin University.

On at least two occasions Ailsa sent across writing about Kartini that she herself had completed or been involved with. In response to her essay published in *Nineteenth and Twentieth Century Indonesia* (a *festschrift* for historian John Legge), Kurnianingrat wrote "So much has been written about Kartini, but your presentation gives it a new angle. Anyhow, I'm reading your article with great pleasure."⁷ Her own thinking about Kartini, she shared with Ailsa, had been decisively shaped by Ailsa's work:

Thomson Zainuddin, privately held. Kurnianingrat's opinion piece, entitled "A Personal View from Indonesia [The Role of the Indonesian Woman]", is also located in Ailsa's personal archive.

3   Jo to Tommy, 6 February 1981.
4   Jo to Tommy, 15 April 1987.
5   Jo to Tommy, 15 April 1987.
6   Ailsa Thomson Zainu'ddin, "Kartini – Her Life, Work and Influence" in Ailsa Thomson Zainu'ddin … [et al], *Kartini Centenary: Indonesian Women Then and Now* ([Clayton, Vic.]: Monash University, 1980), p. 17.
7   Jo to Tommy, undated.

And I have to own up that I have learned to appreciate Kartini much more through your writings. Do you see the irony of it – she wanted to give the Indonesian woman a "real" education, and I had to learn her aspirations through an Australian woman by the name of Tommy Zainu'ddin.[8]

Ailsa, in turn, wrote that her image of Kartini was closely informed by her friendship with Kurnianingrat:

> One thing I must say, in response to your comment that you have learnt to appreciate Kartini much more through my writing, is that my appreciation of her is largely intertwined with my friendship with you. You and Nini and Oom Wach [Frits Wachendorff, head of IPBI] accepted Bett and me as part of the team, no longer outsiders and you are the one and only aristocrat I have ever known. Like Kartini you do not seem to "give a two-pnce [pence] for all that" while representing both "the aristocracy of the mind and the aristocracy of the soul". (This is what I was thinking the other night when I could not sleep – there is a lot of Jo Kurnianingrat in my image of Kartini).[9]

Nini and Chris Rudolph, Frits Wachendorff and Betty Feith were among the mutual friends and acquaintances whose names recur throughout Ailsa and Kurnianingrats' correspondence, as were Mary Johnston and Ann Pryosusilo (both Mary and Ann lived in Indonesia for many years after initially travelling up under the auspices of the Volunteer Graduate Scheme). Following a trip to Jakarta in January 1984, Ailsa sent a letter thanking Kurnianingrat and her family for their "marvellous hospitality ... It really was a haven of peace to be there and the time went very quickly, far too quickly for my liking."[10] In her reply, Kurnianingrat wrote "The photos look wonderful; the house seems so much grander than it really is. But most important, they really bring back the days that you both were here. I really loved to have you with us, and when Mary joined us it was a happy crowd."[11] A photograph of Ailsa which Kurnianingrat received in mid-1987 drew this response: "Nobody can miss the typical Tommy-grin! And whatever Din teases you with, you are still like that, but mellowed. Your friends in Indonesia all agree that you are much more charming now than

---

8   Jo to Tommy, 14 December 1987.
9   Tommy to Jo, 26 and 29 December 1987.
10 Tommy to Jo, 19 February 1984.
11 Jo to Tommy, [April/March 1984].

you were when young (and innocent?)"[12] For Ailsa and Kurnianingrat, as for Harumani and Betty, a valued part of their friendship lay in their shared past, including their time at IPBI in Jakarta in the 1950s.

After beginning to write her memoir in May 1991, Kurnianingrat did much of the writing between June and November of that year. During that time she sent drafts to Tommy, who would, in turn, reply to both Kurnianingrat and Harumani with her thoughts and questions. Kurnianingrat did further writing in mid-1992. During a visit to Jakarta at this time made by Ailsa's husband Din and her elder daughter Nila, the latter helped Kurnianingrat type up the material. In her letters to Ailsa, Kurnianingrat gave her consent for Ailsa to edit and revise the manuscript, and she also accepted her friend's offer to write an introduction in the event that the memoir be published, although she stipulated that Ailsa not "say all the nice and flattering things that you so often say about me, because that is a far too rosy picture of the real me".[13] Ailsa promised to do her best in this respect, adding that what she would write would not be flattery, but rather "the truth as I see it".[14] In a letter from March 1993, Kurnianingrat requested help finding a suitable ending to her narrative, and the next month, Ailsa wrote promising to send notes based on her own memories of IPBI to supplement Kurnianingrat's account of the Inspectorate. Before either of these things could happen, Kurnianingrat suffered a stroke which would prove fatal. Ailsa's respect and affection for her friend would find expression in her obituary for Kurnianingrat, published as the Epilogue to the present volume.

The letters presented in Part Three are but a very small selection of the body of correspondence that flowed between Ailsa and Kurnianingrat over many years, as well as from the smaller number between Ailsa and Harumani. They have been selected and transcribed by Ailsa and Ann from the file of correspondence between Ailsa and Kurnianingrat entitled "Jo – Correspondence and Autobiography/Biography" (1955–1993) which is privately held in the papers of Ailsa Thomson Zainuddin. As noted in the introduction to this volume, each of the correspondents was known in different contexts by different names. In these letters, Harumani signs herself and is addressed as Nini, Ailsa as Tommy and Kurnianingrat as Jo.

---

12 Jo to Tommy, undated.
13 Jo to Tommy, 24 July 1992.
14 Tommy to Jo, 2 August 1992.

CORRESPONDENCE

"A CONVERSATION WITHOUT WORDS"

Extracts of Correspondence between
Kurnianingrat Ali Sastroamijoyo,
Ailsa Thomson Zainuddin
and Harumani Rudolph-Sudirdjo,
1990–1993

Rawamangun

5 January 1990

Dear Tommy,

Last night I had a dream about you and your sister (who was in fact Betty Feith) visiting us in Jakarta. We went to my brother's place which was (in the dream) just one house away from ours. I showed you his back garden where he grew lots of fruits and you and Betty showed me the shawls you had been crocheting for choir practice!! They were beautiful too. Betty's was black and yours was white!!

I think I had the dream because the afternoon before Jo and I had been talking about you. You have been very much in my mind – I think you know that Jo's eyes are getting worse. She can hardly see and has to be helped in quite a lot of things. She has started Braille and has got some practice material from Holland (friends introduced her to people from a Society for the Blind in Holland, she went there in August). But to do the writing and reading exercises she needs somebody to dictate the lessons to her and to listen when she reads them back. It's very difficult to find someone who can read Dutch and has time to spare. Rini is willing but she doesn't read Dutch, although she understands it a little. During the Christmas holidays I have been able to help but I'll start teaching again soon.

Jo is trying to fill her time practising her Braille (for this she needs help) listening to the "talking" books she got from Holland

and the cassettes she got from you and from some other friends. But yesterday she mentioned that life was very boring for her. She's got nothing interesting or stimulating to do. I have suggested earlier that she write articles (or essays) for the "corner" in one of the English newspapers (*Jakarta Post* or *Jakarta Times*) that they publish here. But for that you have to be up to date and know about current events – which is rather difficult for someone who has to rely on somebody else for current news.

Well, yesterday I had a brilliant idea! Do you remember *Yesterday's Daughters* that I got from you? Jo could write something in that style. I've promised her to bring her the book and read her parts of it. But Jo needs some prodding and I thought you could do the prodding. You know I've always admired Jo for being able to find interesting topics to talk about and to talk about coherently and convincingly. I think her letters should be interesting reading too. Well, as you and Mary do [sic] have received letters from her I thought you might be able to convince her that she could do it. So will you do it Tommy?

As I read the letter back, I see that I have really jumped immediately into the thing I wanted to ask and I haven't wished you a happy New Year. Well, I do wish you and Din and your children and grandchildren a happy and successful year. Is there a chance to see you again sometime in the near future?

[...]

All my love,

Nini

"A Conversation Without Words"

[January 1990?]

Dear Nini,

It was a surprise and a delight to receive, in the one mail, letters from both you and Jo. I knew from her last letter and from Mary [former volunteer graduate, Mary Johnston] that her eyes were very much worse and I had actually not quite known what to do about replying, whether by letter or by tape. Mary and Anne [former volunteer graduate, Ann Pryosusilo] seem to think that tapes are unlikely to arrive unless someone sends them LTH from Indonesia so when I put letters on tape they then sit around until they are woefully out of date and they also sound very stilted. Jo wrote about receiving tapes from the Netherlands but perhaps those ones come in some special fashion not available from here.

Your dream was unusual and intriguing. It has to be a dream world, I assure you, if I am crocheting in it – knitting would be more typical of both of us though I've never tackled a shawl. I leave that to my real sister. Bett and I as sisters was quite appropriate, just as I think of you and Jo as very like sisters (to each other and to us).

Yes, I think your idea is a brilliant one. I was trying to encourage Jo to think of writing an autobiography but she said that some of it was too painful to recall. It is also a very long haul to contemplate as she would know because of Pak Ali's book. On the other hand vignettes from her past would be marvellous. She was talking to me about her life as a girl and the parallels with Kartini, while in the paper she wrote for the republication of the articles on Kartini which Sisters, a women's publishing company here (since – alas! – defunct) had talked about publishing was a delight to read as, of course, are her letters. She could also reflect on books she has read and regards as significant. I would love more details of her life in Sydney or in Ithaca as well as of her schooling, her work during the Revolution, sketches of people she has met in life or in literature. The list is endless. She could write either in the format of *Yesterday's Daughters* or perhaps in the form of letters. If it were easier for her it might also take the form of interviews just as I collected her memories of Molly Bondan though that, like the Braille, would require an interviewer. Perhaps she could be persuaded to soliliquise [sic] if she can still manage a tape recorder. The final collection might finish up being a series of biographical vignettes, each complete in itself but also part of a larger whole. Yes, it is a brilliant idea and I'll certainly be prepared to do some gentle prodding. [...]

Love from,

Tommy

1 January 1991

Dear Tommy,

As you see, the first letter of the year goes to you. Did my Christmas and New Year's greetings arrive on time? I hope you had a pleasant time with children, grandchildren, and, of course, husband. It is always difficult to go back to routine after a time of festivities. For me it makes no difference now that every day is a holiday.

That is the reason why I find it rather difficult to keep up my correspondence; there isn't much to tell. Every day I do Braille exercises, reading or writing. I always have to find a victim to dictate to me or to check my reading, which is not so easy because I started with the Dutch Braille system that I got when I was in Holland. ... My "relaxation" exists in listening to cassettes, so you can understand how happy I was with the ones you sent me. From the Braille Institute in Den Haag I also get regular shipments of cassettes containing books read to those who cannot read the normal way. The ones I get are in English or Dutch. I heard for instance *Sons and Lovers* read in 15 cassettes; it was wonderful! It is as if I am reading the books myself, and sometimes, when I have been too greedy, and have been listening too long to the cassettes, my eyes feel heavy as if I had been reading too much. ... However, I must confess that my brains need more stimulance, more to digest, and I feel this lack very much. Do you have any suggestions how a woman of 71, with very bad eyesight and hard of hearing could make herself useful?

[...]

Lots of love from

Jo

"A Conversation Without Words"

21 January 1991

Dear Jo,

[...] Now that you need more stimulation you really should consider again doing some autobiographical or reflective writing. When we talked about it in Jakarta I could understand very well that you might find it too painful and therefore too difficult to write an autobiography but why couldn't you write a series of sketches, stories, vignettes? (My Word Spell tried to turn "vignettes" into "vanities" but that is exactly what they would **NOT** be.) You could write autobiographically or they could be semi-fictional, based on your own experiences or stories of or about your family. I wish I had been able [to] record your account of the parallels between your life and Kartini's. I would love further glimpses of life in a Sundanese *kabupaten* and recollections of your school days. You could also record your experiences with the Dutch family (families?) with whom you boarded; your [...] experiences in Sydney; life in Ithaca and the Indonesian community at Cornell; recollections of other people you have known – George Kahin; Pak Ali; Oom Wachendorf; – if they are sketches then you can select what you recall and omit anything that is too painful. Speaking as a historian, I would regard such a project as most useful and of intrinsic value anyway. Speaking as a friend (and fan of long standing) they would be invaluable. I have, of course, no other reason to argue for them being in English except my own desire to read them although writing them in letter form could help you envisage an eager audience. Manning Clark, my former boss and our best known historian, gave me the advice to envisage a person to whom one was telling the story as the way to start writing when I asked how to start my *Short History [of Indonesia]*.

[...]

[from] Tommy Ailsa [sic]

Greetings from Din

[No date]

Dear Tommy,

What a pleasant surprise to hear your voice over the telephone. Unfortunately I'm always dumbstricken when I get an overseas call, maybe because of the costs it entails. That's why I kept telling you: "Go on talking." But you weren't an especially good conversationalist either that day and you must have paid a lot for the long gaps between us. Anyhow, thank you so much for the call.

    I had a light heart attack, but it filled my lungs with water. Now we know the water come there because the heart was weak; but the doctors and we too thought of cancer of the lungs. Thank God it was not that. And when I was beginning to feel better I enjoyed my stay in hospital. Somehow I thought of the prisoners of war who slept in barracks one on top of the other and when one of them got dysentery the others had to suffer too. And here I was, lying between crisp clean sheets and being taken good care of.

    God has apparently granted me a little more time on this earth. I'm sure it is with a special purpose, and I do want very much to give of myself. Instead others give me a lot of themselves and I am at the receiving end, especially because I'm still not entirely cured from the bronchitis I got; hence the terrible coughs you must have heard over the telephone. [...]

    I promised to start writing the story of my life. Goenawan Mohamad promised to find me a dictaphone which was easy to handle, but so far he hasn't been able to find one. However, I started to plan the thing in my head. [...]

    Tommy, thank you so much for your concern about me and all the good wishes you sent me.

Lots of love,

    Jo,

PS *This letter has been so faultlessly typed because Bu Titi, Bu Cing's sister typed it for me.*

"A Conversation Without Words"

24 March 1991

Dear Jo,

[...] The special purpose might very well be to allow all of us who are indebted to you to have some chance of repaying the debt we owe – though, in my case anyway, according to the proverb, they are not the kinds of debt which can be repaid. Number one priority is for you to be entirely cured from the bronchitis and to gain in strength. The other purpose, which I feel sure is special, is the project. I'm looking forward to the first instalment and I hope that Goenawan Mohamad has managed to find a suitable dictaphone and that you are enjoying the planning stage.

[...] my love and best wishes for your health, happiness and creativity,

[Tommy]

[April? 1991]

Dear Tommy,

[...] This letter is the first product of my three weeks' training in blind typing, so I am afraid Rini will have a lot to correct. [...]

We are nearing the end of the fasting month. This year I don't fast, and I am sure I won't have the feeling of having a real Lebaran. It will be just a series of gatherings with relatives and friends but for me it won't be the end of the fasting month. I have tried to do the other things one tries to do during the fasting month without abstaining from eating and drinking, such as trying to control one's emotions and thoughts, but I can't think I have really succeeded. It is strange, you know, Tommy; I am fully aware that I live on borrowed time and try consciously to do something with it, give more of myself to others. Instead I find that others give me so much attention and love, and you are one of them, and I am always at the receiving end.

[...]

Lots of love,

Jo

15 April 1991

Dear Jo and Nini,

[...] I still believe that, with what you call borrowed time, you can be giving a great deal by passing on to others the wisdom and experience you have gleaned over the years and I still maintain that you are deservedly at the receiving end because so few of us have had the opportunity to repay even in part what we owe you. I was reflecting on some of this instead of replying to my mail over the past weekend – because this letter has actually jumped the queue of unanswered letters. I was about to have an early night on Saturday, planning to be up reasonably early and start on letters but, at 11.00 p.m. just as I was about to go to bed, my eye lighted on the book which Mum had used for her reminiscences – calling it:

"The short and simple annals of the poor"
And random jottings as remembered

Grandma, Thelma B. Thomson

I then decided to add to it the letters I received from friends in 1980–1981 when they/you heard of Mum's death and, reading them through, I could really see how many friends she had of all generations and I read again the letters such as yours which helped them to acknowledge the separation and helps now to recall her image. So I delved a bit further and came upon the letters Mum and Dad had written when I was in Canberra and later when I was in Indonesia. They were so delighted to meet you all. It was just the right setting for today's mail – your letter, Jo, and one from a friend in England whose birthday is the day before (and many years after) mine. [...]

I am including the *Spoken word cassette catalogue* I wrote [to Polygram for] so please let me know what you would like – more poetry? plays? Shakespeare? Austen? Dickens? Nini, could you let me know and let me know the number and title because now you have the catalogue and I don't. I should have asked for two!

Love to both and to families and friends,

[Tommy]

> Jakarta
> [Before 25 May? 1991]

Dear Tommy,

Both your letter[s] of 24th March and the one written on the eve of Lebaran have arrived safely. I do appreciate your prompt replies, especially because I know how busy you are. And thank you also for the Lebaran greetings, and for the catalogue of "Spoken Word".

Do you realize how much you do for me? And I accept everything happily and gratefully, but strange enough, with no feeling of indebtedness. I wish you would have the same feeling towards me if I have done something to help you in the far past, although I really don't know what it is. But please, drop the feeling of indebtedness, and let us just enjoy the give-and-take between friends.

[...] I had to stop typing this morning, because I had to join a very enjoyable discussion group. Among other things we were talking about the limitations of man. It was driven home to me that God sends us what is best for us, so that we can learn from it. In one of the Indian books, I think it is the *Baghavad Gita*, it says, "What has happened was for the best; what is happening, is for the best; what will happen, will be for the best." [...]

[...] It is a little bit disappointing that Goenawan has not managed to find a dictaphone that is easy to handle for me. But now I am energetic enough to try and type my story out, or ask someone to take my dictation. Anyhow, I promise that you will have at least one chapter when you come back from Alaska. Only, I am not sure that I will have so much to tell to make it a book. Well, we'll just see how it goes.

To my surprise I find that I have managed to fill more than three pages with my typing. I hope I don't sound too long-winded. Anyhow I must stop now. This letter will not be corrected by Tini [Rini?], who is still fast asleep, so I am afraid you will have to do a bit of guess work where I have made mistakes.

[...]

Lots of love,

Jo

Jakarta
[June? 1991]

Dear Tommy,

[...] As promised, I am sending you the first chapter of my story. You are free to make any alterations, cuts, change the title, because I am only talking myself out. I'll try to send you the rest regularly by instalments, as soon as possible. Because I have [thrombosis], and I don't know how long I will last.

All my love, to you and the family,

Jo

[...] *Tommy, your friendship means a lot to me. Thanks for the many tokens of friendship during all these years. If, by any chance, this story could be published, could you let Rini have [royalties].*

Clayton, Victoria
29 July 1991

Dear Jo and Nini,

We arrived home from Alaska a week ago – Sunday 21st July, to be exact [...] [On the arrival in the mail of draft chapters:] I popped into a café and, sipping cappuccino, I read them through with growing delight – indeed with a whole range of emotions, including something very close to tears, except that one can't really yield to such feelings on one's own in a café. Jo, you write with such delicate understatement that it is a delight to read and re-read. [...]

31/7/91

Chapter four was a very special chapter which I found most moving. I think that having Rini and Ruli for your imagined audience gives a strong unity to your account. I remember when I was about to start writing *A Short History of Indonesia* that I asked the late Manning Clark, my mentor, how I should start writing. He said to imagine that I was sitting opposite someone I knew and telling the story to that person, which, of course, is exactly what you are doing to such good effect. I feel very privileged to be entrusted with this material and to have had the friendship of both of you over so many years. I'll write at greater length before Bett leaves for Jakarta in a few weeks.

[from Tommy]

20 August 1991

Dear Jo and Nini,

[...] I can now report that the day after Bett left I received chapter five, "The Japanese Occupation". It was most appropriate because I collected it from downstairs last Friday on the eve of Independence Day 1991. It also indicated that you must have received my letter of 29 July.

[...]

Lots of love,

[Tommy]

Jakarta
17 September 1991

Dear Tommy,

First of all my apologies for not writing to you sooner. So many emotional things happen one after another that it is really breathtaking. It has slowed down my correspondence and my reminiscences greatly.

Herb and Betty came and went; we met only once, having dinner at Nini's house. They had to do a lot of travelling and had to see many people.

[...] Now I am looking forward to your and Din's arrival. Maybe you have been wondering why I did not comment at it at all. It was certainly no lack of enthusiasm, but the thought if I would still be there when you came. But things are getting better, and though I am now a thin old woman I feel much stronger, and hope to see you in January. And of course you must stay in your hacienda-style Indonesian home.

[...] Tommy, attached is an improved page 8 of the Japanese occupation. I have added some more details, about the last stage of the period. I hope to send you the next chapter next week, and then I'll begin with the chapter on my stay in Australia. It will be the last chapter, for it brings Rini and Ruli to the later years of the Republic, a time they are familiar with. I don't think it can be published, there is too little material. But I am glad you suggested that I should write about it. It was a kind of therapy for me, I had something definite to do. Can't you suggest anything for me to do after this?

[...] Two weeks ago I celebrated my 72nd birthday. In Indonesia it definitely has its advantages to be old. At least people take your requests seriously. I asked relatives and friends not to give me any presents, but if they wanted to contribute something to bring something that we could eat together. My youngest sister organized things; she asked certain people to bring certain things, and we got a very nice and varied menu together. Without my doing anything; in fact I was still too tired to exert myself. But the several hostesses were very busy and enjoyed themselves, and everybody felt at home. When I had a good look at the group I noticed that with the exception of Titi, Cing's older sister, and her sister in law, they were the people that used to come to Gang Tengah. The same people at a further stage in their lives. So it was an exchange of information, and it was an animated gathering.

[...]

Give your family my love. I am looking forward to January.

Love,

Jo.

Clayton, Victoria
7 October 1991

Dear Jo and Nini,

This is a reply to Jo's letter of 17 September, a response to the two parts of the fascinating chapter on the early years of the Republic and an attempt to share with you the celebration of Mary's life which took place today [...]

The conference at Wollongong was a History of Education one on autobiography and biography in educational history so it was most appropriate that I should have received the first part of Ch 6 "The Early Days of the Republic" just before I left and that the second part was waiting for me on my return but I was dismayed to read that you are thinking of finishing the memoirs so soon. Even though it brings you to a period with which Rini and Ruli are familiar from their point of view that is no reason for stopping. On the contrary, precisely because they **are** familiar with it from one perspective, it is important for them to see it also from another as an outcome of the past. ... The IPBI plans and the whole development of education in the Republic, the language policy and its implementation, the British Council and Michigan people, are part of the educational history of the Republic, including some degree of neo-colonialism of the American and, I suspect, Australian variety. It is of interest because, from your perspective, you can present it as emerging from the past, bridging the gap between colonial and post-colonial. The post-independence youngsters will have no sense of it as being built up so recently. So don't stop after Australia. This task is **NOT YET FINISHED**.

I've never thought to ask you, Jo, whether you would have met Kartini's grandson when you were in Australia. Did you overlap at all? Of course I realise that if he were in the Snowy Mountains and you in Sydney that would be unlikely. **Please**, don't stop after your stay in Australia. I would have said that anyway but I say it with much greater urgency and authority after attending the conference. The account of your birthday gathering – the people who used to come to Gang Tengah, the same people at a further stage of their lives looking back comparing life then and now perhaps might be the framework for the concluding chapter.

[...]

Love to you both from both of us,

Tommy

PS I realise I haven't said how much I enjoyed the account of the Revolution. I found it exciting and fascinating.

Jakarta
26 October 1991

Dear Tommy,

[...] About these reminiscences, I am glad you suggested that I write them down. It gave me something useful to do, and I am glad to find that I can still use my faculty to think. But, to be honest, I don't know how to end my narration satisfactorily.

You suggest that I talk about educational programmes, about IPNi [IPBI], but that would be quite different from what I have been doing so far; just writing a simple narration. Besides, I am afraid that it's all I can do at present; Just write down what is in my head, without doing any looking up or having to draw any conclusions. I am afraid you'll have to help me find a decent ending. Maybe we shall have to wait until you and Din are in your hacienda-style Indonesian home, and plot something.

Enclosed I am sending you a small addition to the last page of the chapter on the Early years of the Republic.

Lots of love,

[Jo]

Clayton, Victoria
5 November 1991

Dear Jo and Nini,

[...] Life in Sydney [i.e. Jo's account of her year in Sydney in 1950] was all too brief and absolutely fascinating – fleas, vicious lapdogs and the differences in values as expressed in psychological tests. I hope this is only the first instalment of "Australian Experiences". Does it follow directly after "The Early Years of the Republic" which it seems to do as it finishes with the scholarship? I've only just realised (being a bit slow with numbers) that this last chapter is numbered 9 and the previous one was no. 6, yet I don't think any have gone astray.

[...]

Love to you both from both of us,

[Tommy]

"A Conversation Without Words"

8 May 1992

Dear Jo,

I was so glad to receive your birthday greetings because it prolonged the birthday celebrations but also because it was from you in the midst of such a busy time. [...]

10/5/1992

We had a very pleasant lunch today with Goenawan and two friends. One of them was Pam Sayers who was Administrative Secretary at the Centre of Southeast Asian Studies when Goenawan was here five years ago and the other was Stuart Robson, the Associate-Professor who is head of Indonesian at Monash and on the editorial committee of the Centre of Southeast Asian Studies. He is the one who read your manuscript and who thinks that it would be appropriate for the Centre to publish it when it is finished. So Stuart, Goenawan and I had this common topic of interest which Pam found interesting too.

Goenawan was talking again about a tape recorder for you to use. That made me recall the tape I made when we were discussing the next chapter. I could type it up or else send you a copy of the tape itself if either would be of any use for your next chapter. Stuart thinks it would need an introduction for Australian readers which I would be very happy and honoured to write if you agree. He would like to have even more detail about life in the *kabupaten* – the texture of life there; the images and impressions; the sights and sounds; the differences between the past and the present. They both agreed that the story should continue and Goenawan wants you to include life with Pak Ali so you can't just stop when you return from Cornell. [text crossed out]

When we took Goenawan back to Ormond College, each of us farewelled the other by saying that now we must reply to your last letter so, even though it will soon be midnight, I'm determined to finish this. We really were quite apprehensive about inviting him in the first place because we really thought that a newspaper editor would be so busy meeting important people that he would not have time for anyone else. Now we are also hoping to meet his wife when she comes to join him and have arranged to take them out to the airport when they leave for Leiden on 22nd.

[...]

Love from both of us,

[Tommy] [...]

Jakarta
22 July 1992

Dear Tommy,

[...] As you see, I have typed an additional chapter. Nini has not given her comments about it yet, and I would like you to add whatever you think necessary to the IPBI section. Then Nila has discovered that

I had to leave the typewriter to see to a few things, and I don't remember where I left off. I think it was to tell you that in my copy the third page of the Japanese occupation is missing. again an interruption, and I have lost the course of my thoughts.

[...]

Lots of love,

Jo

Jakarta
24 July 1992

Dear Tommy,

[...] You told me that there was a possibility of my reminiscences being published, and that it would be necessary to have an introduction or explanations for the Australian reader. You offered your help to do that, and I wrote that I would be honoured if you could but on one condition, that you would not say all the nice and flattering things that you so often say about me, because that is a far too rosy picture of the real me.

I have typed an additional chapter about life in the *kabupaten*, and you are free to cross out whatever you think superfluous. Because of this additional chapter I had had to revise the chapter before and after it. Then Nila told me that page 3 of the Japanese occupation was missing, and I would be grateful if you could send me that one. I have also sent you the first chapter of the second part, and I would be very happy if you could find an appropriate title for it. And, what is more, if you can add or correct [any]thing in the IPBI section, that would be wonderful. I have asked Nini to do the same, so we may get a slightly different chapter 1 of Part Two. I am still waiting for inspiration to write the next chapter, about my stay in America, which was quite different from my stay in Australia probably because I was much older at that time.

[...]

Lots of love, until another letter Tommy,

Jo

2 August 1992

Dear Jo,

As usual I have two of your letters to my one – three including the one that did not arrive. I was delighted to receive the new chapter and the revised earlier one [...]

9/8/1992

[...] I am so glad that Nila has had the chance to meet you all and I'm also very glad that you did make good use of her time there and that you were able to put her at her ease (though hardly surprised as it has always been one of your skills). That reminds me of your reference to my introduction/explanation. I'll promise not to say **all** the nice things and I assure you that I don't and won't say anything flattering, only the truth as I see it.

[...]

[Tommy]

18 February 1993

Dear Jo,

When I checked in my Notebook I found that my last letter to you was in October although the belated Christmas Bulletin should have brought you up to date a little and perhaps would have explained why I am again answering **two** of your letters at once, which I seem to have done far too often in our correspondence. I can speak with some authority on the matter of our correspondence as one of the tasks which has been occupying me over the past month is sorting out all my letters, some as far back as about 1945. They include the Bulletins I wrote when I was at IPBI and my letters to my parents. Sorting correspondence seems to be a never ending task, as you might expect from a hoarder such as I am. One problem has been the temptation to re-read them and to re-live various stages of my past life.

Before I answer your letters let me quote from my October letter to you. I wrote:

> What I should do is find some of my Bulletins written while I was at IPBI – but that is then **my** recollections rather than yours – although I would also like to incorporate your letter to us when I asked you to write about the Volunteer Graduates for our special *Djembatan* issue. I'd like to use the article which you wrote accompanying the talks given at the Kartini Centenary at Monash if they had been published by Sisters. It is even more strikingly apt today as hard-line feminists draw battle lines just as the characters in Marilyn French's novel were doing.

Now I **have** found the Bulletins as well as many letters from you, starting with some from Ithaca [...] What I could do is type out or perhaps read on to tape (which would be easier for you to use?) some of my recollections of IPBI between now and May when Bett and Herb hope to visit Indonesia and when Bett could reminisce, tape and/or type some of the IPBI and Ithaca material. [...]

[...]

My love to you and to Rini and Nini. Din will join the 70 year olds in October and I'm not so very far behind.

[Tommy]

[28? March 1993]

Dear Tommy,

This is the last day before Lebaran, and there are a lot of things to be done yet, but I really feel the need to talk to you. First of all, thank you for your letter. So many things have happened in the meantime but I'm afraid this will not be exactly a response to it. You mentioned the possibility of Herb and Betty coming here; I am really looking forward to it … it is nice of her to suggest that she may be able to help me to finish the last chapters into shape. At the moment there is not one person who can help me type things. [...]

Anyhow, [there is] no one who can help me finish the last chapters, and I think I should not wait too long. By the way, you said you could type your ideas about IPBI; if you don't mind my using them, I would be very happy. Don't tape it: it will be nicer to have them on paper – I am still old-fashioned.

Thank you also for the phone call; surprisingly this time we did know what to say to each other. [...]

I am sorry to write you such dreary letters, but this is kind of talking to myself, and I know that you won't pity me but give me your understanding.

Well Tommy, I hope to hear from you again soon.

[...]

Lots of love, and *alam kangen*,

Jo

21 April 1993

Dear Jo,

[...] Sunday was a Very Busy Day. The Volunteer Graduates had a reunion at the home of Ken and Bep Thomas and we were all asked to bring something for the midday meal. [...] I know she [Betty Feith] is very interested in your project and would love to be involved in it. I shall look out some of my letters to Mum for life in the [IPBI] office. Do you remember the occasion when Bett and I decided to turn on an Australian morning tea, despite gentle warnings from various people that it might surprise us? It did as, up to that point, we hadn't bought any Australian style biscuits and, as I recall, we didn't do so again either!

[...] Jo, you can never write to me too often and it is a joy to be in touch with the doings of our friends, both the ups and the downs.... Whenever you feel the need and have the time please write. It always makes me wish I were right there again.

23/4/1993

[...] I hope to send the tape and some IPBI material with Bett. Now I send all my love and best wishes,

[Tommy]

1 June 1993

Dear Tommy,

[...] Thank you so much for your last letter. I meant to answer it much sooner, but like a typical *orang jompo*, a superannuated person, I had a few weeks of feebleness, in which I did not do much else but rest. I did not even feel like talking to you on paper, and as I now never force myself to do things I just did not do anything but listen to cassettes. So, what I mean amongst other things is that you don't have to feel obliged to reply to all my letters, although every letter is quite welcome. When you come to think of it, I just fill a need, do it more to please me than the person I write to.

[...] As far as I myself am concerned, I got the nicest surprise in my life when the government raised the pensions, and because of Pak Ali's achievements he leaves me a widow's pension which enables me to get through the month even without the extra income from teaching. I don't know how long the monthly pension will suffice, because the standard of living rises all the time, but at least temporarily my mind is at rest.

[...] Unfortunately there is no one to check my typing. I hope what I have put down on paper does make sense: sometimes Rini finds lines that make no sense at all.

So, Tommy, don't worry about what turn it is to write; when I feel the need you will get another letter. My warmest regards to Din, Lisa, John and children. I'll write to Nila tomorrow.

All my love,

Jo

In August 1993, Ailsa heard from Harumani that Kurnianingrat's physical and psychological condition had substantially deteriorated after a stroke which resulted in her being hospitalised for two months. As well as being paralysed, Kurnianingrat had lost the ability to recognise previously familiar faces and her powers of communication were substantially reduced. Ailsa's diary entry for 23 August 1993 begins "It has come – the news I have been expecting and dreading – a letter from Nini to the four of us", meaning to herself, her husband Zainu'ddin and Betty and Herb Feith.[1]

31 August 1993

Dear Nini,

Your letter arrived just a day or so before we set off for Sydney [...]. I rang Herb immediately after I had read the letter myself, to read to him but didn't manage to contact Bern [former volunteer graduate, Bernard Lionnet] before we left though I shall do so as top priority when we return next week. Thank you so much for writing. It was exceedingly hard to write because, as far as I know, she did not receive my last letter in time. The tape which Bett and

---

1   See Ailsa Zainuddin's Jottings and Cuttings Book 1993 (1) 23 March to 31 August, in Papers of Ailsa Thomson Zainuddin, privately held.

Herb made is clear and very lucid. I have brought it with me to Sydney to share with Nila, with whom, to her great sorrow, I also shared the news and your letter. Now I am very glad that Nila and Din went to Indonesia last July so that Nila, as an adult, was able to know Jo and to help her a little with her writing. I only wish I could have been there too and am so grateful for the opportunity to stay in January 1992.

I can well understand that you couldn't keep from crying when you saw Jo. I could hardly keep a level voice to read your letter to Herb, and even as I am typing this, the screen is a little blurred. It is so hard to believe and, from that point of view, I can almost pretend that really it can't be true. [...]

The question of what to do with Jo's writings is one I really wish I could talk over with you. I am a little uneasy about Herb's grand scheme for something like a full-scale biography. He envisages research assistants in Indonesia and interviews with people who knew other aspects of Jo's life and work from the ones I knew. It doesn't seem quite right somehow or at least not appropriate for me to undertake although I would be glad to hear that someone was undertaking such a task.

Our original plan was quite a modest one, a monograph with her narrative and an introduction from me which somehow satisfied my own desire to express my gratitude and admiration without contravening her express request that I didn't make a heroine of her. I find a certain difficulty about how to proceed because, although the text is in English, yet it is written to and for her grandchildren. In the Australian context her [...] experiences in Australia and her contribution to the Volunteer Graduate Scheme would both make points of focus for anything published here. I would certainly like to write to Widarti Gunawan or, better still, have a long talk with her. It would probably be good to try to plan an outline but it is very difficult to contemplate right now because my anger – "*Why* should this happen to Jo of all people?" – and grief get in the way of clear thinking.

[...]

Lots of love

[Tommy]

"A Conversation Without Words"

7 November 1993

Dear Tommy/Din, Betty/Herb and Ann,

It has been almost a month now since Jo passed away and even now it is still difficult for me to write about her. It was only after she was gone that we, the children and I, really realised that she was gone. Before that, although there was almost no communication, we still could go to the hospital, we still could go home with the idea – we went to see Jo. The children said – "Another part of Bapak (Chris) is gone" and indeed I miss her not only as my friend but also as part of Chris. During the first *tahlilan* (prayers on the day that she passed away) and on the day of the funeral I realised that she had been a special person for so many, many people. Some ex-students had taken the night express from Jogja to be at her funeral. And these people were only a few years younger than Jo! Then I also knew, Herb, that no one would be able to finish the book she was writing, there were/are too many facets of her life for one person to write about.

Jo passed away peacefully. She was a bit restless but Jetty [Yetty] (a younger sister) who was with her calmed her down. Jetty was able to find a young man (visiting a sick relative) who was able to recite (sing) the *azan* for her, so accompanied by the *azan* Jo passed away peacefully.

Love,

Nini

20 October 1993

Dear Nini,

[...]

9/11/1993

This letter has been sitting in my machine ever since I began it. We were swept up into Din's 70th birthday celebrations, which wasn't entirely easy for me as I kept thinking of the world without Jo. [...]

Herb wrote to George Kahin who had heard the news. Herb sent me a copy of his letter to George and the reply.

15/11/1993

Your letter, written 7 November, arrived today. I was very grateful to receive it especially as you indicated that it was difficult to write. I could not trust myself to read it to Bett, Herb and Anne but shall make them each a copy. [...]

While I agree with your comment to Herb that no one would be able to finish the book that Jo was writing yet I also feel that it might be possible to publish what she has written, perhaps augmented by the tapes of conversations with Din and me last February and with Bett and Herb the day before her final stroke – both of which I have – and maybe some extracts from her letters about the book which I could draw on for the introduction which she asked me to write. She was thinking in terms of publication but I don't think either she or I were contemplating anything along the lines of Herb's suggestion. I would certainly indicate that the text itself was incomplete and that there are many other facets of her life and, as you wrote, many other people for whom she had been a special person. It is too soon to be able to contemplate it just yet though. [...]

I have left the false starts to this letter to indicate that Jo has been very much in our minds over the past month. The HEGG meeting will be exactly a month later so Bett and I will be thinking of you all and of Jo specially as we meet. I was/am still very sad that Jo did not receive my last letter. Her last one to me was written on 1 June, arrived on 9 June and was answered that night but had not arrived when Bett was there. [...]

My brief attempt at a letter on 9 November mentioned Herb's letter to George Kahin in which he said "Are you inclined to write about Jo for *Indonesia*, George? If not you might consider asking Tommy Zainu'ddin to do it." George wrote that he and Audrey "are glad she's prepared to do it". Herb, warned by Bett that I might be a bit taken aback by that when I knew nothing about it, had put a little yellow sticker on George's letter saying "I do hope you feel you'd like to do this. As the copy of my letter shows, I *didn't* say you would." My first reaction was dismay but then I thought that perhaps I should/could/would-if-asked. I do wish that I had read Jo's essays from Cornell days. George also said in his letter that both he and Audrey had always held Jo in very high regard

"And I particularly remember her considerable courage in putting me in touch with Dr Leimena and especially – together with Jo Abdurachman – in getting those important documents to me (right under the nose of the Dutch military police) when I visited Jogja again in early January 1949 when it was occupied by the Dutch."

[...] Oh Nini I'm **so** glad that she [Nila] and Din went to Indonesia and met you all and specially that she had a chance to meet Jo, who was so good to her mother in the pre-natal period when she would invite me home for a meal, a siesta, a *mandi* [bath] and great conversation on days when Din was working late at the office. Nila was delighted too.

Thank you again for your letter, which has enabled me to write mine. You have been wonderful in thinking of us and keeping us in touch even though it hasn't been easy for you.

Love to you and the children as you grieve for Jo and Chris. It is so hard to think of the world without them.

[Tommy]

EPILOGUE

IN MEMORIAM

JO KURNIANINGRAT SASTROAMIJOYO

September 14, 1919 – October 18, 1993

Ailsa Thomson Zainuddin

[This obituary first appeared in *Indonesia*, Volume 58, October 1994.]

In August 1954 I arrived in Jakarta as a new member of the Australian Volunteer Graduate Scheme for Indonesia pioneered by Herb Feith. He was returning to the Ministry of Information while Betty Feith and I were about to join the English Language Inspectorate of the Ministry of Education, Instruction, and Culture formed in 1953 to introduce English, in place of Dutch, as Indonesia's first foreign language, a colossal if unspectacular task. The Inspectorate was headed by Mr Fritz [Frits] Wachendorff, a part-Minangkabau Indonesian nationalist and linguist, who had clear ideas about how to achieve this switch in language and also about the problems of teaching English as first foreign language. As an individual he could sometimes be impatient with delays and did not suffer fools gladly. His colleagues were Mrs. Nini Rudolph, who had studied as a Fulbright scholar at Barnard College and Columbia University Teacher Training College, and his deputy, Miss Jo Kurnianingrat, then in her mid-thirties, who always dressed immaculately in *kain* and *kebaya*. Only later did we appreciate that, in immediately inviting us to call her "Jo," she had followed our custom rather than hers to put us at ease. We soon noted that she achieved the same amount of work and discipline from the office staff without raising her voice, creating a relaxed atmosphere through her restrained dignity and air of authority. We learnt much later what we never suspected initially, how hesitant they were about employing two unknown foreigners on their team.

When preparing for my first visit to Indonesia, I had carefully studied George Kahin's *Nationalism and Revolution in Indonesia* but failed to connect his reference to "two courageous Indonesian girls, Jo Abdurachman and Jo Kurnianingrat" (page 338) with this gracious, considerate woman assisting our acclimatisation in a new job and a new society. After the

Dutch repudiation of the Renville Treaty by renewed military action against the Republic, the two young women helped an American – George Kahin himself – convey to the outside world the final pre-invasion speeches the Republican leaders were prevented from broadcasting. Kurnianingrat, with other Indonesian women, established clandestine "rice kitchens" for civil servants unwilling to collaborate with the Dutch (page 397).

We knew "*ningrat*" indicated aristocracy. Jo was the only aristocrat we young Australians had ever met, let alone known as a friend. When, through reading Kartini's *Letters of a Javanese Princess*, I "met" and later wrote about this other *bupati*'s daughter, there was much of Jo Kurnianingrat in my image of Kartini. Jo, like Kartini, seemed interested only in "two kinds of aristocracy, the aristocracy of the mind and the aristocracy of the soul – of those who are noble in spirit." Some found her aristocratic bearing and self-restraint intimidating. Although unintimidated myself, it took a decade before I realised she was not, as I had believed, taller than I was.

In 1980 Jo wrote, in an article unfortunately still unpublished:

> I was born in an environment similar to that of Kartini, pioneer of women's emancipation in Indonesia, but forty years later. In the 1920s, the *kabupaten* no longer confined girls within its walls; it was a centre from which youngsters went forth to pursue their studies. Many cousins of mine, boys as well as girls, came to live in the *kabupaten* and we grew up together as equals. Never were the girls made to feel that the boys were superior and the younger did not have to humble themselves before the older. Whereas Kartini craved the opportunity to get Western schooling, we were encouraged to learn as much as possible about Western culture.

This began early. When she was three she attended the village school alongside her father's *kabupaten* at Ciamis and was sent, when four, to board with an Indo-European family in Tasikmalaya to learn Dutch. At five, with sufficient Dutch to enter European primary school, she was sufficiently advanced for the second form. At seven she was sent to Bandung. At the school run by the Ursuline order, she had no friends among her classmates, so spent her leisure time at the cinema, becoming a film fan, learning German, and improving her spoken English. She boarded with Dutch-speaking families during the week but spent weekends at the Bandung *kabupaten* to keep in touch with her Sundanese background.

After completing junior high school she undertook teacher training, obtaining her Hoofdacte. In about 1938 she began teaching at a

Dutch-Chinese school in Jakarta. Through Dahlan Abdullah, an elderly Sumatran colleague, she learned about the nationalist movement and began observing some of the injustices from which she had, till then, been protected. She also became engaged to a cousin, Jusuf Prawira Adiningrat, a law student, son of the Patih of Weltevreden but, although her father was prepared to accept her choice of partner – as Kartini had envisaged but had not achieved – Jo was then "transferred on request" (of her father!) to the Purwakarta European primary school where she could be properly chaperoned by siblings! When the Japanese invasion threatened, they agreed that Jus would join Jo in Purwarkata should the Japanese come. This he attempted to do but, after a long, agonising wait, she discovered that, on his way, he had been killed by villagers who thought he was Chinese. Almost fifty years later she wrote, "Isn't it strange that, after all those years, Jus's family still consider me one of them? To them I am still the older sister I would have been had he not died."

During the Japanese Occupation her father's pension ceased. Jo, seeking employment in Jakarta, met Dahlan Abdullah, whose pre-war anti-Dutch stance enabled him to find her a job at the Municipal Offices. Later she taught psychology at a Teacher Training School for Girls (Sekolah Guru Puteri or SGP) in Yogya. Initially, teaching in Indonesian was hard. She first translated each lesson, then learnt it by heart. In her memoirs she commented wryly that this was "a good way to master Indonesian" and, fortunately, the students asked no questions.

Under Dutch and Japanese rule contact with the outside world was minimal. After independence, when the Republican Government transferred to Yogya, "all of a sudden it was as if the doors to the outside world were thrown open." In 1946 Jo began teaching senior high school English, also reading the Voice of Free Indonesia's English language broadcasts to that outside world. With her fluent English, aristocratic bearing, and quiet dignity she was in demand at state dinners for foreign visitors. She has recalled "the general atmosphere of real friendship. We were all equals, only some got more important tasks to perform than others; but we appreciated each other. Nobody, no matter how high in rank, felt superior. Nobody felt poor in spite of the many deprivations." At the same time she emphasised that family networks continued to link those on opposite sides of the independence struggle. Of her father, whose pension was restored by the Dutch, she wrote, "I could not help being glad for him; he had suffered enough in his old age."

In 1947, "flabbergasted but elated" to be chosen, Jo went to Jakarta as a secretary in the Indonesian delegation to the Renville negotiations, a nerve-racking but exciting introduction to secretarial duties. Back in Yogya she was woken on December 19, 1948 by the Dutch bombing of the airport as they launched their second military attack. Many students, both young men and young women, left to join the independence fighters. The Dutch closed Republican schools but few Indonesians were willing to attend Dutch-run schools. Instead clandestine lessons continued at the homes of former high school teachers. When not teaching, Jo undertook administrative work for the Indonesian Red Cross. Her house was also a depot for parcels for the guerrilla troops. Twice she narrowly escaped detection by Dutch soldiers.

When the tide turned in favour of the Republic and life became more settled, Ali Sastroamijoyo, Minister of Education, offered Jo a scholarship for one year's study in Australia. "Not even in my wildest imagination," she later wrote, "had I ever dreamed of going to study abroad. It was really a miracle!" She left for Sydney in November 1949, studied psychology, saw many schools, read extensively, visited Victoria and Tasmania, and made many friends, as well as totally confusing one Scout Leader whose odd behaviour, she learned, was because he "had not expected to see such a sophisticated woman from Indonesia."

Two years after returning home she became first deputy head of the small but active English Language Inspectorate, which co-ordinated the work of two British Council officers and a team of Ford Foundation teachers in planning and trying out an English language syllabus for Indonesian post-primary schools and institutions. It also controlled the two-year English courses for secondary teachers throughout Indonesia and ran conferences for expatriate teachers. One met at Puncak in 1955 as delegates swept past to the nearby Bandung Conference, chaired by Prime Minister Ali Sastroamijoyo.

By 1956 the original IPBI team had dispersed. Jo went to Cornell University on a Ford Foundation scholarship to study English literature and linguistics. She took full advantage of her two years in the States, attending or auditing both regular and summer courses on various periods and genres of English literature and aspects of linguistics – as well as learning Russian – while writing her thesis on Shakespeare in Indonesia. Initially she missed her network of friends in Indonesia – "people here are so busy that they have not got time to be really friendly," she noted – but she enjoyed the independence of her own self-contained apartment. By her second year she was a central figure in the growing Indonesian community at Cornell, adding entertaining and even visiting the sick to her busy schedule.

On her return she taught in the English Department of the University of Indonesia, taking over as head in June 1960. In 1970 she married the widowed former Prime Minister and Nationalist Party leader, Ali Sastroamijoyo (b. 1903). She wrote: "This change in my life was the greatest surprise for myself. I never planned to give up my life as I had shaped it, but you see that things always turn out quite different from what we expect." Five years later Pak Ali died. Jo wrote: "Now that I belong to the older generation I'm expected to pay more attention to all family events and affairs, both in Pak Ali's and in my own big families. It's surprising how much of my time goes into it." A year later she reflected that "my ideal of a quiet life has not come true yet. Especially with the grandchildren growing up I have to give a lot of attention to them." They remained her concern for the rest of her life.

With courage and dignity she faced the handicaps of increasing age. She continued private teaching, though failing eyesight and hearing made this progressively more difficult. She began learning Braille. She was persuaded to write "Other Worlds in the Past" as a last story for her grandchildren and maintained contact with her extended families and her many friends worldwide. Although she insisted that she was "just an ordinary woman with no outstanding achievements at all," my own first impressions – of her innate dignity; her calm poise; her sensitivity to the needs of others; the sense she gave that the whole of living was an art which she had mastered – have only been confirmed. The fortitude with which she faced life and the role model she provided to other young women were far from ordinary. She was an independent woman whose life and example contributed significantly, although unobtrusively, to the new Indonesian nation, while she was also a central figure in the networks of family, students, and friends whose lives she enriched.

GLOSSARY

adipati	official title for regent
ASCM, SCM	Australian Student Christian Movement
alun-alun	large square in front of the houses of regents and district heads
AVA	Australian Volunteers Abroad
bekicot	snails
betjak	pedicab, tricycle
bupati	district head, regent
Ceuk	(Sundanese) older sister
Cultuur Zaken	Culture Business
djembatan	bridge, also the name of the quarterly magazine of the Volunteer Graduate Association
Darul Islam	armed Islamic movement aimed at establishing an Islamic state (lit. House of Islam)
Ibu	term of address, Mrs; mother
IPBI (Inspeksi Pengajaran Bahasa Inggeris)	English Language Inspectorate
Hoofd Djaksa	Chief Prosecutor
jambu	various species of rose-apples, guavas, cashews etc
jeruk	citrus fruit
jeruk Garut	a kind of tangerine
kabupaten	regency; residence of the regent
kain	fabric worn as clothing; wrapped skirt
kampong, kampung	small village; in an urban context, an unplanned, unserviced area inhabited by an Indonesian community
Kang	older brother
kebaya	woman's blouse worn with sarong
kléwang	short sword
Kraton	the royal palace, residence of the ruler and centre of the early Javanese kingdoms
kris	ceremonial, sacred, wavy-edged dagger
Landwacht	Home/Country Guard
Ma	term of address, mother
manggistan	mangosteen
mantri oeloe-oeloe	irrigation official
merdeka	freedom
Newman Society	Federal Catholic student organisation
NICA	Netherlands Indies Civil Administration
NUAUS	National Union of Australian University Students

OSB	Overseas Service Bureau
Pak, Pa	Mr; father
pancuran	jet of water; shower; tap
Pangeran	honorific for Javanese ruler
PKI (Partai Komunis Indonesia)	Indonesian Communist Party
pasanggrahan	government guest house
patih	Javanese official below regent
pegawai	civil servant, also used as a synonym for Volunteer Graduate
pencak silat	the art of self-defence
pendopo	large, open verandah in front of important Javanese residences for receiving visitors
PETA (Pembela Tanah Air)	Defenders of the Homeland
Plantersbond	Planters Union/Association
PMI	Indonesian Red Cross
priyayi	member of the Javanese gentry, often in the higher civil service
raden ayu	Javanese title for married aristocratic woman
RAPWI	International Red Cross
rujak	fruit salad with sweet, sour sauce
Sarikat Islam	Islamic Brotherhood
Sarikat Rakyat	People's Union
sawah	irrigated rice fields
selendang	strip of material worn by women across one shoulder (for carrying)
sembah	respectful greeting
serimpi	dancing
SMA (Sekolah Menengah Atas)	Senior High School
SMP (Sekolah Menengah Pertama)	Junior High School
Tentara Pelajar	Student Army
udeng	(Javanese) a square piece of cloth for making one *blangkon* (headgear)
VGA	Volunteer Graduate Association
VGS	Volunteer Graduate Scheme
wayang	shadow play with leather puppets
WSCF	World Student Christian Federation
WUS	World University Service

ABOUT THE AUTHORS AND EDITORS

Betty Maynard Feith (née Evans)

Betty Feith is a teacher with a lifetime involvement in church and other service, particularly with refugees and the advancement of peace and human rights. Born in Melbourne in 1931, Betty attended Methodist Ladies' College, Kew, before studying history and education at Melbourne University, and she later graduated with a Master of Educational Studies from Monash University. Betty worked at the English Language Inspectorate, Jakarta, in 1954–56, under the auspices of the Volunteer Graduate Scheme, a programme she co-founded. She has taught at schools and tertiary institutions in Melbourne and Indonesia, and her courses on Asian and Indonesian Studies at Burwood and Toorak Teachers' Colleges in the 1970s were among the first of their kind in Victoria. She has been closely involved with the Australian Student Christian Movement, the Christian World Service and the Uniting Church of Australia's Division of Social Justice in Victoria, among other organisations. Her association with Indonesia has been shared with her husband, Herb Feith, and with the couple's three children.

Harumani Rudolph-Sudirdjo

A teacher whose career spanned English language education, training and curriculum development, Harumani Rudolph-Sudirdjo has been described as having belonged to "a small educationally privileged generation of teachers who played a key role in the great democratising wave of education for all" (Belben, "Harumani Rudolph-Sudirdjo: 'Learning and Teaching through Changing Times'," *Network* 2(1) July 1995). Born on 7 December 1922 in Bandung, Harumani attended Dutch schools, and graduated with a teaching diploma from the I. E. V. Kweekschool in 1941. She took up a Fulbright scholarship to study at Barnard College, Columbia University, in 1951–52, and graduated with a Bachelor of Education from the University of Indonesia in 1967. Harumani was a member of the English Language Inspectorate, Jakarta, from 1955 to 1966. She also worked in junior and senior high schools, the University of Indonesia, and many other organisations. She married Chris Rudolph in 1953, and the couple had five children. Harumani died in 2014.

Ann McCarthy

Ann McCarthy was raised in New Zealand, and has a background in archival work at Archives New Zealand and also at the e-Scholarship Research Centre at the University of Melbourne, where she was a member of the team that worked on the archival records of Diane Elizabeth Barwick, anthropologist, historian and Indigenous rights supporter (available from http://www.austehc.unimelb.edu.au/guides/barw/barw.htm). Ann studied history and English at Victoria University of Wellington, and her Masters thesis, completed at the University Melbourne under Patricia Grimshaw and Katherine Ellinghaus, was a postcolonial analysis of an early novel by a Native American woman – *Cogewea*, by Mourning Dove (Okanogan). Ann's current PhD project, which is informed by the work of philosopher Agnes Heller, explores the emotional households of fictional characters, drawing on two 1940s Australian novels.

Kurnianingrat Ali Sastroamijoyo

Teacher, lecturer and public servant, Kurnianingrat Ali Sastroamijoyo worked extensively in English language education and training in the early years of the Indonesian Republic, and she is also remembered for the active part she took supporting the nationalist cause during the Revolution. Born into a Sundanese *bupati* family in 1919, Kurnianingrat attended schools in Tasikmalaya and Bandung, and she graduated with teaching diplomas from the I. E. V. Kweekschool, aged 18. In 1950 she spent a year in Australia observing the school system, and in 1956 she took up a Ford Foundation scholarship to study for a Master of Arts at Cornell University. During the 1950s she was second in charge of the English Language Inspectorate in Jakarta, and in this role helped to oversee the establishment of English as Indonesia's first foreign language. She later joined the English Language Department at the University of Indonesia, becoming head of the Department in 1961. Kurnianingrat married former Indonesian Prime Minister, Ali Sastroamijoyo, in 1970. Kurnianingrat died in 1993.

Ailsa Gwennyth Thomson Zainuddin

Ailsa Thomson Zainuddin is a writer and scholar who has specialised in the history of education. Born in Melbourne in 1927, Ailsa studied English and history at Melbourne University, and received her MA for a thesis entitled "The *Bulletin* and Australian Nationalism". In 1954, Ailsa travelled to Jakarta under the Volunteer Graduate Scheme, working at the English Language Inspectorate. In 1965 she joined the Faculty of Education, Monash University, where she carried out pioneering work in relation to Southeast Asian history of education, and the history of education for girls and women. Ailsa was awarded a PhD from Monash University in 1983 for her centenary history of Methodist Ladies' College, Kew, the school she herself attended, and which she maintained an association with for over fifty years. Ailsa's published works also include *A Short History of Indonesia*, and an Indonesian cookery book. She retired from Monash in 1992. Ailsa and her husband Zainu'ddin (Minangkabau), whom she married in 1954, have two daughters.

BIBLIOGRAPHY

*citation carried over from "An Episode in Education for International Understanding: The Volunteer Graduate Scheme in Indonesia 1950–63 – 'Putting in a Stitch or Two'", by Betty Feith. Masters thesis, Monash University, 1984.
^cited document is reproduced in full in this book

Archival and Manuscript Material

Assorted Documents
*Buchori, Mochtar. Field Work and Public Service Programs for University Students in Developing Countries, Qualifying Paper, 1970.
Doig, Ian. "Recollections of Indonesia 1954–55", 2003. Personal account, 72 pages.
*Feith, Herbert. "Growth and Development in Asia: Some Criticisms of Conventional Approaches". Lecture presented to Asian Leadership Development Centre, World Student Christian Federation, Tonzan, Japan, October 1972.
*Feith, Herbert. "How Asia Changed Me". Paper presented to the Fifth National Conference of the Asian Studies Association of Australia (ASAA), University of Adelaide, 13–19 May 1984.
Feith, Herbert. Letter to American Committee on Africa, 23 April 1959.
*Li, Lincoln. "A Personal View of the Blainey Debate". Paper presented to Plenary Session, Fifth National Conference of the Asian Studies Association of Australia (ASAA), University of Adelaide, 13–19 May 1984.
*Obituary for Noela Powell (née Motum), 1984.
*"Racism in the 1980s: A Response", Ministerial Discussion Paper. Victorian Ethnic Affairs Commission, Division of Research and Policy. East Melbourne Office of the Minister for Ethnic Affairs, 1984.
Tirtawinata, Dr. R. H. (Ambassador for Indonesia). Speech delivered to the Volunteer Graduate Scheme Conference, University of Melbourne, 23 August 1956.
*"Women's World Day of Prayer", annual pamphlet by Ecumenical Women's Committee, Women's World Day of Prayer Committee (WWDOPC)
*Zainu'ddin, Ailsa Thomson. "How Have I Been Affected in My Life and Thinking by My Experiences in Asia?" Paper presented to the Fifth National Conference of the Asian Studies Association of Australia (ASAA), University of Adelaide, 13–19 May 1984.

Records of the National Union of Australian University Students (NUAUS)
^"A Pilot Project in Southeast Asia – The Australian Volunteer Graduate Scheme for Indonesia", hand-out, 1959.
*Sub-Committee for Graduate Employment in Indonesia, later Standing Committee. Agendas and minutes for meetings 1953.

*The following mimeographed material pertaining to the Volunteer Graduate Scheme was sent out from the NUAUS Office, most of it labelled not for publication:

Ashton, Thelma. "Opportunities for Librarians in Indonesia", September 1955, 2 pages.
Bailey, Vern. "Comments on the V.G.S.", February, 1960.
Bailey, Vern. "Opening for Medicos in Indonesia", October 1955, 4 pages.
Doig, Ian. "Hints for Pegawais – For restricted circulation", [1956], 6 pages.
Doig, Ian. "Indonesia – an Opportunity for Australians", no date, 3 pages.
Feith, Betty. "English Language Teaching In Indonesia", 1956, 11 pages.
Feith, Herb. "Indonesia – A Challenge", June 1954, 3 pages.
Feith, Herb. "Indonesia since Independence", reprinted from *Nation*, New York, 29 August 1953.
Feith, Herb. "Report by H. Feith to Students and Graduates Interested in the NUAUS Scheme for Graduate Employment in Indonesia", September 1951, 9 pages.
Frankel, Alison. "Pharmacy in Indonesia", September 1954.
Meeking, Chas. "Our Graduates are Giving Vital Help to Indonesia", reprinted *West Australian*, 20 August 1954.
McMichael, O. "Graduates to Indonesia", no date, 3 pages.
Wills, Elaine. "Adventure in Indonesia", October 1960, 2 pages.
Zainu'ddin, Ailsa. "Review of the Volunteer Graduate Scheme, 1960", 11 pages.
"New Zealand University Students Association Volunteer Graduate Scheme", October 1959, 12 pages.
NUAUS News Bulletin (throughout the 1950s)
"P.E.G.A.W.A.I. (Plan for the Employment of Graduates from Australia to Work as Indonesians) i.e. Graduate Employment Scheme for Indonesia – Report to Intending Pegawais under P.E.G.A.W.A.I. (pegawai – employee)", August 1952. Open letter prepared by Oliver McMichael in collaboration with Gwenda Rodda and Herbert Feith. 12 pages.
"The Scheme for Graduate Employment in Indonesia: An Account of the way the Scheme works, and a Letter from Indonesia to Interested Volunteers", National Union of Australian University Students. November 1953. 21 pages.
"The Scheme for Graduate Employment in Indonesia: An Account of the Scheme and a Letter from Indonesia to Interested Volunteers", National Union of Australian University Students. Second Edition, December 1954. 21 pages.
"The Volunteer Graduate Scheme for Indonesia: An Account of the Scheme and a Letter from Indonesia to Interested Volunteers", Volunteer Graduate Association for Indonesia. Third Edition, December 1956. 21 pages.
"Report of the Committee for Graduate Employment in Indonesia to the 1954 N.U.A.U.S. Council", 7 pages.

Records of the Overseas Service Bureau (OSB)

"An Australian Peace Corps?" One-page hand-out, 4 March 1964.
*Bulletins, Newsletters and Reports (Australian Volunteers Abroad Programme), 1963–1983.
Memorandum of the Overseas Service Bureau Committee. Travel Grant to Ivan Southall, June 1963.
*Overseas Service Bureau. National Committee Monthly Minutes, 1961–1967.

Records of the Volunteer Graduate Association (VGA)

Djembatan Quarterly Newsletter of the Volunteer Graduate Association for Indonesia, Union House, University of Melbourne (Ed. Ailsa Zainu'ddin 1957–1963). Cited articles:
>   Anderson, Don. "Backstage", 2(1), September 1958.
>   Bayly, John. "Foreword – Full Circle", 2(4) Special Issue, September 1959.
>   Doig, Ian. "Life as a Pegawai", 2(2), December 1958.
>   Feith, Betty. "Colonialism Dies Hard", 2(4) Special Issue, September 1959.
>   Feith, Herb. "The Indonesian Political Scene", 1(1), July 1957.
>   Graham, Sylvia. "Teaching in Tondano (Sulawesi)", 1(2), November 1957.
>   ^Kurnianingrat, Jo. "An Indonesian Opinion on the VGS", 2(4), Special Issue, September 1959.
>   Motum, Noela. "Lemonade with the President", 1(1), July 1957.
>   Rodda, Gwenda. "Hidup Sederhana", 2(4) Special Issue, September 1959.
>   Thomas, Ken. "Reflections on Going Home", 1(3), February 1958.
>   Webb, Jim. "A New Approach to Asia", 1(4), June 1958.
>   Whitfield, Harry. "Gadjah Mada", 2(1), September 1958.
>   Whitfield, Harry. "The Old Ways and the New", 3(1/2), December 1959.
>   Zainu'ddin, Ailsa. "It's Dangerous to Go to Indonesia", 1(1), July 1957.

From the editorial column of *Djembatan*:
>   "They Also Serve", 2(4) Special Issue, September 1959.
>   "Invitation to Adventure – A History of the VGS", 2(4) Special Issue, September 1959.
>   "The First Ten Years", 5(2), October 1963.

*Minutes (incomplete) – Monthly Meetings of the National Committee, 1953–1964.
Minutes of the Volunteer Graduate Association for Indonesia National Committee – Special Meeting, 20 February 1960, Kew, Melbourne.
*Newsletter to Present and Past Volunteers, 1962–1966 (Eds, Betty Feith 1962–1964, Janys Foster 1964–1966).
*^"What is a PEGAWAI?" Illustrated flyer, no date.

Records from the Papers of Herbert Feith, 1946–2001. National Library of Australia, MS 9926 (transfer pending; see "Archival Sources" in the Introduction to this volume).

*Engel, Frank. "The Origins of the Overseas Service Bureau – An Address by Frank Engel – Australian Volunteers Abroad Briefing, Jan. 1983".
^Feith, Betty. "An Episode in Education for International Understanding: The Volunteer Graduate Scheme in Indonesia 1950–1963 – 'Putting in a Stitch or Two'". Master of Educational Studies thesis, Monash University, 1984.
Feith, Betty. "History of the Volunteer Graduate Scheme – Talk for AVA briefing – January 1983". Typescript, 16 pages.

Records from the Papers of Ailsa Thomson Zainuddin, Privately Held

Records Pertaining to Indonesia and the Volunteer Graduate Scheme

"Building the Future: The Life and Work of Kurnianingrat Ali Sastroamijoyo" (1992–1996). File comprises draft biographical article plus two interview transcripts.

"Harumani Rudolph-Sudirdjo – Biographical Documents (CV; Belben Article)" (1992–1995).
"Jo – Correspondence and Autobiography/Biography" (1955–1993)
"Kurnianingrat Ali Sastroamijoyo" (1919–1993). File comprises biographical notes and transcribed extracts (10 pages, typescript).
"Ollie McMichael Correspondence" (1952–1982 [2002])
^"Other Worlds in the Past" by Kurnianingrat Ali Sastroamijoyo. Written 1991–1993 (42 pages, typescript, with reviewer's comments).
"A Personal View from Indonesia [The Role of the Indonesian Woman]" by Kurnianingrat Ali Sastroamijoyo. Unpublished paper, 1980. (9 pages, typescript).

From Ailsa Zainuddin's Daily Journals
Jottings and Cuttings Book 1993 (1) 23 March to 31 August.

Published Material

Abeyasekere, Susan. *Jakarta: A History*. Singapore: Oxford University Press, 1987.
*Adams, Cindy. *My Friend the Dictator*. Indianapolis: Bobbs-Merrill, 1967.
*Armstrong, Bill, ed. *The Aid Debate: A Collection of Statements, Articles and Comments on the Question of Overseas Aid*. Fitzroy, Victoria: Action for World Development, August 1982.
Asian Studies Association of Australia Newsletter, Vol. 7, No. 2, November 1983.
*Beeby, C. E. *Assessment of Indonesian Education: A Guide in Planning*. Wellington: New Zealand Council for Education Research, 1979.
Belben, Gillian. "Harumani Rudolph-Sudirdjo: 'Learning And Teaching Through Changing Times'," *Network*, Vol 2, Issue 1, July 1995.
Bondan, Molly. *In Love With a Nation: Molly Bondan and Indonesia – Her Own Story In Her Own Words*. Edited by Joan Hardjono and Charles Warner. Picton, NSW: C. Warner, 1995.
Bondan, Molly. *Spanning a Revolution: The Story of Mohamad Bondan and the Indonesian Nationalist Movement*. Jakarta: Pustaka Sinar Harapan, 1992.
Bushell, Alma, ed. *Yesterday's Daughters: Stories of Our Past by Women over 70*. Melbourne: Nelson, 1986.
Clark, Keren. *The Two-Way Street: A Survey of Volunteer Service Abroad*. Wellington: New Zealand Council of Educational Research, 1978.
*Coast, John. *Recruit to Revolution: Adventure and Politics in Indonesia*. London: Christophers, 1952.
Control or Colour Bar? – A Proposal for Change in Australia's Immigration Policy, Melbourne: Immigration Reform Group, 1960.
*D'Cruz, J. V. *The Asian Image in Australia: Episodes in Australian History*. Melbourne: Hawthorn Press, 1973.
*Eldridge, Philip. "Australian Aid to Indonesia: Diplomacy or Development?" *Australian Outlook*, Vol. 25, No. 2, 1971.
*Eldridge, Philip. "Australian Aid to Indonesia: A Preliminary Assessment", *Ekonomi dan Keuangan Indonesia*, Vol. XXII, No. 4, December, 1974.
*Eldridge, Philip. *Indonesia and Australia: The Politics of Aid and Investment Since 1966*. (Development Studies Centre, Monograph No. 18). Canberra: Australian National University, 1979.
Feith, Herbert. "Molly Bondan: Pioneer, Mentor and Role Model", in *Half a Century of Indonesian-Australian Interaction*, edited by Anton Lucas (8–16). Adelaide: Flinders

University Dept of Asian Studies and Languages, 1996.
*Feith, Herbert. "The Political Crisis in Indonesia", *Australia's Neighbours*, Australian Institute of International Affairs, May, 1957.
Gelman Taylor, Jean. Editor of and with an introduction to *Women Creating Indonesia: The First Fifty Years*. Clayton, Vic: Monash Asia Institute, 1997.
*Goldman, R. J. "The Implications of a Multicultural Society for Australian Education", in *Australia's Multicultural Society* (Meredith Memorial Lectures). Bundoora, Vic.: La Trobe University, 1978.
Hoffman, Elizabeth Cobbs. *All You Need is Love: The Peace Corps and the Spirit of the 1960s*. Cambridge, Massachusetts and London, England: Harvard University Press, 2000.
Howe, Renate. *A Century of Influence: The Australian Student Christian Movement 1896–1996*. Sydney: University of New South Wales Press, 2009.
Immigration: Control or Colour Bar? – The Background to "White Australia" and a Proposal for Change, Immigration Reform Group. Edited by Kenneth Rivett, with a historical chapter by David Johanson. Melbourne: Melbourne University Press, 1962.
"In Memory of Herb Feith", Interview by Margaret Coffey, *Encounter*, Radio National, 9 March 2003, www.abc.net.au/radionational/programs/encounter/in-memory-of-herb-feith/3533384, accessed 12 July 2016.
*Inglis, Amirah. *Amirah: An Un-Australian Childhood*. Melbourne: William Heinemann Australia, 1983.
*Kahin, G. McT. *Nationalism and Revolution in Indonesia*. Ithaca, New York: Cornell University Press, 1952.
Kartini, Raden Adjeng. *Letters from Kartini: An Indonesian Feminist 1900-1904*. Translated by Joost Coté. Clayton, Vic: Monash Asia Institute, Monash University in association with Hyland House, 1992.
Lagu-Lagu Dari Indonesia: Songs of Indonesia. Collected and translated by Ailsa Zainu'ddin; music transcription by Helen McMahon; illustrations by Jonathan Waud. South Yarra, Vic.: Heinemann Educational Australia, 1969.
*Li, Lincoln. "Blainey's Lesson of History on Immigration Challenged", *Monash Reporter*, No 5–84, July 4 1984, 5. (Review of "Racism in the 1980s: A Response", as listed above in Archival and Manuscript Material.)
*Lockwood, R. *Black Armada*. South Sydney, NSW: Australasian Book Society, 1975.
**The Missionary Review*. The Methodist Church of Australasia, Department of Overseas Missions, 1892–1977.
**New Hope for Asia: The Colombo Plan for Co-operative Economic Development in South and South-East Asia*, Economic Information Unit of the United Kingdom Treasury. Prepared by the Commonwealth Office of Education for the Department of External Affairs, Canberra, 1951.
*Pittock, A. Barrie. *Racism in Australia: An Introductory Perspective*. Address delivered at Australian Council of Churches Conference, 1971. Melbourne: Australian Council of Churches, 1971.
A Place in the World: Stories from Australian Volunteers International, Australian Volunteers International. Foreword by José Ramos-Horta, Introduction by the Hon Justice Michael Kirby. Melbourne: Melbourne Books, 2007.
*Preiswerk, R., ed. *The Slant of the Pen: Racism in Children's Books*. Papers presented as part of Geneva Programme to Combat Racism, 1978. Geneva: World Council of Churches, 1980.
Purdey, Jemma. *From Vienna to Yogyakarta: The Life of Herb Feith*. Sydney: University of New South Wales Press, 2011.

Purdey, Jemma. *Scholarships and Connections: Australia, Indonesia and Papua New Guinea* (Working Papers, Series Two, No 46). Geelong: Alfred Deakin Research Institute, Deakin University, 2014.

Reid, Anthony. *The Indonesian National Revolution 1945–1950*. Hawthorn, Victoria: Longman, 1974.

*Salter, M. J. *Studies in the Immigration of the Highly Skilled*. Canberra: Australian National University Press, 1978.

Sastroamijoyo, Ali. *Milestones On My Journey: The Memoirs of Ali Sastroamijoyo, Indonesian Patriot and Political Leader*. Edited by C. L. M. Penders. St Lucia, Qld: University of Queensland Press, 1979.

Soedarpo, Mien. *Reminiscences of the Past*. Edited by Mildred Wagemann. Jakarta: Sejati Foundation, 1994.

*Southall, Ivan. *Indonesia Face to Face*. Melbourne: Lansdowne Press, 1965.

Southall, Ivan. *Indonesian Journey*. Melbourne: Lansdowne Press, 1965.

Sutherland, Heather. "Notes on Java's Regent Families: Part 1". *Indonesia*, No. 16 (October 1973): 125–31.

*Tiffin, Rodney. *The News From Southeast Asia: The Sociology of Newsmaking*. Singapore: Institute of Southeast Asian Studies, 1978.

*"Vibro". Quarterly Newsletter on Community Development, published by Yayasan Indonesia Sejahtera/Indonesian Welfare Foundation. Solo, Indonesia.

Wesley, Laurie, ed. *Celebrating the New Zealand University Students Association's Volunteer Graduate Scheme for Indonesia*. Auckland: Laurie Wesley, 2013.

*Zainu'ddin, Ailsa. *A Short History of Indonesia*. Melbourne: Cassell Australia, 1968.

Zainu'ddin, Ailsa Thomson. "Building the Future: The Life and Work of Kurnianingrat Ali Sastroamijoyo", in *Women Creating Indonesia: The First Fifty Years*, edited by Jean Gelman Taylor, 156–202. Clayton, Vic.: Monash Asia Institute, 1997.

^Zainu'ddin, Ailsa Thomson. "In Memoriam: Jo Kurnianingrat Sastroamijoyo, September 14, 1919 – October 18, 1993". *Indonesia*, No. 58, (October 1994): 115–19.

Zainu'ddin, Ailsa Thomson ... [et al]. *Kartini Centenary: Indonesian Women Then and Now*. [Clayton, Vic.]: Monash University, 1980.

INDEX

Abdullah, Dahlan 100, 128, 129, 133
Abdurachman, Jo 142, 145, 148, 151
  and George Kahin 201, 205
Abu Bakar Lubis viii
Adiningrat, Jusuf Prawira 137, 138, 140, 148, 153
  courtship of Kurnianingrat 129–130
  death 131, 207
AIA Vic. *see* Australian Indonesian Association of Victoria
Algadri, Hamid 102, 147, 148, 149, 152
American Committee on Africa 43–44
  see also Feith, Herb
Anderson, Don 36 n40, 45 n49
  and Australian Indonesian Association of Victoria 62
  "Backstage" (*Djembatan*) 32 n32
  as chairman of Melbourne Committee 32
  as chairman of VGA 62
  and *Control or Colour Bar?* 63 n82
  see also Volunteer Graduate Association
The Arabian Nights 108, 117
ASCM *see* Australian Student Christian Movement
Ashton, Thelma *see* Rungkat, Thelma
Australian Government (Commonwealth)
  and Kurnianingrat's scholarship 99
  and VGS intergovernmental agreement 19–20, 45, 73, 77, 79
Australian Indonesian Association of Victoria 41, 62, 64
  see also Anderson, Don; Zainu'ddin
Australian Student Christian Movement 38
  attracting new volunteer graduates 32 n32, 37
  and beginnings of VGS xii, 18, 71
  conferences 18, 45 n49
  and OSB 7 n2
  see also Indonesian Student Christian Movement; Volunteer Graduate Scheme
Australian Volunteers Abroad 67 n89
  establishing of ix, 12, 13
  see also foreign aid, Overseas Service Bureau, Volunteer Graduate Scheme
Australian Volunteers International x, xvi n2, 7 n2
  and Overseas Service Bureau x
AVA *see* Australian Volunteers Abroad
AVI *see* Australian Volunteers International

Ball, William McMahon 7 n3, 19, 72

Bayly, John J.
  and forming of the Volunteer Graduate Scheme 16–17, 18
  as member of Melbourne Committee 72
Bibib (Kurnianingrat's sister)
  support for the Republic 145
Bondan, Molly
  Herb Feith and viii, 7 n3, 19
  Kurnianingrat and 179
  on the Volunteer Graduate Scheme xix
  volunteer graduates and ix, 19 n7, 21 n11, 34 n36, 56 n68

civil service, Indonesian
  employment of volunteer graduates in 17–20 *passim*, 29–32 *passim*, 36–37, 46–47, 51–54 *passim*, 79, 82–84
  see also Indonesian Government; Indonesia, Republic of
Clark, Manning xxi, 172, 181, 186
Colombo Plan xvii, 37, 51 n58, 62
Columbia University
  Harumani and xix
Control or Colour Bar? 63 n82
Cornell University
  Betty Feith and xvi, 61, 63
  Herb Feith and xvi, 43
  Kurnianingrat and xvi, xix, 18 n4, 102, 169, 181

Dicky (Kurnianingrat's brother)
  support for the Republic 145
Djembatan
  ceasing publication 45–46
  editor 32
  and editorial policy 34 n36
  as official publication of Volunteer Graduate Association 12–13, 16 n2, 32, 41
  see also Volunteer Graduate Association; Volunteer Graduate Scheme; Zainuddin, Ailsa Thomson
Dutch–Chinese Primary School, Glodok, Jakarta
  Kurnianingrat's work at 128–130

Engel, Frank
  and VGS aims and ethos x, 7 n2, 18 n6
English Language Inspectorate *see* IPBI
European school, Purwakarta
  Kurnianingrat's work at 130

– 223 –

Feith, Annie image 7
Feith, Betty xx–xxi, 7–8; images 1, 2, 3, 4, 7, 9
  and ASCM xx, 213
  "Colonialism Dies Hard" (*Djembatan*) 31 n29, 56 n68
  as history teacher xxi, 8, 61, 213
  marriage xx, 8, 15
  as secretary of Melbourne Committee 7, 14, 72
  as volunteer graduate xvi, 7, 69, 92–94, 167–169
    friendships xvi, xix–xxi, 93, 167, 174–175
    return to Australia 61–62, 63
  see also Feith, Herb; IPBI; volunteer graduates
Feith, David image 7
Feith, Herb images 1, 7
  coins phrase "putting in a stitch or two" 25
  on political scene in Indonesia (1957) 35
  publicises VGS at Cornell 43
  and VGS aims and ethos x, 25–27, 32, 43–45, 48, 56 n68
  as volunteer graduate 19-20, 51
  1951 visit to Indonesia xi, 7 n3, 19–20, 21 n11
  see also American Committee on Africa; Bondan, Molly; Feith, Betty; Volunteer Graduate Scheme; volunteer graduates
foreign aid
  and paternalism viii, 17, 21 n11, 26, 28–29, 54, 99-93
  post-war environment and vii, 29
  VGS as new mode of vii–x, 13, 16–20, 29-33, 48–49
  see also Australian Volunteers Abroad; Australian Volunteers International; Overseas Service Bureau; Volunteer Graduate Scheme

Gadjah Mada University 43 n45, 140, 141
Gadog, visit by Kurnianingrat to 122–123
Gelman Taylor, Jean
  Women Creating Indonesia 96, 98, 102
  Gone with the Wind 144
Gungwu, Professor Wang 66

Haji Agus Salim 149
"Hallo, Hallo Bandung" (song) 113, 142, 148
Hamengkubuwono IX, Sultan of Yogyakarta 134–135, 140, 149
Hatta, Bung *see* Hatta, Mohammad
Hatta, Mohammad 138, 139, 140, 149, 151
Harumani *see* Rudolph-Sudirdjo, Harumani
Hoedt family 98, 117, 121

Ibu (Kurnianingrat's mother) image 6
  marriage 107
  see also Gadog, visit by Kurnianingrat to; Sastrawinata, R. A. A.
Ibu Gedong *see* Sastrawinata, R. A. A.
  death 152
  marriage 107
  as Raden Ayu 109, 111, 112, 113, 114, 119, 125
Ibu Saodah image 7
I. E. V. Kweekschool
  Harumani's attendance at 167, 213
  Kurnianingrat's attendance at 98, 125–127, 214
Immigration Reform Group 63 n82
Indonesian Government *see* civil service, Indonesian; Indonesia, Republic of
  in exile 149, 151–152
  and VGS intergovernment agreement 18–19
Indonesia, Republic of
  Dutch military actions against 142–152 *passim*
  early years of 138–152
  Japanese occupation of 131–138 *passim*
  proclamation of independence 138–139
  see also civil service, Indonesian; Indonesian Government; Sastroamijoyo, Kurnianingrat Ali; Volunteer Graduate Scheme
Indonesian Student Christian Movement 72
  see also Australian Student Christian Movement
Indonesian-Australian relations 56 n68
Inspeksi Pengajaran Bahasa Ingerris *see* IPBI
IPBI images 2, 3, 4
  disbanding of 169, 208
  employment of volunteer graduates at 92–94, 167–169
  friendships formed at xvi, xix, 92, 167
  language policy 168–169, 208
  role of 167, 205
  see also Feith, Betty; Pryosusilo, Ann; Rungkat, Thelma; Rudolph-Sudirdjo, Harumani; Sastroamijoyo, Kurnianingrat Ali; Wachendorff, Frits; Zainuddin, Ailsa Thomson

Japanese occupation of Indonesia *see* Indonesia, Republic of
Jayusman, Achmad 101, 138, 140, 169
Johnston, Mary
  as volunteer graduate 67 n89, 69
  friendships 174
Jo Kurnianingrat *see* Sastroamijoyo, Kurnianingrat Ali
Julius, Bernice 157–159, 161

INDEX

Kahin, George 19 n9, 61, 199, 200–201
   commends Kurnianingrat xvii–xviii, 18 n4, 201, 205–206
   see also Abdurachman, Jo; Sastroamijoyo, Kurnianingrat Ali
Karno, Bung *see* Sukarno
Kartini, R. A.
   Ailsa's work on 172, 173–174
   Kurnianingrat, parallels with 96, 174, 179, 181, 206, 207
Kirby, Michael 5
Der Kongress Tanzt 123

Labor Club
   and Volunteer Graduate Scheme vii, 6, 38
Leimena, Dr Johannes
   Kurnianingrat and 201
   and volunteer graduates 19, 21 n11, 23

McDonald, Ann *see* Pryosusilo, Ann
McMichael, Oliver 32
   letters home of 2, 14, 19 n8, 20–22 *passim*, 23, 28 n24, 51 n59
   as volunteer graduate 19, 20 n10, 21 n11, 70–75, 99 n5
   see also Sugoto, Dr R.; volunteer graduates
McMichael, Ollie *see* McMichael, Oliver
Mohamad, Goenawan 182, 183, 185, 191
Monash University xi, 191
   Ailsa Zainuddin and xxi, 194, 215
   Betty Feith and xxi, 2, 213
   Centre of Southeast Asian Studies 62, 63, 172, 191, 194

National Union of Australian University Students
   attracting new volunteer graduates 37
   and forming of the Volunteer Graduate Scheme 18, 79
   see also Volunteer Graduate Scheme, National Union of Indonesian Students
National Union of Indonesian Students (PPMI) 72, 79
Netherlands East Indies
   civil service 54, 106
   evacuation of Government to Australia 130
Netherlands Indies Civil Administration *see* NICA
Newman Society
   attracting new volunteer graduates 37
New Zealand Volunteer Graduate Scheme xvi n2, 70, 80
NICA 150, 151
NUAUS *see* National Union of Australian University Students

Office of Education, Australian Government
   and Kurnianingrat's visit to Australia 152, 153, 155, 156, 157, 159, 161, 163, 164
O'Neill, Hugh
   and Indonesian Arts Society 62
   and teaching of Southeast Asian architecture 62
   and VGS ethos x
   as volunteer graduate 34 n36, 70
OSB *see* Overseas Service Bureau
Overseas Service Bureau
   administration of VGS and ix, 12, 13, 87
   ethos and principles x
   forming of 12, 13, 45–46
   see also Australian Volunteers Abroad; Australian Volunteers International; foreign aid; Volunteer Graduate Scheme; Webb, Jim

Peace Corps
   and the Volunteer Graduate Scheme vii, xvi, 56 n68, 87
Pryosusilo, Ann
   marriage 67 n89, 70
   as volunteer graduate 37 n41, 93, 169
   friendships formed 174
   see also IPBI; volunteer graduates

Red Cross xx
   Australian xvi n2
   Indonesian (PMI) xviii, 142, 144, 148, 150, 208
   International (RAPWI) 142, 144, 145
Renville Agreement 147, 206
   see also Sastroamijoyo, Kurnianingrat Ali
Rodda, Gwenda 14; image 1
   "Hidup Sederhana" (*Djembatan*) 30 n29
   Kurnianingrat and 18 n4, 92
   as volunteer graduate 19, 21 n11, 23, 70, 76–78
   see also volunteer graduates
Roem, Dr Mohammad
   as member of Indonesian Government in exile 149
   volunteer graduates and 21 n11, 72
Rubbo, Michael 44–45
Rudolph, Chris image 8
   friendship with Kurnianingrat xx, 167, 174, 199
Rudolph, Nini *see* Rudolph-Sudirdjo, Harumani
Rudolph-Sudirdjo, Harumani images 3, 4, 5, 8
   background xix–xx, 213–214
   and Indonesian Revolution xx, 103 n9
   and IPBI 167-169
   friendships xvi, xix–xxi, 167, 174–175

– 225 –

and Kurnianingrat's memoir
  correspondence with Kurnianingrat and
    Ailsa regarding 177–201
  initial proposal regarding 177–178
  see also IPBI; Sastroamijoyo, Kurnianingrat
    Ali
Rungkat, Thelma *see* IPBI; volunteer graduates
  marriage 69
  as volunteer graduate 37 n41, 69, 93

Sarikat Rakyat movement 119–120
  Ciamis riot 120–121
  see also Sastrawinata, R. A. A.
Sastrawinata, R. A. A.
  as Bupati of Ciamis 106–108 *passim*,
    110–114 *passim*
  death 166
  marriages 97, 107
  and Sarikat Rakyat riot 98, 120–121
  and "Western-oriented education" for his
    children 99–100, 127
Sastroamijoyo, Ali
  and Kurnianingrat's Australian scholarship
    152
  marriage to Kurnianingrat 102, 209
  as member of Indonesian Government in
    exile 149, 152
  Milestones on my Journey 149, 151
Sastroamijoyo, Kurnianingrat Ali images 3,
  4, 5
  Australian Government scholarship 99,
    152
  Australian visit 152–164
  birth 107
  childhood 107–119, 121–125
    attends village school 108
    life in the kabupaten 107–114
    sent away to learn Dutch 115, 116
  and Cornell University xix, xvi, 208
  death 199–201
  Ford Foundation scholarship 169
  on foreign aid 92–94
  and George Kahin 148, 149
    passes speeches to Kahin 150
  and Indonesian Revolution 138–152 *passim*
    political views among her family on 153
    and "rice kitchens" 151
  see also Indonesia, Republic of
  and IPBI 166–169
    employment of volunteer graduates at
      92–94, 167–169
  friendships xi, xvi, xix–xxi, 93, 167, 175
  courted by Jusuf Prawira Adiningrat
    129–130
  marriage to Ali Sastroamijoyo 209
  and national movement for independence
    100, 129

and Renville negotiations *see* Renville
  Agreement 145–147
schooling 97, 98
  high school 122, 123–124, 125
  primary 116, 117, 118, 121, 206
as teacher
  during Japanese Occupation 134–137
  of English language 98, 140–141
  in Indonesian language medium 136,
    207
  in occupied Yogyakarta 150, 208
Sundanese pryayi background
  attitudes towards Western culture 96,
    99–100, 110–111, 127, 129, 206
  respect shown to elders 111
  and Voice of Free Indonesia 141, 144
  see also Indonesia, Republic of
writing of "Other Worlds in the Past"
  correspondence with Ailsa and
    Harumani regarding 177–201
  drafts sent to Ailsa 186, 187–188, 190,
    192–193
  health and vision problems during 177,
    180, 182–183 *passim*, 186, 187–188
    passim, 196, 197
  satisfaction derived from 188, 190
  see also Adiningrat, Jusuf Prawira;
    Indonesia, Republic of; IPBI; Rudolph-
    Sudirdjo, Harumani; Sastrawinata,
    R. A. A.; Sastroamijoyo, Ali; Zainuddin,
    Ailsa Thomson
SCM *see* Australian Student Christian
  Movement
Senior High School, Yogyakarta
  Kurnianingrat's work at 140–141
Southall, Ivan 14, 47 n53, 59–60
  Indonesia Face to Face 19 n7, 24 n8, 27 n23,
    31 n29, 47 n53, 57 n69
Sugoto, Dr R.
  and Kurnianingrat 99 n5, 157
  Oliver McMichael and 21 n11, 75, 99 n5
Sukarno 33, 47
  and Indonesian Revolution 138–140
    passim, 149, 151–152
  volunteer graduates and 23
Sutan Syahrir 140, 149
Sydney University
  Kurnianingrat's attendance at 155, 156, 161

Teacher Training School for Girls (SGP),
  Yogyakarta
  Kurnianingrat's work at 134–136 *passim*,
    140, 207
Thomson, Ailsa *see* Zainuddin, Ailsa Thomson
Tirtawinata, Dr R. H.
  on the Volunteer Graduate Scheme 33,
    64, 80

– 226 –

INDEX

University of Indonesia
  Harumani and xx n8, 102, 209
  Kurnianingrat and xviii, xx
University of Melbourne
  and forming of the Volunteer Graduate
    Scheme 7 n3, 17, 19, 82
  see also Feith, Herb; Webb, Jim; Zainu'ddin

VGA *see* Volunteer Graduate Association
Voice of Free Indonesia *see* Sastroamijoyo,
  Kurnianingrat Ali
Voluntary Service Overseas (VSO)
  and the Volunteer Graduate Scheme vii,
    xvi, 87
Volunteer Graduate Association
  Australian Indonesian Association of
    Victoria and 62
  Djembatan and 16 n2, 46 n52, 32
  forming of 12–13, 32
  and Melbourne Committee 32, 41
  role of 46 n52, 12–13, 84
  see also Anderson, Don; Volunteer Graduate
    Scheme
volunteer graduates
  and Asian Studies in Australia 61–64
    passim, 66
  and Australian Embassy 54–55, 56 n68, 77
  availability of work 38–39, 44 n47, 48–51
  backgrounds 6, 13, 38, 49, 64–65
  consensus among 38, 39, 41
  culture shock 13–14, 38, 51–59
  Indonesian language and 3, 21 n11, 24,
    57–58, 61–64 *passim*
  return to Australia 58–59, 61–67
  White Australia policy, opposition to 63
  and work ethic 14, 24, 38–39, 48–50, 51–54
  see also Feith, Betty; Feith, Herb; Bondan,
    Molly; civil service, Indonesian;
    Johnston, Mary; Leimena, Dr Johannes;
    McMichael, Oliver; O'Neill, Hugh;
    Pryosusilo, Ann; Rodda, Gwenda;
    Sukarno; Rungkat, Thelma; Volunteer
    Graduate Scheme; Zainuddin, Ailsa
    Thomson
Volunteer Graduate Scheme
  and Australian Student Christian
    Movement 2, 5, 6, 18, 37, 38, 45 n49, 71
  attracting new volunteers 32 n32, 37
  beginnings vii–x, xii, 16–20, 82
    and NUAUS and ASCM conferences 18
    and World University Service conference
      viii, 16–17
  and "foreign expert" 3, 17, 27, 28, 30,
    55–56, 92–93
  and intergovernmental agreement 19–20,
    82
  Jakarta Committee 5, 13, 41

following up volunteer applications
  37–39, 46–47
and problem of lack of suitable work
  38-39, 49, 50
literature of
  Djembatan 12–13, 32–36 *passim*, 39,
    41–46 *passim*
  informal newsletter 46
  letters home and 20–23, 36
  and NUAUS 23–33 *passim*, 37, 49
Melbourne Committee 5, 6, 13, 14, 15, 32,
  41, 42, 45, 71–72
and National Union of Australian
  University Students viii, 12, 26 n21, 37,
  45 n49, 71, 83, 84
and Overseas Service Bureau ix, x, 12, 13,
  14, 45–46, 87
philosophy and ethos 20–36
  countering misperceptions of Indonesia
    ix, 23–24, 27–28, 33–36, 40–41, 47, 66
  influence of Indonesian supervisors and
    colleagues upon ix, 21 n11, 23, 24,
    28–29
  moral tones and themes of 25, 27, 28, 33
  as new mode of international
    development vii–x, 13, 16–20, 29–33,
    48–49
  "putting in a stitch or two" 2, 25, 45, 50,
    52–53,
  salary equality ix, 13, 17, 27–33 *passim*,
    42–44 *passim*, 49, 54–57 *passim*
  support for Indonesian nation-building
    viii–ix, xv, 12, 13, 20–27, 44, 48–49
as progenitor of "peace corp" idea vii, xvi,
  87
and Volunteer Graduate Association
  12–13, 46 n52, 84
see also Australian Student Christian
  Movement; Australian Government;
  Djembatan; foreign aid; civil service,
  Indonesian; Indonesian Government;
  National Union of Australian University
  Students; Overseas Service Bureau;
  Volunteer Graduate Association;
  volunteer graduates

Wachendorff, Frits 99, 167–169 *passim*, 174,
  205, images 3, 4
Webb, Jim 14, 45, 56 n68, 59
  "A New Approach to Asia" (*Djembatan*) 32
    n32
  as honorary secretary of the VGA 14, 32
  as OSB director 6, 45, 46 n52, 87
  and VGS ethos x, 86–87
  as Warden of Union House, University of
    Melbourne 45 n50, 46 n52
  see also Overseas Service Bureau

White Australia policy *see* volunteer graduates
Wiltens, André 124, 125
Wiranatakusumah, R. A. A.
  Kurnianingrat and 117–118, 148
The Women's Room 172, 194
World University Service 16, 17 n3

Yesterday's Daughters 172, 178, 179

Zainuddin, Ailsa Thomson xx–xxi; images 1, 2, 3, 4, 7, 9
  and ASCM xx
  and *Control or Colour Bar?* 63 n82
  as *Djembatan* editor 32, 34 n36, 39, 41, 42, 44, 85–86
  "It's dangerous to go to Indonesia" (*Djembatan*) 4, 34–35, 59 n71
  and Kurnianingrat's memoir
    correspondence with Kurnianingrat and Harumani regarding 177–201
    responds to drafts received from Kurnianingrat 186–190 *passim*
  as volunteer graduate xvi, 92–94, 167–169, 205
    friendships xvi, xix–xxi, 93, 167, 174–175
  marriage xx–xxi, 215
  see also IPBI; Sastroamijoyo, Kurnianingrat Ali; volunteer graduates; Zainu'ddin
Zainu'ddin image 7
  and Australian Indonesian Association of Victoria 62
  as Indonesian diplomat xxi
  and University of Melbourne 62
  see also Zainuddin, Ailsa Thomson
Zainu'ddin, Lisa image 7
Zainu'ddin, Nila 175, 192, 193, 197, 198, 201, image 7
Zainu'ddin, Tommy *see* Zainuddin, Ailsa Thomson